Privacy

"A wonderful exploration of the multifaceted work being done to protect the privacy of users, clients, companies, customers, and everyone in between."

—Peter Wayner, author of *Translucent Databases*

"Cannon provides an invaluable map to guide developers through the dark forest created by the collision of cutting-edge software development and personal privacy."
—Eric Fredericksen, Sr. Software Engineer, PhD., Foundstone, Inc.

"Cannon's book is the most comprehensive work today on privacy for managers and developers. I cannot name any technical areas not covered. No practitioners should miss it."

—Ray Lai, Principal Engineer, Sun Microsystems Inc., Co-author of *Core Security Patterns* and author of *J2EE Platform Web Services*

"Every developer should care deeply about privacy and this is the best book I've read on the subject. Get it, read it, and live it."

—Keith Ballinger, Program Manager, Advanced Web Services, Microsoft

"J.C. Cannon's book demonstrates that information and communication technology can contribute in a significant way to restoring individual privacy and raises more awareness of the complexity and importance of this societal problem."

—Dr. John J. Borking, Former Commissioner and Vice-President of the Dutch Data Protection Authority

"If you are planning, implementing, coding, or managing a Privacy campaign in your Company or your personal computing, there is no more relevant reference. J.C. Cannon nails the issues."

—Rick Kingslan, CISSP, Microsoft MVP-Windows Server: Directory Services and Right Management, West Corporation

"It's often been said that security is a process, not a product. Privacy is no different! Unlike other privacy books, J.C. Cannon's book has something valuable to convey to everyone involved in the privacy process, from executives to designers and developers, many of whom aren't thinking about privacy but should be."

—Keith Brown, Co-founder of Pluralsight and author of *The .NET Developer's Guide to Windows Security* and *Programming Windows Security*

"J.C. Cannon's new book on electronic privacy is an important addition to the available works in this emerging field of study and practice. Through many humorous (and occasionally frightening) examples of privacy gone wrong, J.C. helps you better understand how to protect your privacy and how to build privacy awareness into your organization and its development process. Keenly illustrating both the pros and cons of various privacy-enhancing and potentially privacy-invading technologies, J.C.'s analysis is thorough and well-balanced. J.C. also explains many of the legal implications of electronic privacy policies and technologies, providing an invaluable domestic and international view."

—Steve Riley, Product Manager, Security Business and Technology Unit, Windows Division, Microsoft

"Privacy concerns are pervasive in today's high-tech existence. The issues covered by this book should be among the foremost concerns of developers and technology management alike."

—Len Sassaman, Security Architect, Anonymizer, Inc.

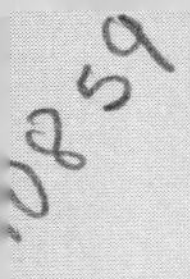

Privacy

What Developers and IT Professionals Should Know

J.C. Cannon

Addison-Wesley

Boston • San Francisco • New York • Toronto • Montreal
London • Munich • Paris • Madrid • Capetown
Sydney • Tokyo • Singapore • Mexico City

The publisher offers discounts on this book when ordered in quantity for bulk purchases and special sales. For more information, please contact:

U.S. Corporate and Government Sales
(800) 382-3419
corpsales@pearsontechgroup.com

For sales outside of the U.S., please contact:

International Sales
international@pearsontechgroup.com

Visit Addison-Wesley on the Web: www.awprofessional.com

ISBN: 0-321-22409-4

Text printed on recycled paper

1 2 3 4 5 6 7 8 9 10—CRS—0807060504

First printing, [September, 2004]

Library of Congress Cataloging-in-Publication Data

Acknowledgements

When Michael Howard wrote his first two books, I had an office across from his. When I saw the artwork for his first book on his door, I asked him about it. It interested me to discuss the process of writing books with him. He was very accommodating and encouraged me to write this book. Although there was a lot of pain involved is getting this book completed, my hat's off to Michael for pushing me to get this book completed and even helping me review it.

While working on the second edition of their book, Michael's coauthor, David LeBlanc, asked me to write a chapter on privacy for their book. Later on, Ben Smith asked me to write three chapters in the book he was writing, *Microsoft Windows Security Resource Kit*. These experiences encouraged me to write my own book. Little did I know how hard it would be.

Other Microsoft authors such as Rob Howard, Mindy Martin, and Frank Redmond III, with whom I had an opportunity to work, also influenced my decision to write my first technical book. I owe them a debt of gratitude for persuading me to tell my story.

Many of the ideas around privacy reviews at Microsoft came from Jeffrey Friedberg and the work he did pioneering privacy reviews with the Digital Media Division at Microsoft. The privacy-analysis design techniques are an extension of Jesper Johansen's work on security threat-modeling analysis. I also want to thank the members of the Microsoft Corporate Privacy Group, Windows Privacy Council, Privacy Development Council, and BAMTech alias for their guidance.

I started down the road to privacy when Richard Purcell hired me into Microsoft's Corporate Privacy Group and taught me the basics of privacy. When Richard left Microsoft to start his own privacy venture, I had the pleasure of having Peter Cullen as my new boss. Peter has become a great mentor for me and also took time to review this book.

Early in my privacy career I was fortunate enough to meet Ann Cavoukian and buy my first privacy book, *The Privacy Payoff*. Ann is the consummate privacy professional and serves as the voice of clarity to all of us in the privacy field. I continue to reference her book on a regular basis. I was delighted when she agreed to write the foreword for my book.

I would like to thank Mike Gurski, Eric Fredericksen, J. D. Meier, Joel Rosenblatt, Len Sassaman, Mark Ellis, Peter Wayner, Rick Kingslan, Stefan Brands, Steve Riley, and other unnamed reviewers for spending time reviewing my book.

Karen Gettman, of Addison-Wesley, deserves special praise for sticking with me after the many slipped schedules and not-so-positive reviews. I would also like to thank Elizabeth Zdunich and Amy Fleischer for responding to my many questions on how to put this book together. I am deeply indebted to Ronald Petrusha who spent a great deal of time helping me with the final review of my book. I would like to thank Christy Hackerd and Keith Cline for performing the copyediting. I would also like to thank the many other people of Addison-Wesley who assisted with the production of this book.

On a personal note, I want to thank my wife Renée, and my friends Reggie Brown and LaVonne Vaskevitch for consoling me after some of the long nights working on my book. Having the support of your family and friends is invaluable on any important endeavor.

About the Author

J. C. Cannon is a privacy strategist in the Corporate Privacy Group at Microsoft. He works as a technical strategist for the team, focusing on ways to apply technology to applications that will give consumers better control over their privacy and enable developers to create privacy-aware applications. J. C. works closely with Microsoft product groups and Microsoft research, and gives presentations to developers from other companies on building privacy in to their applications. Prior to this role, J. C. was a program manager for Active Directory for two and a half years. In this role, he worked with developers and independent software vendors on integration strategies for Active Directory and applications. He has written several white papers on Active Directory integration, which are on MSDN, and has given presentations on Active Directory integration techniques at major Microsoft conferences.

Before coming to Microsoft in 1998, he spent ten years as a software consultant helping companies integrate Microsoft technologies into their applications and businesses. Previous to becoming a consultant, J. C. worked as a software developer for companies in the United States, England, France, and Sweden. J. C. started his career in software in 1979 after ending his six-year career in the U.S. Navy, where he fixed avionics for A6 aircraft. Three of those years were spent working on the flight deck of aircraft carriers. J. C. received his Bachelor of Science degree in mathematics from the University of Texas at Dallas.

Contents at a Glance

Table of Contents

Dedication

To Davon and Dakar hoping you will always pursue your dreams and to Reneé who helped me find mine.

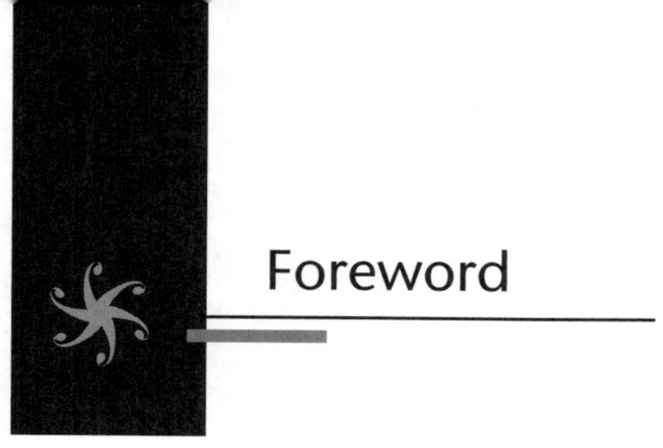

Foreword

Dr. Ann Cavoukian

Historically, technology has taken the form of a double-edged sword. Opinions regarding its potential benefits have ranged from Luddite distrust to nerdish enthusiasm. But taken as a whole, technology has largely facilitated the greater well-being of society. The exceptions have occurred when insufficient care was taken in understanding a technology's potential dangers and, accordingly, minimizing the negatives while maximizing the positive features of a particular application.

The world is now changing dramatically as a result of advances in technology. Its unparalleled adoption in both the public and private sectors is raising heightened concerns, particularly in the areas of the collection and management of personal information. The use of personal information can provide great benefits, including improved services for customers and increased revenues and decreased costs for businesses; it can, at the same time, raise unwanted externalities for individuals in the misuse of their personal information and loss of privacy. We are witnessing what could be characterized as a growing societal angst regarding this concomitant loss of privacy. Survey after survey finds that individuals, in both their capacity as citizens and consumers, wish to preserve their privacy and are exercising some form of control over information relating to themselves. Increasingly, people are making their decisions based on an equation of trust and will pursue various avenues of recourse if their trust is abused. That equation, simply stated, is: demonstrate trust, and maintain the lifelong value of the customer; break trust, and lose the customer.

That trust will inevitably be tested in the management and control of one's personal information. For the most part, organizations have concluded that a commitment to respecting people's privacy through sound privacy policies makes good business sense and ensures compliance with the privacy laws that may affect their organizations. However, the privacy functionality of a technology that is used to collect and manage personal information is the ultimate acid test of trust. And this is the Achilles' heel for many organizations.

Unfortunately, unlike Achilles, organizations tend to ignore this vulnerability and may be doomed to suffer the consequences. J.C. Cannon gives enough examples throughout his book, *Privacy: What Developers and IT Professionals Should Know*, to focus one's attention on the privacy meltdown that results when technology does not live up to a company's stated privacy policy. To reduce this vulnerability, I have long advocated for the concept of privacy by design—the need for privacy to be designed into an information management system, right from the beginning. Certainly, designing privacy functionalities into a system can indeed be a daunting task for the uninitiated. What is needed is a defined development process, as well as examples of databases that have accomplished the task of building in privacy, whether by including privacy enhancing features or through privacy solutions that manage the data from the code level up. Only then, when those things are established, can a developer or organization successfully build privacy into their technology solutions. Part III of this book fills the current void by providing the necessary detail required for a developer to actually build privacy into a given technology.

Privacy Enhancing Technologies

Privacy Enhancing Technologies (PETs) are at a crossroads. To date, apart from some research activity and a few trial balloons, PETs have not gone mainstream. Conventional thinking on this can be summed up in two words, *nullus prettii*—no commercial potential. However, nothing could be further from the truth—it all depends on your perspective. PETs can play a vital role for both governments and businesses wishing to gain and maintain the trust that is so vital to their respective enterprises. PETs can provide the backbone for an ongoing trust relationship with both citizens and customers. Then why, you might ask, hasn't this backbone developed yet?

The challenge for the PETs breakthrough in the area of commercial applications is twofold. In order for an organization to focus on developing or using PETs, a basic understanding of privacy is necessary. While this has presented a significant barrier in the past, I am pleased to report that this no longer appears to be the case. However, when it comes to implementing the privacy controls available today, technology often creates its own barriers of usability and lack of privacy functionality. It is not uncommon to be baffled by how to use or simply turn on a privacy feature. Part I of this book, entitled "Privacy for Everyone," provides a good look under the hood of some of these technologies and a critical examination from a privacy perspective of Microsoft Windows, the dominant operating system for the foreseeable future. In addition, thanks to this book's extensive list of links and very clear descriptions, the reader can easily find the major and minor technologies and solutions that have privacy-enhancing or protective functionalities.

The second challenge for PETs is that organizations must first internalize a set of privacy "mantras," as Cannon calls them. They bear repeating here:

- Provide prominent disclosure
- Put users in charge of their data
- Seek anonymity
- Recognize that less is more when it comes to collecting and managing personal information

These are some of the cardinal rules that an organization must implement with a fair degree of rigor and commitment. Lip service just won't do it any longer.

At this juncture, most books on privacy draw a number of insightful privacy conclusions regarding legislation, policy, communication, education, and commitment. What few books have done to date is walk developers through the necessary steps to actually build privacy functionalities into the solutions they are expected to deliver. Cannon's book goes the extra mile and accomplishes this goal, fulfilling a service that is critically needed. It is especially Part III, "Privacy and the Developer," that will become thumb-worn by the technology experts who will be well positioned to put the information to good and practical use. Optimally, Part III will act as a catalyst to help introduce PETs, or their equivalent functionalities, into the mainstream of technology solutions. Thus the reason why this book is so very important—it may just succeed in nudging PETs into the mainstream, in which case, we all win.

Read this book and profit.

Dr. Cavoukian is the Information & Privacy Commissioner of Ontario and the co-author of two books on privacy, *The Privacy Payoff: How Successful Businesses Build Customer Trust* and *Who Knows: Safeguarding Your Privacy in a Networked World.*

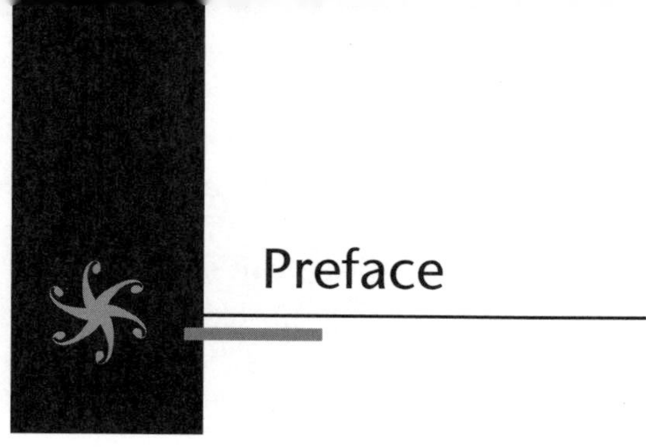

Preface

"Is it secret? Is it safe?"
GANDALF TO FRODO
LORD OF THE RINGS, THE FELLOWSHIP OF THE RING

The movie *Marathon Man* contains a scene in which the protagonist is tied to a chair and being asked over and over again "Is it safe?" He doesn't know how to answer the question and starts to squirm when the interrogator takes out a set of dental tools and walks toward him. This is the discomfort that many consumers feel when considering whether to complete an online form or download software from the Internet. Not knowing whether it is safe to share your information or use technology can be frustrating. There should be no ambiguity when it comes to a person's safety. It should be clear what will happen to a person's data when clicking the Submit button on a form or dialog. You should be able to trust that the new software you installed on your computer won't take data from your computer and send it across the Internet.

When a dentist is looking in your mouth or a mechanic is looking under the hood of your car, do you wonder whether they are looking for their next Porsche payment or trip to Hawaii? Do you wish there were an easy way to trust their intentions? In the same manner, you probably wish there were an easy way to trust the privacy statement that is obtained from a Web site or the end-user license agreement from an application before you used them. You should not have to feel obliged to perform a Google search before trusting a company.

The term *solutions*, as used throughout this book, refers to applications, tools, software services, interactive Web pages, and any other products created with a programming or script language. I don't want anyone to think that I am focusing on only a specific type of technology or platform to provide answers to today's privacy issues.

This book will help you learn to use technologies that will help you protect your privacy and to build solutions that can help protect the privacy of others. More than that, you will learn to build your own privacy infrastructure to permit the creation of trustworthy software and services and help you respond effectively to privacy incidents.

Disclaimer

I currently work at Microsoft in their Corporate Privacy Group. Most of what I know about privacy and much of the technology discussed in this book I learned while working there and with other groups at Microsoft during my six-year tenure. However, the opinions expressed in this book are entirely mine and the other contributors to this book, not those of Microsoft. Although many of the practices described in this book come from Microsoft practices, there are subtle differences between some of the practices described here and the ones followed at Microsoft. I even included descriptions of technology from companies other than Microsoft to give you a broader view of the privacy technologies that exist today.

My focus on Microsoft technologies in this book is not a statement that they are the only means or best means for developing privacy solutions; it is only indicative of the fact that I spent more than 15 years working on those technologies.

The information provided in this book should not be considered legal advice. Any practices that might affect the image of your company or that could expose you to litigation should not be implemented without consultation from your company's executive and legal departments.

Organization of the Book

The book consists of three parts, each with its own specific focus. Although all readers will benefit from reading the entire book, some readers may want to concentrate on areas that are of greatest interest to them.

Part I is *Privacy for Everyone*. It provides an overview of privacy, which will assist readers with understanding privacy policy, privacy-invasive and privacy-enhancing technologies, and protecting oneself from privacy intrusions.

Part II is *Privacy and the Organization*. It gives instruction on how to build a privacy organization, which looks at selecting personnel, getting training, and evangelizing privacy throughout the company. This part also looks at building a privacy response center to respond to privacy issues that might arise in a company.

Chapters 4 through 9 discuss issues that are important to consumers in protecting their privacy online. Consumers will learn about ways to protect themselves from spam, how to use P3P, and about privacy-invasive technologies.

Part III is *Privacy and the Developer*. This part goes into more technical topics that will be of interest to developers building privacy-enhancing technologies and companies looking to include privacy awareness into the way products are built. The Platform for Privacy Preferences Project is discussed along with protecting database data. This part includes a couple of sample applications that provide instruction on how to use role-based access control to protect access to data based on the category of the data and the role of the user wanting to access the data.

I Privacy for Everyone

1 An Overview of Privacy

To be invisible will be my claim to fame...
A man with no name
CURTIS MAYFIELD

Mary walked along the Champ de Mars on the evening of July 14th hoping to get a closer look at the festivities. However, as she squeezed through the crowds, Mary could feel her demophobia about to get the best of her. The multitude of eyes watching her as she crossed the grounds began to pierce her skin. The rockets whizzing past her head exacerbated the situation for her and at times left her frozen with fear. If only she could be invisible and enjoy the evening in peace, she would have felt much more comfortable. Eventually, she returned home to watch the remainder of the event from a site on the Internet, not realizing that there were many more people watching her than there had been when she was walking along the Champ de Mars. The dilemma of maintaining one's privacy while interacting with the outside world affects us all. No matter how well we disguise ourselves, it's not quite like being invisible. True privacy permits a person to be effectively invisible whether one is in public or surfing a site on the Internet.

We live in a world surrounded by technology—technology that has the potential to watch our every move. However, when we surf around the Internet, run applications, and use the latest technology, we are unable to feel the normal eeriness one feels from being watched, due to the detached state in which technology places us. When someone watches you electronically, it's not easy to discover the culprit. Taking a quick look around does not expose the surveillance activity. After being exposed electronically, one does not usually find out that his or her privacy has been invaded until long after the intruder has absconded with yet another identity, set of secret documents, or sensitive information that one would rather not become public. Eventually a notification is received in the mail or by a call from a financial institution.

Who's Watching Our Data?

When using an application, you do not think about someone looking over your shoulder as you type. When you are surfing the Internet, think about being at a Rolling Stones concert where you are walking among thousands of people. At any point in time, someone could see what you are doing and listen to what you are saying. It is even possible that someone may get close enough to lift something from your pocket. Using your computer online is a lot like that. Think of the Internet service provider (ISP) that you use for e-mail and Internet access. They must certainly keep logs of Internet traffic, typically for tuning, performance monitoring, and in some cases forensics; and this is where privacy issues can come into play. How much do you know about what they are logging? They also make periodic backups of their systems to permit them to recover from catastrophic failures. These backups are sure to include your e-mails, files that you may have attached to the e-mails, your Web site files, and anything else you may be keeping on their servers. Do you think any of the administrators get bored some nights and browse through the files that they are there to protect, maybe on occasion even making a copy of something juicy they find?

Now that you understand the exposure that exists at your ISP, what about all the people and institutions to which you send e-mails? They all probably use ISPs that log information and have their *own* internal servers that store data. Each one of these places has system administrators who are responsible for the data that is transmitted and stored in their companies. Think of the thousands of people that your data electronically passes by every day. Think of all the possibilities for a poorly written program, poor security, and bad practices to cause your sensitive information to be exposed to the world. If this scares you, it should. Browsing through a file, searching a database, or monitoring data going across a network cable is pretty simple with today's technology.

Browsing the Internet and using e-mail programs are just a couple of the many technologies that we expose ourselves to almost every day. There are literally thousands of applications in use today on many platforms, some being provided to us by unscrupulous people and some by well-meaning companies with employees who are doing things of which the companies are unaware. We would probably be surprised if we knew what was really happening behind the scenes. In some ways, applications are just too complex for their own good. It's this complexity that can cause us to let our guard down when it comes to protecting our data. Notepad and Paint are two programs that do a great job, and they are simple enough that we don't have to worry about what is happening behind the scenes.

Some financial packages and image-editing programs have so many features that it's hard to keep track of which ones are activated. If all you want to do is keep your checkbook balanced or print color pictures from your digital camera, you shouldn't have to worry about features that may be communicating with the Internet. Let's take a look at some more notable applications and what may not be so obvious to you.

Technologies That Communicate with the Internet

Developing software solutions today requires a special sensitivity to consumers' desire to be in control of their personal data. When consumers use your solutions, they should feel there are no hidden features that are exposing their information. There should be adequate controls to protect their personal data, usage patterns, and browsing habits. In addition, privacy controls and risks should be prominently disclosed before a user starts to use an application. Failure to explicitly consider privacy issues can have undesirable consequences. Windows XP and Windows Media Player 8 were the subject of several negative news articles, mostly because consumers were not adequately informed of the privacy risks and how to control them. Some time after the release of Windows XP, Microsoft allayed the fears of administrators by producing a white paper that explained all the features of Windows XP that communicate with the Internet and how they could be managed.[1] A similar paper was created for Windows 2000.[2] The white paper for Windows Server 2003 was available at the time the operating

1. The paper, "Using Windows XP Professional with Service Pack 1 in a Managed Environment," can be found at http://www.microsoft.com/technet/prodtechnol/winxppro/maintain/xpmanaged/00_abstr.asp.

2. http://www.microsoft.com/downloads/details.aspx?FamilyID=b27e5699-d9c9-4573-ae5b-5904d51a523a&displaylang=en

system was released.[3] When Windows Media Player 9 was released, it was lauded[4] for its vast improvement in providing consumers with clear ability to control privacy settings.

Did you know that when you use certain applications, such as RealOne Player,[5] Microsoft Word 2003,[6] and Quicken 2003,[7] you are sometimes sending information to the Internet? For example, the information you seek help on and the media to which you are listening? These applications can also download information from the Internet and place it on your computer. Every time you place a CD in your player to listen to music or insert a DVD to watch a movie, RealOne Player will optionally enhance the experience by providing details about what you are listening to and watching. Isn't it nice to have the album cover displayed and each track listed when you play a CD? What you may not realize is that you have to inform RealOne Player's Web site about the titles of your content before the background information can be downloaded. Microsoft Word uses the Internet to find the most current information in response to searches you initiate using help or the Clip Art tool. Quicken can transfer your account information and help you track your investments. However, in each of these cases you are potentially sending sensitive information to the Internet. Even if each of the companies that collect this data has the most rigorous security procedures and privacy policies in place, they are only as good as the people who execute them.

In each of these cases, you have the power to control how these applications communicate with the Internet. Make it a point to investigate the privacy settings of the applications you use. Sadly, these settings aren't always easy to find. RealOne Player calls them Internet settings. On the Microsoft Office XP version of Word's Security dialog, a privacy section

---

3. http://www.microsoft.com/downloads/details.aspx?FamilyID=d217e2ff-6871-404d-9931-c13ab669766f&displaylang=en

4. Joe Wilcox, "Microsoft puts privacy policy on display," August 27, 2002, CNET News.com.

5. Find out what data RealOne Player sends to the Internet at http://www.real.com/products/player/more_info/moreinfo.html?ID=317&DC=Unk&LANG=en&PN=RealOne%20Player&PV=6.0.11.830&PT=Free&OS=Win&CM=&CMV=&LS=&RE=&RA=&RV=.

6. Find out what data Microsoft Word 2003 sends to the Internet at http://office.microsoft.com/assistance/preview.aspx?AssetID=HP010499591033&CTT=4&Origin=CH010393691033.

7. Find out what data Quicken 2003 sends to the Internet by selecting the Privacy Statement item under the Help menu when running Quicken.

helps you clear metadata from your document. However, to control how Microsoft Word communicates with the Internet is much harder. This control is much improved in Microsoft Word 2003. Quicken 2003 has online services embedded into almost every feature that comes with the application. Trying to get a good understanding of what it is doing would be a daunting task for a financial expert, let alone the typical consumer. At least it has an easy-to-find privacy statement beneath the Help menu, something most applications don't have.

I think that companies and developers may somehow have a hard time visualizing why privacy awareness would be worthy of more than a cursory investigation. For security vulnerabilities, the goal is to protect users from attackers trying to exploit them. This is a noble cause because the damage produced by these types of issues has cost companies and individuals a great deal of time and money. With privacy vulnerabilities, it is more about protecting users from the application itself. For example, think about the data that is collected by the applications you use on a daily basis. Is the application sending this data across the Internet? Is there an easy way to protect or clear this data? If you are still having a hard time conceptualizing what a true privacy issue might look like in the news, perform a Google search for the article "Microsoft Word Bytes Tony Blair in the Butt."

Investigating Applications

Above I provided examples of applications that could send your data to the Internet. There are many more. Before using an application, read over its privacy statement. If there isn't one, demand one from the creator of the application. Although a privacy statement can't ensure that an application will honor it, you will at least have recourse if you are misled. One other thing you can look for is the application's privacy settings and a description of how to use them. Also Google the application to see what people are saying about it.

Make sure that the Web sites you visit have a privacy statement and have implemented the specification defined by the Platform for Privacy Preferences Project (P3P).[8] P3P provides a quick way for your browser to evaluate the privacy policy of a Web site. P3P is covered in detail in Chapter 9.

---

8. The home page for the Platform for Privacy Preferences Project is http://www.w3.org/P3P/. The P3P specification can be found at http://www.w3.org/TR/P3P/.

To determine whether a Web site has integrated P3P, in IE 6.0 select the View menu and pick the Privacy Report command. On the Privacy Report dialog, select a Web site and click the Summary button. If a privacy statement displays, P3P has been at least partially implemented. In Netscape 7.0, select the View menu and pick the Page Info command. On the Page Info dialog, select the Privacy tab and click the Summary button. A privacy statement should display if P3P has been at least partially implemented.

I don't want to mislead you into thinking that a privacy statement or P3P integration automatically makes a Web site or a company safe. Companies can use misleading language, change their policy after collecting your data, or just lie about their data handling practices. Even if a company is committed to protecting your privacy, there could always be an individual at the company who might go against corporate policy and steal your information or release it to a third party inappropriately.[9] If a company posts a privacy statement on their Web site or uses P3P to express their privacy policy, and if a consumer is harmed because of a violation of that privacy policy, the consumer may pursue legal means for restitution (and stands a good chance of winning if the privacy policy is subsequently found to be misleading or incorrect). When I state that a consumer can be harmed, I mean that the consumer's privacy could be violated by unwanted contact or by having his or her identity stolen, which could lead to financial loss.

When you are out in public, you can take precautions to protect yourself. You can wear a disguise to protect your identity, use a cell phone with encryption capabilities to protect your conversations, or hire a bodyguard to keep people away from you. However, what does one do to acquire that same level of protection when running an application, sending an e-mail, or visiting Web sites?

This is one of the many questions this book answers, not only for users of applications, but also for developers of applications. Just as solution providers have a responsibility to deliver reliable, secure solutions, they should also be concerned with solutions that assist in the protection of user privacy. This can be done through encryption, security settings, spam filters, and other means. Sometimes all a user requires is conspicuous disclosure so that at a minimum it will be clearly understood what data about the user is being collected and how it is being used.

9. Ryan Singel, "JetBlue shared passenger data," Wired News, September 18, 2003.

Defining Privacy

The term *privacy*, at the most rudimentary level, is about complying with a person's desires when it comes to handling his or her personal information. That is, it refers to the right of individuals (e.g., consumers or business partners) to determine if, when, how, and to what extent data about themselves will be collected, stored, transmitted, used, and shared with others. This includes their right to browse the Internet or use applications without being tracked unless permission is granted in advance. It also includes the right to be left alone.

Even pseudonymous tracking can be an issue if there is a possibility the tracking information could be correlated with other more sensitive data. For example, a globally unique identifier (GUID) used to track a user could be associated with the same IP address used to collect the user's e-mail address at another site. If you are able to identify the owner of the data that you are collecting based on examining the data, then it is not truly anonymous. A good example of this is anonymous surveys that a lot of companies conduct. For example, suppose a survey asks for your ethnicity and you are the only Native American at the company being surveyed; in this case, the survey isn't anonymous for you. A famous printer company got in trouble with the German government for collecting so-called anonymous data without the users' permission. In this case, users would fill out the registration information, which included the printer serial number. Each of the printers would occasionally send information back to the company on its usage habits. Because both sets of data included the serial number, they were both deemed to be personal information because they could be correlated. Even though the data was stored in different databases and never referenced against each other, the fact that they could be correlated was enough for the German government to force the company to change this data usage practice.

Direct marketing companies and phone solicitors are now forced to consult a national do-not-call database before phoning people these days. It is pretty serious when the government has to create an enormous system just to keep people from calling you. The same mechanism is being planned for spammers. Many spammers are finding themselves being dragged into court and paying hefty fines for sending unsolicited e-mails.[10] Companies are making a fortune creating software and systems to stop you from receiving e-mail you don't want. Who would ever have thought that blocking e-mail

10. Margaret Kane, "EarthLink wins spammer suit," CNET News.com, July 19, 2002.

would become a cottage industry? Let's throw in software that permits you to browse the Web and send e-mail anonymously and, of course, software that stops popup ads from appearing; you probably would have scoffed at the ideas of investing in these ideas a few years ago, but perhaps now you wish you had paid more attention to them.

Answering the Call for Privacy

The need for privacy can be understood, even though its definition sometimes eludes us. More and more, privacy affects how we do business. It used to be that being vigilant about taking the credit card carbons after making a purchase was enough. Now there is almost a fear about using online technology that was to be a boon to the way we live our lives. This fear is affecting online business in a negative way. If you saw the movies *Enemy of the State* or *Minority Report*, you probably noticed a lot of cool technology that would be great to share among family and friends. However, having those advanced technologies without safeguards in place could put us in more of an Orwellian society than an age of infinite possibilities. Every new technology seems to come with a caveat that we are often too busy or naïve to comprehend. For technology, maybe privacy just means coming with a leave-me-alone button.

In each of the cases where unwanted contact is viewed as an annoyance, simply informing users of your intent before collecting user data or contacting them could mitigate privacy concerns. For example, suppose you are at home and about to sit down for dinner when you notice someone walking around in your backyard poking at the ground with a stick. You open the sliding glass door leading to your backyard and yell out, "Excuse me, can you tell me what you are doing in my yard?" He replies, "Don't mind me, I'm just checking your yard for moles." At this point, you are not sure whether you should call the police or just toss him out yourself. Then your spouse interrupts you, "Honey, I forgot to tell you that I called someone to come by today and find out what those mounds in our backyard are." With that explanation, you close the door and sit down to dinner. How would you have felt if, before you looked out the window, your spouse had remembered to tell you that an inspector would be in your backyard? You would probably have felt a lot more comfortable about seeing him.

This is the level of disclosure that solution providers and application developers need to provide if they want customers to feel comfortable using their solutions. The simple act of informing customers in clear language of your intentions with regard to data usage can lower barriers to sales and clear the air of any feelings of distrust. If the phone call, e-mail, or knock at the door is expected, you will be much more successful at building a network of loyal customers. So the question is how does one ensure that the technologies one is building or the systems that are being pulled together from multiple technologies are being created in a way that does not diminish consumer trust? What standards or practices exist to make it easier to build trustworthy solutions, and what is the best way to integrate them into your current business practices?

That is the essence of this book; looking at privacy-fortifying technologies and practices and investigating positive ways in which to develop, deploy, and use them. We will look at ways to build a company that is viewed as trustworthy and that delivers products that can be trusted. As a consumer, you will become more aware of the privacy-invasive technologies that exist and how to better shield yourself from them—and better yet, how to use them in a way that is beneficial to you. The thought of people using hidden tracking devices might seem inappropriate to you. However, when they help you find a lost pet, you can see the value in them. If you are able to control who has access to the tracking data, the technology turns into an enabling one rather than an invasive one.

The Path to Trustworthiness

The path to trustworthiness is a long one. Don't expect to be able to instantly stop the way you develop solutions and start cranking out technology that consumers will just embrace with open arms. It takes time to build trust, so be patient. Resist the urge to make a big announcement about becoming a company that people can trust; just become one. Think of a restaurant that you frequent on occasion. The food and service are mediocre, but it's close by and cheap, so you tolerate the less-than-perfect conditions. Then one day you go to the restaurant and notice a sign on the door that says, "From now on, we are going start providing good service and delicious food." So you walk in the door a bit excited and notice that the food and service are about the same. How do you feel about the place now, the same or a little worse? You would probably stop going altogether. What if you went there one day and were greeted at the door by name, and the meatloaf that you order occasionally was better than Mom used to make? In this case, wouldn't you want to start telling your friends about the place?

Building software and services people can trust doesn't just help you, it also helps the industry as a whole. The more people trust the systems that they use, the more they will use them. Or as Barbara Lawler, Hewlett-Packard's Chief Privacy Officer, put it, "The stronger the trust, the stronger the customer relationship. And the stronger the relationship, the stronger the bottom line."[11] Likewise, the more that you complain about bad practices, the greater impact you will have on changing the products that companies produce. Look at all the applications coming out with antispam features and parental controls. Almost every Web site has a privacy statement now. You probably didn't even notice that browsers have integrated P3P.

Regardless of our relationship to computer technology, we all have a role to play in advancing the cause of privacy. As developers, we have a responsibility to build solutions that enable consumers to protect their privacy. As IT administrators, we should scrutinize solutions that are being deployed in our enterprise. As consumers, we should be less tolerant of technologies that aren't privacy-aware. If you go to the Help menu of an application and there is no selection for a privacy statement (and if a privacy statement is not easy to find), send an e-mail to the president of the company asking for a copy of the privacy statement.

The Privacy Mantras

Throughout this book, I point out some phrases that developers and administrators should take on as privacy mantras. Repeating these mantras as you interact with customers, build solutions, create Web sites, or create corporate policy will help you become a better advocate for privacy. Consumers should feel that the companies with which they do business support these mantras. They are as follows:

- **Provide prominent disclosure**—Let your customers know what data you collect, store, and share about them in a clear and transparent fashion.
- **Put users in charge of their data**—Users should be able to control how data about them is used. Extend that control to parents and employers where appropriate.

11. Beth Negus Viveiros, "TRUST=REVENUE," Direct, May 15, 2002.

- **Seek anonymity**—Look for ways to reduce the amount of identifiable information that you collect and track.
- **Less is more**—Continually minimize the information that you collect, store, and share. Extend this concept across your company.

Valuing Privacy

As the reader of this book, you probably understand the importance of privacy. But how do you get an entire company to value privacy? It can be extremely difficult in a company that is dependent on customer data for its survival. However, all companies have a code of ethics by which they govern themselves. Many of them have "The customer comes first" as an important tenet. If that is true, then valuing a customer's privacy should naturally be an extension of that tenet. It's then a matter of getting executives to adopt "valuing privacy" as an important company value and encouraging all employees to take on the responsibility to support it. This adoption is what will engender a visible change in your company's practices. Wouldn't it be great to hear an analyst or journalist say about your company, "Valuing privacy is more than their policy; it's the way they do business."

As Ann Cavoukian says very well in her book *The Privacy Payoff*, "Failure to proactively embrace sound privacy practices is risky at best. First and foremost customers expect the protection of their personal information, and when those expectations are not met, they will take their business elsewhere." From this observation, you can see how valuing privacy adds to the bottom line, which is why most companies are in business in the first place.

Conclusion

If you are a technologist looking to build privacy-aware or privacy-enhancing technologies, this book will give you the background and guidance you need to get started and lead you through your journey. This book is also beneficial to managers and executives who would like a better understanding of privacy technologies. The book covers privacy practices you should be following and those you should be avoiding when creating solutions that you want consumers to trust. There is information on building a product group and development processes with privacy in mind.

IT administrators will find helpful tips on how to manage privacy technologies in their enterprises. Chapter 4 is devoted to managing privacy for Microsoft products, which can be helpful to administrators and consumers. It covers the privacy settings for Windows XP, Windows Server 2003, Office 2003, and Windows Media Player 9. Consumers and privacy advocates alike will find a wealth of information here about what privacy technologies exist and how to use them.

Consumers may find the sections on privacy-invasive technologies a bit unnerving. Remember that these technologies can also provide great benefit. Where possible I include suggestions on how to protect yourself from privacy-invasive technologies. When a company has gone too far with regard to the invasion of your privacy, don't put up with it. Benetton and Wal-Mart[12] backed down from their decision to use tracking tags once the complaints started rolling in. And when they go back on their word, it causes bad press for them.[13]

References

If you are just getting started in privacy and would like to understand the history of privacy from a national and international viewpoint, privacy legislation, how privacy affects marketing and commerce, or how to develop a privacy organization and privacy practices for running your company, the book you want is *The Privacy Payoff*, by Ann Cavoukian, Ph.D., and Tyler J. Hamilton (McGraw-Hill Ryerson, 2003).

Another book that takes an in-depth look at international privacy legislation, tools, and process is *Privacy Handbook*, by Albert J. Marcella Jr., Ph.D., CISA, and Carol Stucki, CISA (John Wiley and Sons, Inc., 2003). Another important section of this book is the Country-by-Country Summary, which provides a brief description of privacy in 53 countries around the world.

12. Alorie Gilbert and Richard Shim, "Wal-Mart cancels 'smart shelf' trial," CNET News.com, July 9, 2003.

13. "Chipping away at your privacy," *Chicago Sun-Times*, November 9, 2003.

For consumers, especially parents, who spend a lot of time online browsing and purchasing items from Web sites, other privacy books can provide you with better guidance. If you are concerned about your online privacy and want a better understanding of what risks exist when browsing or purchasing online and how to protect yourself against them, a good book is *Protect Yourself Online*, by Matthew Danda (Microsoft Press, 2001).

2 The Importance of Privacy-Enhancing and Privacy-Aware Technologies

Privacy-enhancing technologies (PETs, not to be confused with the household variety) and privacy-aware technologies (PATs) are new concepts for most people. However, the term *PET* is not really new.[1] Not only is the term PET an established one, there are even workshops that focus on PETs.[2] At least one book has been written devoted to designing PETs.[3] Privacy-enhancing technologies are solutions whose specific purpose is to help consumers and companies to protect their privacy. It also includes those technologies that permit developers, solution providers, and service companies to add privacy enhancements to their solutions.

Privacy-aware technologies are standard non-privacy-related solutions that include features that enable users to protect their privacy. Passwords, file access security, communication inhibitor, and encryption are examples of privacy features that are added to many applications. These types of features, although important, usually are neglected during the design and subsequent development of applications.

1. The term Privacy-Enhancing Technology (PET) was coined by Dr. Ann Cavoukian, Information and Privacy Commissioner of Ontario, Canada, and Dr. John Joseph Borking, associate board member of the Dutch Data Protection Authority, in August 1995 in his paper "Privacy Enhancing Technologies: The Path to Anonymity."
2. Information on the yearly PET workshop can be found at http://petworkshop.org/.
3. Hannes Federrath (Ed.), "Designing Privacy Enhancing Technologies," Springer, ISBN: 3-540-41724-9.

The Goal of PATs and PETs: The Constant Pursuit of Anonymity

One of the main goals of privacy professionals should be the constant pursuit of anonymity for the people and data for which they are custodians. True privacy-enhancing technologies should aid custodians in this pursuit of anonymity. PETs should protect your identity, your actions, your data, and your destinations. Anonymity is not always possible, especially in scenarios where online purchases are involved. However, your mantra when creating PETs should be "seek anonymity."

There are many steps between full identity and anonymity, and PETs should help move you in the right direction. The following is a collection of characteristics that PATs and PETs help to partially realize. They will help you understand the different types of protection that can be found on the path toward anonymity.

- **Anonymity**—Anonymity is the state of being anonymous or virtually invisible; having the ability to operate online without being tracked. For example, you could spend all day browsing the Internet and the Web sites you visit would have no idea who you were or which computer you were using to access the Internet.
- **Pseudonymity**—Pseudonymity has characteristics similar to anonymity in that you are not identifiable, but you can be tracked through an alias or persona that you have adopted. Free mail services such as hotmail.com and juno.com can provide pseudonymity to their users.
- **Unlinkability**—This refers to the inability to link pieces of related information. This could mean isolating multiple transactions made using the same credit card or medical treatments from the patient requesting the treatments. The ability to link transactions could give a stalker an idea of your daily habits or an insurance company an idea of how much alcohol your family consumes over a month. Using a one-time credit card number for each one could minimize linkability. Treatment isolation could occur by purchasing treatments in advance using cash and then getting access to treatments using an anonymous treatment card.
- **Unobservability**—This refers to the inability to be observed or tracked while you are accessing a service or browsing the Internet. Anonymous Web services permit you to browse the Internet without being tracked.

- **Address privacy**—When you connect to the Internet you are assigned an IP address, which can be used to track and contact you. Even if you are assigned a dynamic IP address every time you connect to the Internet, your Internet service provider's (ISP) logs can be used to track which IP address was assigned to you. Using an anonymous service can mitigate this issue.
- **Location privacy**—When accessing location-based services or requesting mapping information, your location can be deduced based on the location of your mobile device or the address you are requesting on a map. Check with your mobile service provider to determine whether you can set your privacy settings to keep from being tracked on your mobile device.
- **Authorization privacy**—To gain access to a sports club, users are often required to have a membership. This can be used to track how often a member uses the facilities, even though it is important only to know that the bearer deserves access to the facility. In the same manner, grocery stores should not need to know your name in order for loyalty cards to be beneficial to the store. Service providers should be able to permit pseudonymous access to their services.

Privacy-Enhancing Technologies

PETs serve a similar purpose as blinds on windows, a mask on robbers, and the bank where you keep your money. For the most part, they are designed to protect you online, but there are some that permit you to protect yourself while you are working offline in circumstances where you are sharing a computer either at work or at home. The following section identifies some important PETs.

Anonymizers and Pseudonymizers

This section looks at different technologies and Web sites that permit you to surf the Internet anonymously or pseudonymously.[4]

4. A long list of publications dating back to 1981 that cover various ways in which you can protect your identity and information when communicating electronically can be found at http://freehaven.net/anonbib/.

Anonymous E-mail Sites

Several Web sites permit you to browse and send e-mail anonymously. For example, the following Web site will permit you to send an anonymous e-mail to someone at no cost: http://cyberatlantis.com/anonymous_email.php.

Most anonymous e-mail sites charge for the service. Some have the added benefit of being able to fake the return address so receivers of the e-mail will think that it came from someone else. Although this may protect the identity of the sender, it can expose innocent people to false accusations. In actuality these services are pseudonymizers because the service provider knows your identity:

- http://www.advicebox.com/
- http://www.sendfakemail.com/
- http://www.mutemail.com/
- http://www.iprive.com/imail.shtml

Several types of routing mechanisms permit anonymous Internet browsing and e-mail service. The following sections provide information about these mechanisms that can help you maintain your privacy while on the Internet.

Mix Networks

These types of networks are used to send anonymous messages from point A to point B using a predetermined route that incorporates several nodes. The message itself is encrypted using keys from each of the routes in turn so that only the last destination nodes can read the message, and each node is aware only of the nodes next to it in the chain. This prevents any observer from determining what is being transmitted or the source and destination of a message. An observer watching multiple nodes would not be able to track a message during low-traffic periods, because each node holds messages until several messages have been received and releases them in random order. The site http://www.anonymizer.com/ provides this type of anonymous service. The downside to using a mix network is that they are generally one-directional. Also, if a node is down, your message can get held up because all the nodes in your route won't know the final destination.

Onion Routing

Onion routing is the adaptation of a mix network to facilitate online applications. The packets with layered encryption are referred to as onions, and nodes are called onion nodes. Onion networks can support e-mail, HTTP, and FTP applications, among others. This type of service can be found at http://www.onion-router.net/.

Crowds

Crowds, as its name implies, is a type of routing that groups Web requests together into a crowd of sorts. The requests that are grouped come from a geographically diverse group of requests. When your request is finally delivered, it can be delivered by any number of people who are in the crowd. This prevents Web servers from determining the source of a specific request. One advantage that crowd routing has over mix routing is that each node knows the final destination of a message, so if a node goes down the message can be rerouted. Of course, this means that the mechanism is not as private as a mix network. You can find more information on crowd routing at http://www.research.att.com/projects/crowds/index.html.

JANUS Routing

JANUS routing is used to mask the identity of the receiving Web site. That is, the Internet address is known, but the server that hosts the site would not be known. This permits people to have Web servers whose identities are protected. All routing to and from the Web server goes through the JANUS service provider. The URL for the Web site and all page links are encrypted to hide the identity of the true links. The site http://www.rewebber.de/about/janus.php3.en provides information on the implementation of a JANUS service.

History-Clearing Tools

Almost every application you use these days keeps track of what you are doing to permit you to easily go back to a previous file or Web site. Netscape, Opera, and Internet Explorer browsers come with a clear-history feature. Applications such as Microsoft Word permit you to clear and adjust the size of the recently used file list. There are also tools that specialize in clearing your tracks. The site historykill.com named their site after their history-erasing tool.

Popup Blockers

Popup ads are ads that show up in a separate browser window when you are visiting or leaving an Internet site. Figure 2.1 is an example of a popup ad. Sometimes multiple ads display. Ironically, some of these ads come from companies that want to help you block the ads. A popup blocker prevents these ads from being displayed. These are considered PETs because they help prevent the invasion of your privacy by unwanted ads. You can get a sense of the importance of a technology by checking the number of returns from a Google search. Searching for "popup blocker" returned more than 50,000 results. Who would have figured that this would have turned into such a booming business?

The Avant browser blocks these popup ads, as does the IE6 browser that has been updated with Service Pack 2. Several tools can help you block annoying popup ads, too. A small sampling of the popup blocker tools that are out there include STOPzilla, PopSwat, AdShield, and Popup BeGone (see Figure 2.2 for a sample popup for popup blockers).

Antispam

For the most part, spam is unsolicited bulk advertising e-mail. Spam has to be one of the most annoying things about being online other than popup ads. Most Internet service providers, such as MSN and AOL, come with spam-blocking tools built in to their e-mail tools. You can also buy these tools separately and in packages (as listed below). Because this is such a big area, one whole chapter of this book focuses on spam. See Chapter 5 for more information about spam.

Figure 2.1 Popup ad from historykill.com

Popup Dialogs and the Messenger Service

Popup dialogs, such as the one in Figure 2.2, are different from the standard popup ads. They are displayed using the **net send** command. This is an old network command that was used to communicate between computers before e-mail or Internet Messenger existed. If you are getting these types of ads, it's because a program on the Internet is just executing **net send** commands against a range of IP addresses hoping to connect with an unprotected computer on the Internet. These messages are harmless, but annoying.

To see how displaying these dialogs works, go to the command line and enter **net send * "hello"**. You should see a dialog appear with the word hello in it. You can replace the asterisk with your IP address if you know it. To avoid this annoyance, disable the Messenger service. You can do this by bringing up the Services console by entering **services.msc** on the command line or in the Run dialog. Find the Messenger service, open its Properties dialog, and disable it. This will not affect your Internet Messenger application.

Spyware

Spyware is a type of devious software that monitors your browsing habits or steals information from your computer. Many of these applications merely display ads to you based on the Web sites that you visit. Although the ads can be annoying, what's more annoying is that many of these applications are not easy to remove. You can find a number of anti-spyware tools at http://www.spychecker.com/software/antispy.html.[5]

Figure 2.2 Popup dialog from byebyeads.com

5. http://www.spychecker.com/spyware.html

An abbreviated list of spyware, as indicated by the SimplyTheBest spyware site,[6] includes the following:

- Alexa
- BargainBuddy
- Cydoor
- Flyswat
- Gator
- Mattel Brodcast
- Morpheus
- Xupiter
- Windows Messenger Service

Cookie Managers

So what are cookies and why are they so troublesome? Cookies are small text files that are placed on your computer by a Web site. They permit you to store login information, preferences, and history information in order to improve the browsing experience for Web sites that you frequent. Cookies are owned by Web sites and can't be viewed by other Web sites, so in general they are harmless. The danger comes in when banner ads place a cookie on your computer. Because they can appear on any page at any Web site, the Web site for the banner ad is able to track every Web site you visit that has one of their ads. With the use of cookies, they are able to piece together an image of who you are and what you like. The Netscape, Opera, and Internet Explorer browsers all have cookie-management features. You can also buy separate tools such as the one offered by historykill.com that offer advanced features such as the following:

- Deletion of all history files, including index.dat, which is a file that contains your browsing history
- Deletion of temporary Internet files
- Clearing recent file lists
- Encryption and overwriting deleted files to prevent recovery

6. http://simplythebest.net/info/spyware.html

Secure File Deletion

One of the most overlooked sources of privacy vulnerabilities is from hard drives that are given away as part of old systems. Even government agencies have been guilty of leaking sensitive information by not properly destroying files contained in the hard drives of old systems. Deleting files, and even formatting drives, does not always sufficiently remove data from a hard drive. It typically requires special programs to securely remove data. You can find a list of deletion software at http://www.webattack.com/shareware/security/swerase.shtml.

Online Privacy Protection Suites

Several companies offer tools for protecting your online privacy and clearing your tracks to prevent colleagues and family from knowing where you have been. These run the gamut between free software with simple features to complex enterprise-ready packages. These packages include software for firewalls, spam prevention, file deletion, cookie management, popup ad blocking, history removal, and anonymous Web access. They can be found at the following URLs:

- http://download.com.com/2001-2017-0.html?tag=dir
- http://www.anonymizer.com/
- http://www.historykill.com/
- http://www.websitetrafficbuilders.com/internet-privacy-spyware-blocker-ghostsurf.htm
- http://www.thefreesite.com/anonymous_freebies/
- http://privacy.net/software/
- http://www.zeroknowledge.com/
- http://enterprisesecurity.symantec.com/content/productlink.cfm?EID=0
- http://www.mcafee.com/myapps/default.asp

Privacy-Aware Technologies

A privacy-aware technology, or PAT, is one that was designed, developed, and permits deployment with privacy in mind. This means that when a standard product is developed, not only are features for usability, performance, and security taken into account, but thought is also given to empowering consumers and companies by providing them with features that will help them protect their privacy and understand the privacy risks involved with using an application. For example, when you use the RealOne Player to play DVDs, information about what you are viewing could be sent to the real.com site. Not only should you be informed about this, but also there should be an easy way for you to avoid this transmission of data if it concerns you.

Every application being sold today should be a PAT. Even if there are no privacy risks to using an application, that should be clearly stated to users. The biggest concern that users have about using software is not knowing what is happening behind the scenes and how to control it. Consumers should have the ability to easily understand and manage all data that an application sends or receives. This section looks at why PATs are important and at the different types of privacy features that go into building PATs.

The Importance of Privacy-Aware Solutions

The cost of not taking privacy into account when building applications is too great to ignore. One survey shows that in 2001 online and offline retailers lost *$6.2 billion* in sales because of privacy issues.[7] A separate survey found that *64 percent* of consumers reported leaving a Web site they had been browsing because of privacy reasons.[8] Think about your own trepidation when it comes to using your credit card online or with a small retailer. You are not alone when it comes to being concerned about your online privacy. This concern spills into the use of applications. The power of the Internet has encouraged many developers to add Internet connectivity to their solutions, often times unknown to users. This can be disconcerting to users who have used these applications in the course of handling sensitive data. When development companies are not up front about data that might be exchanged with the Internet, consumers can lose trust in a company. A 2003 survey found that consumers are less likely to purchase software from a company they do not trust even if that software is cheaper and has better features than a similar one from a competitor.[9]

7. Survey by UCO Software, Inc. released November 7, 2001.

8. Survey by Culnan-Milne Survey on Consumers & Online Privacy Notices released December 2001.

9. A listing of privacy surveys can be found at http://www.privacyexchange.org/iss/surveys/surveys.html.

Finding Business Value in Privacy-Aware Solutions

So what is the business value of making privacy an integral part of building solutions? A privacy-aware solution doesn't necessarily encourage customers to purchase your product, but it can help remove barriers caused by privacy issues that might discourage product sales. It provides one more differentiator to set you apart from your competitors. Customers are more cautious these days about the applications they install. What you really want to do is remove any surprises. You want to avoid comments from your customers such as the following:

- I didn't know they were collecting my data.
- I didn't know they were doing that with my data.
- I didn't know I was agreeing to these e-mails or phone calls.
- I didn't know they were going to track me in that fashion.
- I didn't know they were storing history information.

These types of complaints can cause general distrust for your products and a decrease in customer loyalty. You want to prevent your customers from being surprised about what your solution is doing and avoid providing the media with ammunition for a future attack against your solution. Here are a few benefits to investing in privacy:

- Increases customer trust.
- Avoids negative articles from journalists.
- Avoids costly litigation caused by breaking privacy laws.
- Lowers barriers to sales by removing questionable features.
- Makes your product better at privacy than your competitors.
- In the end, it's all about selling more software

Privacy Features

Privacy features are what bring privacy awareness to a PAT. So what are examples of privacy features? In general, these are features that can assist your application in protecting its users' privacy. Privacy features can be used to inform and empower consumers when it comes to controlling their privacy. They let people know what is going on with regard to their privacy and enable them to make choices about how their data is handled or how they are tracked and contacted. The following is an abridged list of privacy features that you can implement:

- Privacy statement
- P3P integration

- Privacy settings
- Centralized privacy setting management
- Ability to view data to be transmitted
- Clear tracks and personal information
- Documentation of privacy-related data
- Unsubscribe feature
- Access control
- Encryption

Privacy Statement

Whenever you collect sensitive user information, it is critical to clearly disclose your intentions in a privacy statement. Every application, Web service, and Web site that you build should have a privacy statement that is easy to understand and easy to find. Web sites traditionally have a privacy link located at the bottom of the page that points to the privacy statement. Applications can have an online or offline privacy statement and make it accessible from a "Privacy Statement" menu item under the Help menu.

Privacy statements for an application can be online or offline. Creating an offline privacy statement for an application makes sense when you have a static privacy statement and your application is not required to be online to be used. Use an online privacy statement if the statement may be undergoing change and usage of the application requires it to be online anyway. In general, online statements are better because they make it easier to provide consumers with current information.

TRUSTe

TRUSTe is a consumer advocate company devoted to protecting consumer privacy. The TRUSTe site, http://truste.org/bus/pub_resourceguide.html, provides information on how to create a privacy statement.

P3P Integration

The Platform for Privacy Preferences Project (P3P) was developed by the World Wide Web Consortium (W3C) to permit Web sites to express their privacy policy in a way that was readable programmatically by P3P-enabled browsers and applications. P3P integration involves deploying two XML files to your Web site and placing a set of P3P codes into response headers. By adding P3P integration to your Web site, you can avoid privacy warnings displayed by P3P-enabled browsers when visitors come to your Web site. These warnings appear as an eye in the status bar of the Netscape and Internet Explorer browsers. The AT&T Privacy Bird is an add-on tool for Internet Explorer that chirps to indicate a Web site's level of privacy. See Chapter 6 for more detailed information on P3P.

Privacy Settings

Privacy settings permit users of your application to express their personal "privacy preferences." Where appropriate, create and document privacy settings for your application. For example, users can be permitted to indicate whether they wish to download background information on media they are watching, receive marketing e-mails, or have troubleshooting information sent from their computer. Adding these settings to your application puts users in charge of their information and their privacy.

Make the settings easy to find. Many of the newer applications have had a privacy tab added to the Properties dialog. Figure 2.3 shows the Privacy tab located on the Netscape 7.0 Preferences dialog.

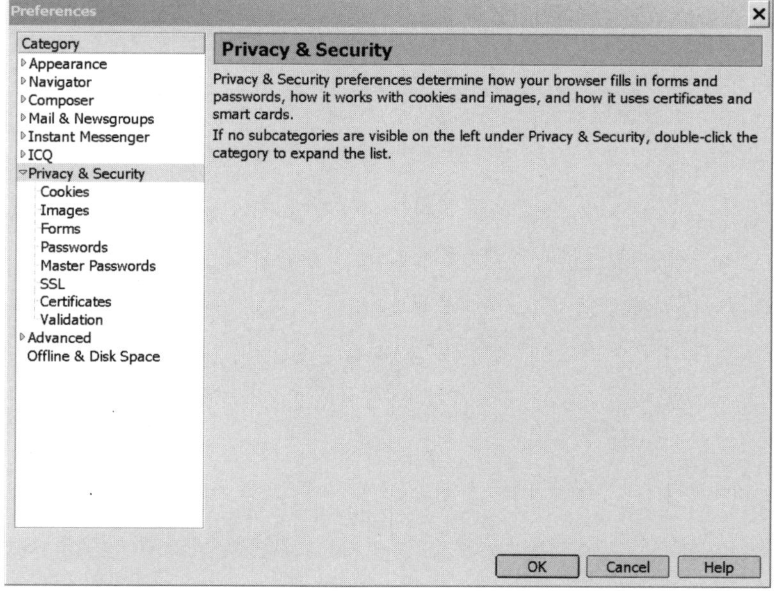

Figure 2.3 Netscape 7.0 Privacy tab

You can also provide quick access to privacy settings by providing a separate command for displaying a privacy settings dialog. For example, add a command that provides access to a privacy report dialog under the Help menu, as shown in Figure 2.4.

How and when privacy settings are presented can be very important and can even increase end-user trust. Windows Media Player 9 Series introduced a new per-user "first-run" paradigm for its privacy settings. Rather than wait until a user discovers the settings in a nested menu, the settings are presented to each user the first time he or she launches Windows Media Player. Reviewers touted the new privacy experience. For example, the *Washington Post* said "[The player has] a refreshingly clear explanation of your privacy options and no sneaky attempts to spam you with marketing pop-ups ... [other software developers] could learn from this." Figure 2.5 shows the Windows Media Player 9 Series per-user "first-run" privacy experience dialog.

Previously we looked at cases where an application collects information on behalf of the application. What if a service provider uses your application to collect information from its customers? Say you are building a customer relationship management application. The service provider using your application will probably collect contact information from its customers. How will the service provider determine whether these customers want to receive e-mail? By adding privacy settings to your application, you permit the service provider to store their customers' privacy preferences with its customers' contact information, which saves them from having to create a separate database.

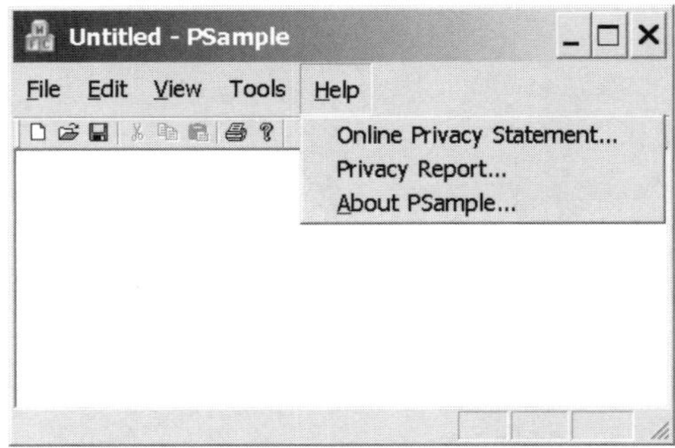

Figure 2.4 An example of a privacy settings command

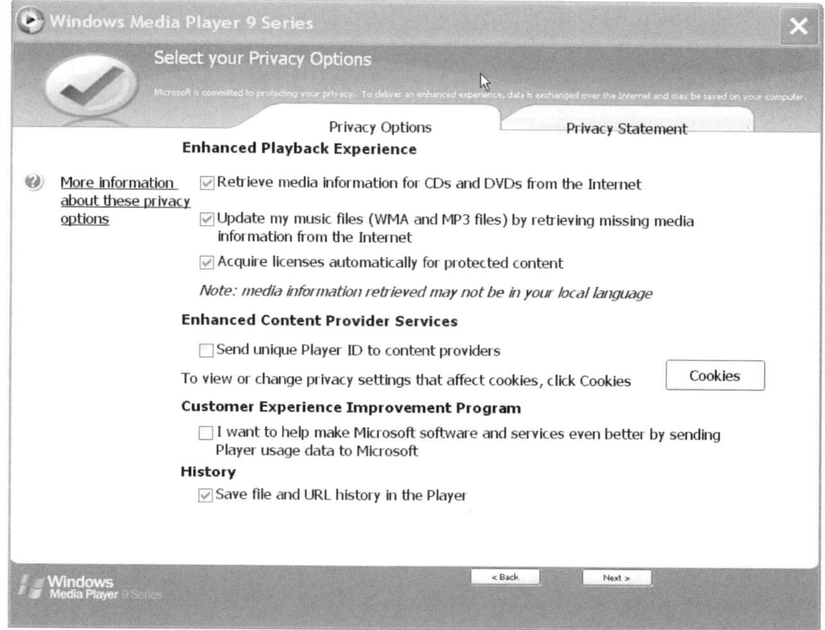

Figure 2.5 Windows Media Player 9 privacy setup dialog

The dialog in Figure 2.6 offers an example of the types of privacy settings that you could add to your application to be completed by end users of your application.

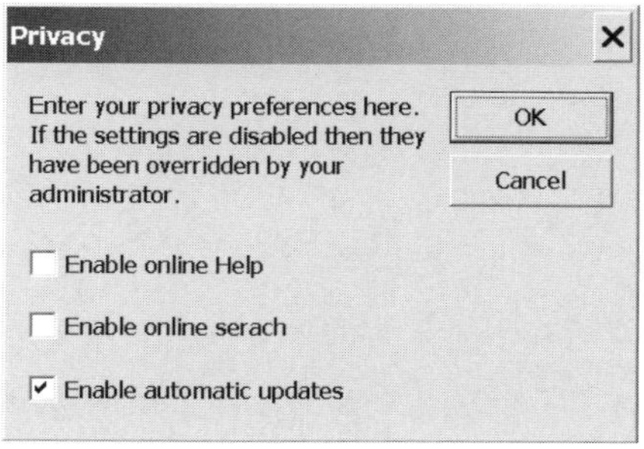

Privacy

Enter your privacy preferences here. If the settings are disabled then they have been overridden by your administrator.

OK

Cancel

Enable online Help

Enable online serach

Enable automatic updates

Figure 2.6 An example privacy settings dialog

Centralized Privacy Setting Management

Privacy settings are important for permitting consumers to control the privacy of their desktops. For computers that are networked within an enterprise, the ability to manage privacy settings in a centralized manner is equally important to permit IT administrators to control the privacy of their enterprise. Consider the situation where a company has more than one thousand workstations. Each of these desktops may have an application that might send sensitive or excessive information to the Internet. Typically users have to adjust their settings based on instructions from their IT department, or a representative from the IT department has to go to each computer and modify the settings. Either of these methods runs the risk of getting something wrong or overlooking a computer. Centralized management of privacy and other settings is invaluable for large enterprises.

Windows-Based Privacy Setting Management

For computers connected to a Microsoft Windows Active Directory domain, Group Policy is a means of providing centralized control of privacy settings.[10] Group Policy provides a means for remotely managing an application's Registry-based settings. Privacy settings for several Windows applications are shipped with the server version of the operating system. Figure 2.7 shows a view of the Windows Media Player privacy settings in a Group Policy editor window that ships with Windows Server 2003.

Applications do not have to ship with the Windows operating system in order to take advantage of Group Policy. Group Policy settings can be deployed using administrative template files.[11] Microsoft Office System 2003 is an example of a product that provides administrative template files with the product. These files are available in the Office 2003 Editions Resource Kit.[12]

---

10. Information about Group Policy and using the Group Policy Management Console to manage Group Policy can be found at http://www.microsoft.com/windowsserver2003/gpmc/gpmcwp.mspx.

11. Information about creating custom administrative templates can be found at http://msdn.microsoft.com/library/en-us/policy/policy/extending_registry_based_policy.asp.

12. Find more about the Office 2003 Editions Resource Kit at http://www.microsoft.com/office/ork/2003/.

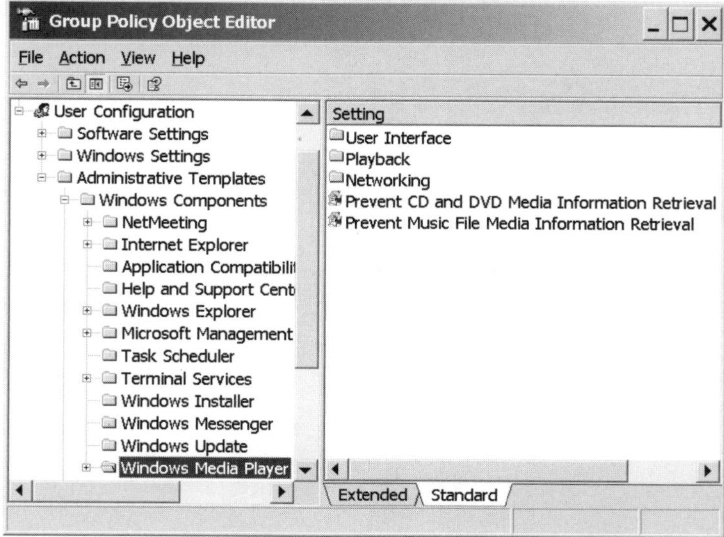

Figure 2.7 Sample of Group Policy privacy settings for Windows Media Player 9

Linux-Based Configuration Management

Red Carpet Enterprise from Ximian, which is shown in Figure 2.8, is an example of a product that provides centralized software deployment and configuration management for Linux-based systems.[13] Ximian provides a browser-based and command-line interface for use by administrators. Software deployments can be configured based on groups of users or computers that are defined by the administrator. Commercial or custom software can be deployed with this product. Deployments can be done manually or programmed to occur automatically.

Ability to View Data to Be Transmitted to the Internet

Many applications transmit data to the Internet. Unfortunately, most of these applications do not permit users to see what is being transmitted. This can and does make users reluctant to use applications or even install an operating system. The Windows error-reporting application is different from most applications because it permits users to see in great detail what is being sent before the data is sent. The error-reporting dialog, shown in

13. The home page for the Red Carpet Enterprise product is http://www.ximian.com/products/redcarpet_enterprise/.

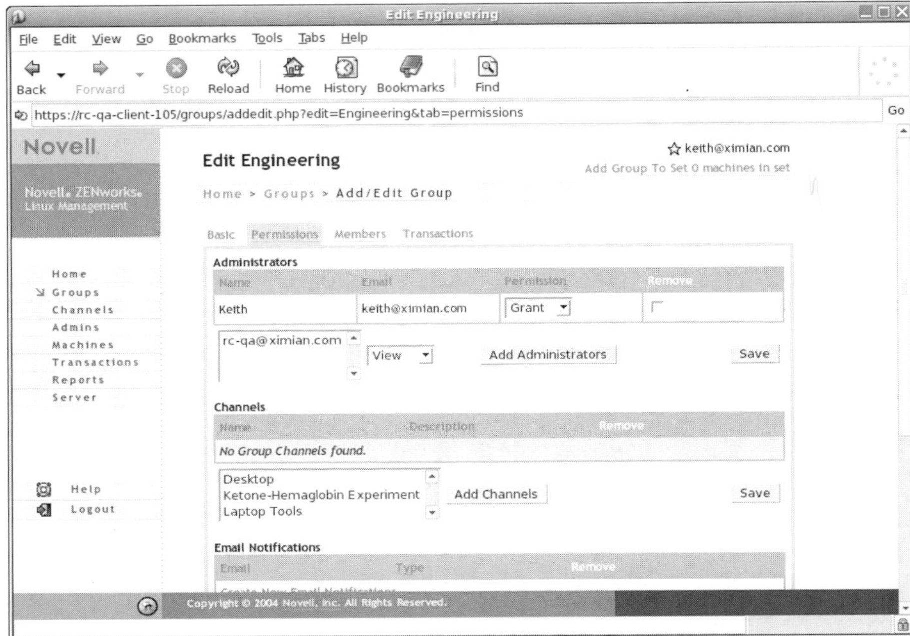

Figure 2.8 Sample of Ximian screen[14]

Figure 2.9, indicates what is being sent, why it is being sent, and the user benefit from sending the data. The user also has the option of not sending the data at all. This is the level of disclosure and control that all applications should provide to customers.

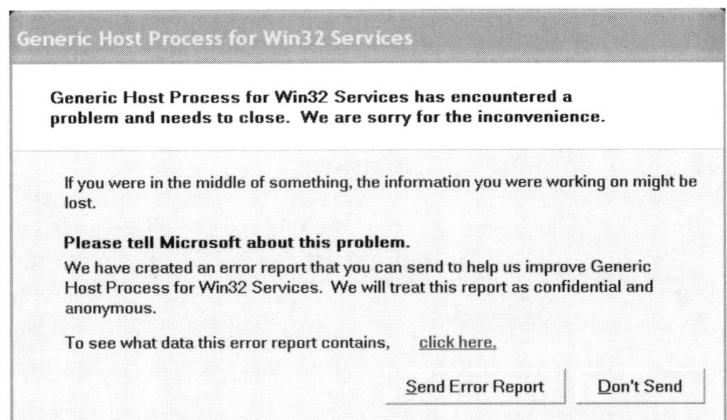

Figure 2.9 The Windows Error Reporting dialog

14. Copyright © 2002-203 Novell, Inc. All Rights Reserved. Used with permission from Novell, Inc.

Widows Error Report also provides users with a settings dialog to permit them to control the applications that will cause error-reporting information to be sent to the Internet. Figure 2.10 shows this dialog. This prevents dialogs from annoying users when they are concerned only about specific applications. It also permits IT administrators to control which applications are sending data over the Internet and can even force Windows Error Reporting to log errors with a server located within the enterprise through the use of associated Group Policy settings.

Clear Tracks and Personal Info

Many applications have features that keep track of files that have been opened, Web pages that have been visited, changes that have been made to a document, or media that have been played. What if users of your application don't want that information tracked or want to be able to clear it when they need to? Are there settings to provide this level of control? This is important in scenarios where users share their computers or want to send a document that may contain hidden data that could later be extracted by recipients of the document. If your application stores a usage history or personal information, provide users with a way to turn off the functionality and remove the information.

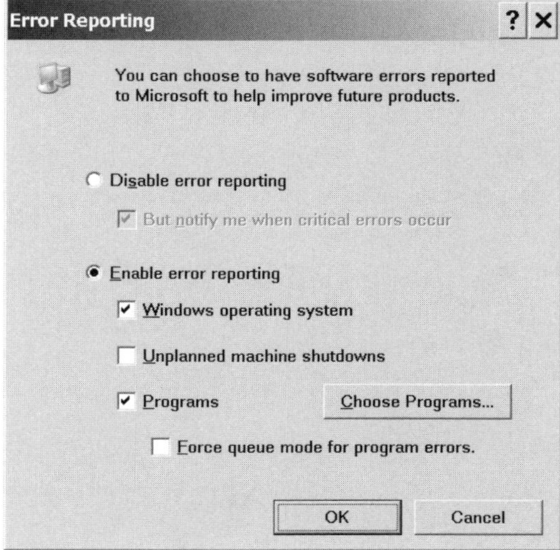

Figure 2.10 The Windows Error Reporting settings dialog

Documentation of Privacy-Related Data

If your application or Web site creates cookies, service quality monitoring (SQM) files, or collects data that is later transmitted from a user's computer, document the contents of these items. (SQM files are used by applications to store usage problems that may occur.) A vague statement about the contents of data files is not enough; be specific. For example, users have requested that Microsoft provide details of the data that is sent during activation. Provide this information in your privacy statement and as part of your help documentation.

Unsubscribe Feature

If your application or service sends e-mails to end users, inside the e-mails provide users with a means to remove themselves from the mailing lists that are used to send the e-mails. If you are developing solutions that can be used to send out e-mails to users, especially as part of marketing campaigns, add a feature to permit users to unsubscribe to these marketing campaigns. This feature should be integrated into the application to make its use as seamless as possible.

Access Control

Most applications need to provide some level of security to prevent access to features and data to those who do not have authorization to use them. Access control for applications is usually implemented by asking users to log in to the application before they can use it. Applications should also provide role-based access to data and features to prevent every user of the application from accessing sensitive features or data when it is not important for his or her job. For example, users of a customer relationship management application who need to send mailings to customers should not necessarily have access to customer credit card or social security numbers. Also provide auditing as part of your security strategy. Auditing helps to prevent administrators from making inappropriate accesses to information by tracking their usage.

Encryption

A vulnerability that many applications have is their accessibility by an administrator. The administrator is often needed for installation and maintenance of an application, but is not required to access the data stored by the application. Permitting administrators to access your application data can pose a risk to sensitive data. For example, a database administrator may have access to a customer's credit card information. To mitigate this risk, provide a feature in your application to encrypt stored data. For information on cryptography and developing cryptographic code, visit http://msdn.microsoft.com/library/en-us/security/security/cryptography_portal.asp.

Microsoft Word comes with encryption to help protect the contents of documents from being viewed by the wrong people. Office 2003 has integrated a feature called Information Rights Management (IRM), which can help ensure that only the proper people are permitted to receive a document via e-mail.[15] The use of IRM permits authors of a document to also manage the following:

- Who can print a document
- Who can copy a document
- Who can forward a document
- Who can modify a document
- The expiration date for a document

Note

Although IRM helps to prevent the accidental release of information, it should not be viewed as the sole, secure means to protect content. For example, any number of tools could be used to copy the content of an IRM-protected document and send it on to someone else.

If you are deploying Web services on a Web site, make sure that Web pages that collect data are protected during transmission using Secure Sockets Layer (SSL). If you are building a Web service, encrypt data before sending it across the Internet. As consumers, you should ensure that the Web page is using SSL before you enter sensitive information into a Web page. The lock icon on the status bar of the Netscape and Internet Explorer browsers can determine this. By double-clicking the icon, you can verify that the certificate it displays matches the URL of the Web site that you think you are visiting.

15. More information on IRM can be found at http://www.microsoft.com/office/editions/prodinfo/technologies/irm.mspx.

Getting Involved in PETs

If you are interested in getting involved in PET research or you are just interested in hearing about what's new in the area of PETs, you should attend a PET workshop. Information about future and past workshops can be found at http://www.PETWorkshop.org. PET researchers and developers also attend the Computer, Freedom, and Privacy conferences. Information about these conferences can be found at http://www.cfp.org.

Conclusion

Privacy is of great concern to consumers these days. Being responsible for a privacy faux pas can irreparably tarnish your company's reputation and cause you to lose customers. As you build solutions for your customers, partners, and employees, provide them with a means to control the collection, storage, and sharing of their information. Prominent disclosure through the use of a privacy statement is the best way to provide users with disclosure of your privacy practices. Provide privacy settings to make it easier for users to control their privacy and implement these settings in a centralized fashion to permit IT administrators to maintain the same control across their enterprise.

As consumers, demand more from the products that you buy. After using a new product, call the customer support department of the manufacturer and let them know how you feel about the investment that you made in their product. If the product lacks privacy features, then it could be unnecessarily exposing your data. Features such as encryption and access control should always be provided for the protection of your sensitive data. Use the anti-spyware tools listed in this chapter to keep your computer free of snooping and annoying applications. Use the anonymizing tools to protect your browsing habits and to protect the identity and content of your e-mails.

These are the privacy questions that you should be asking about software that you install on your computer:

- Does the software provide prominent notice about its data handling practices?
- Are there controls that make it easy for me to mange my privacy?

- Are there controls to permit me to manage my family's privacy?
- Are there controls to permit me to manage the privacy across my enterprise?
- If the company sends my data to their Web site is it protected?
- Is there a way I can contact the company if I have a privacy issue?

3 Privacy Legislation

One of the most overlooked areas of software development is a company's legal liability for producing software whose practices violate privacy legislation. In general, when companies are trying to determine which features to add to the next version of their products, they perform research to find out what their customers want and then pass the requirements on to their development team to find creative ways to integrate them into their products. With all of the power that the Internet provides, it only makes sense for developers to want to Internet-enable their applications. They don't think about how users may feel about their data flowing to the Internet, especially if the user is benefiting from it. Considering there was no precedence for writing Internet-enabled applications, it's easy to see how developers could get carried away with their creativity. Wouldn't you enjoy using intuitive, self-healing applications that provide you with up-to-date information as you are using them?

To provide personalized services or Internet-enriched features to an application, some data about the user has to be sent to the Internet. For example, the title of the media to which the user is watching or listening, the applications the user is running, and the Web sites the user is visiting. Although this may seem like a small price to pay for great features, not only can these cases be considered an invasion of privacy, they could also be against the law. According to the Computer Fraud and Abuse Act, it is not permissible to download data to or upload data from users' computers without their permission. Companies often bury "the permission" in an end-user license agreement (EULA), privacy statement, or terms-of-use document. Although American privacy legislation permits this type of obscure notice, privacy legislation in Germany requires prominent notice and specific consent before transferring any data from a user's computer.

For consumers this can mean a more complicated installation process or features that are disabled by default.

Regulations Changing the Way Companies Do Business

Many companies that did not understand the intricacies of the various pieces of privacy legislation paid an enormous price settling lawsuits and reengineering their products. Abiding by legislation can increase production costs and force developers to be more creative about how they provide information to users while adding additional settings to permit users to control their privacy. In the end, companies will find that extra development expenditures up front are well worth it to avoid costly litigation after a product has shipped. In addition, the cost of litigation can be compounded by the cost of recalls and lost sales. The following sections detail the experiences of some companies that were affected by privacy legislation.

DoubleClick

Early on Web sites started tracking repeat visitors to provide a personalized experience and push targeted ads at the user. With the advent of banner ads came the capability to track users through multiple sites. When DoubleClick did this, they not only tracked users, they also stored personal information about them and sold it to third parties, according to a suit filed by a California woman.[1] MatchLogic ran into similar problems when tracking information on more than 72 million users.[2]

RealNetworks

When RealNetworks came out with their RealJukebox software, it included a unique identifier that permitted them to track what individual users were listening to and recording. Even though they may have done this to provide users access to the type of music they wanted to hear, it was considered an unwarranted invasion of privacy.[3]

---

1. Douglas F. Gray, "DoubleClick Sued for Privacy Violations," CNN.com, January 28, 2000

2. Christopher Saunders, "MatchLogic Faces Privacy Suit," Internet Advertising Report, November 22, 2000

3. Courtney Macavinta, "RealNetworks Changes Privacy Policy Under Scrutiny," CNET News.com, November 1, 1999

Alexa Internet

On the surface the Alexa Toolbar is a great tool that makes it easier for users to perform research while surfing the World Wide Web. However, it was not obvious to users that their current link was being transmitted to the Alexa Web site along with any search strings that were embedded in the address to the current Web page. One could argue that clicking the Related Links button of the Alexa Toolbar was akin to providing consent. Unfortunately, many users didn't see it that way, and as part of a court settlement Alexa Internet had to pay up to $40 to each user who was harmed by the feature.[4]

Microsoft Office 2003

The new version of Office has several Internet-enabled features that bring power and information to the fingertips of its users. However, having these features on by default can be troubling for some users. In sensitivity to German laws about sending data from a user's computer by default, the Office team created a separate version of the product that has the Internet-enabled features turned off by default.

Major Privacy Legislation

This section looks at the major pieces of international privacy legislation that have had an impact on how companies do business, manage their enterprises, and develop software solutions. Whether you are handling personal data from employees, customers, or partners, or writing code or building systems that handle personal data, be sure to review the legislation described here. Although your company may reside in one locale, you may be doing business across country boundaries or transferring personal data with organizations that exist in other countries. In these cases, you should be familiar with the privacy legislation for the locales that may be affected by your data transfers or usage.

4. Danny Sullivan, "Alexa to Pay in Privacy Dispute," SearchEngineWatch.com, June 4, 2001

Note

The information provided here should not be taken as legal advice. Before deploying any solutions, always get your legal counsel to review them.

Organisation for Economic Co-operation and Development (OECD)

I think it only appropriate that I begin this section with a discussion of the set of principles that is considered the basis for privacy legislation worldwide. The OECD consists of 30 member countries, 70 nonmember countries, and several nongovernmental organizations. Early on it was decided that an important task that the OECD should take on was the creation of a set of privacy principles that could be adopted by all member countries. One of the main reasons for developing these principles was to ensure the flow of personal data among countries.[5] To support this desire, on September 23, 1980, the OECD adopted the "Guidelines on the Protection of Privacy and Transborder Flows of Personal Data," also known as the OECD Fair Information Practices. The following is a list of the principles that make up these guidelines.

Accountability

Each organization is responsible for complying with each of the guidelines that make up the OECD Fair Information Practices.

Collection Limitation

Any personal data collected from a data subject should be done so in a legal and fair manner. Only the data needed to carry out stated business purposes should be collected. The consent of the data subject should be obtained before the collection of personal data where appropriate.

Data Quality

Only collect the data that is needed for specific business purposes. Do not keep the data longer than is necessary to fulfill these business purposes. To the greatest extent possible, ensure that the data being collected is complete, current, and correct.

5. http://www.oecd.org/document/18/0,2340,en_2649_201185_1815186_1_1_1_1,00.html

Individual Participation

Individuals should have the right to request that an organization disclose to them the data that the organization has on them in a manner that is simple and inexpensive. The data should be returned in a timely manner in a form that is easy to understand. Individuals should have a way to correct or contest any discrepancies with their data.

Openness

Organizations should be transparent about their policies and practices for handling personal information. A description of the data handling policies and practices as well as the name of the data controller should be made easily accessible to the general public.

Purpose Specification

The purposes for which data is being collected should be specified to the data subject before or at least at the time that the data is being collected. Any additional purposes must be compatible with the original purposes and must be specified.

Security Safeguards

Reasonable precautions must be taken to prevent the unauthorized access, destruction, disclosure, modification, or use of personal data.

Use Limitation

Personal data must not be disclosed, made available or otherwise used except to accomplish the purposes for which it was collected, as specified in the purpose specification. Exceptions can be made in only two cases: with the explicit consent of the data subject, or to comply with the law.

In the absence of any other privacy legislation or policies, the OECD Fair Information Practices should be adopted by an organization. By following these principles in running a business and creating products and services, a company is sure to earn the respect of customers in any country where it plans to do business.

EU Directive on Data Protection

On October 24, 1995, the European Union (EU) issued its directives on data protection.[6] The member countries of the European Union were given until

---

6. http://europa.eu.int/comm/internal_market/privacy/index.htm

October 1998 to pass legislation that supported these directives. The data protection directives placed strict guidelines on the collection, storage, processing, and sharing of data. Many countries quickly passed legislation that adopted the guidelines from this directive. Some countries even created legislation that was even stricter than the directive. Germany is one of those countries. If you are planning to deploy software in Germany, work with a data protection specialist to review your architecture long before you have frozen the design.

An important section of the directive called for a *moratorium* on the transfer of personal data to countries outside of the EU that did not have similar privacy legislation. This would have had a serious impact on American companies doing business with European companies. If you have applications or Web services that transfer data between the United States and an EU member country,[7] be sure that your legal department validates that you are abiding by the EU Directive on Data Protection. See the section "The U.S. Safe Harbor Privacy Principles" later in this chapter for more guidelines on doing business with the EU.

Personal Information Protection and Electronic Document Act (PIPEDA)

PIPEDA is Canadian legislation that governs the collection, use, and disclosure of personal information through the normal course of business.[8] It applies to both paper-based and online content. PIPEDA consists of five parts. Part one covers the basic guidelines for handling personal information. The remaining parts deal with the use of electronic documents in place of their paper counterparts. The act was released in three stages. Stage one was released in January 2001, and covered the use of personal information other than medical information by commercial companies at the federal level, including information about the organizations' employees. Stage two was released in January 2002, and simply added the coverage of health information. The final stage was released in January 2004, and extended coverage to commercial activity that transpires within and between provinces and between provinces and international entities.

7. For a list of member countries, see http://europa.eu.int/abc/governments/index_en.htm.

8. http://laws.justice.gc.ca/en/P-8.6/index.html

Like many pieces of privacy legislation, PIPEDA is based on the principles outlined by the OECD's Fair Information Practices. The way in which it differs from other privacy legislation is that it is consent-based, meaning that consent must be obtained from the data owner before personal information can be collected, used, or disclosed.

The U.S. Safe Harbor Privacy Principles

In response to the EU Directive on Data Protection, mentioned previously, the U.S. Department of Commerce created the Safe Harbor Privacy Principles. Safe Harbor was issued on July 24, 2000, and accepted by the European Commission on July 28, 2000.[9] This means that U.S. companies that subscribe to Safe Harbor would be able to exchange personal data with EU member countries. Subscribing to Safe Harbor means agreeing with its seven privacy principles. Companies building products that collect, store, or transmit data, should make sure that their applications comply with these principles. The seven principles are described in the following sections, along with some best practices for building applications that align with them.

Companies that subscribe to Safe Harbor and later fail to abide by their commitment to it could be fined $12,000 a day by the U.S. Federal Trade Commission (FTC). For this reason, it is important that any of your applications that collect, store, or transmit data abide by these principles.

Notice

Whenever a user's data is to be collected, stored, or shared, the user must be informed of these practices before the data is collected. A privacy statement must be easy to find and easy to understand. The privacy statement must indicate what data you are collecting, the purpose for collecting it, with whom it is shared, what protections are placed on the data, how long it is kept, how users can gain access to their data, and how to contact the company collecting the data to resolve any privacy issues they may have. Web services must provide an easy-to-find link to the privacy statement on a Web page. Applications must provide a privacy statement selection under the Help menu. Applications that do not have a user interface can present the privacy statement during the install process or first-run experience for each user who starts the application.

9. http://www.export.gov/safeharbor/sh_overview.html

Choice

Users must always be given an opportunity to manage any features that handle their data though the use of privacy settings. These settings can be implemented on a privacy dialog or a Web page. They could be transmitted to the company via e-mail, postal mail, or a phone call, and stored in a database for later retrieval. For sensitive data, the privacy settings must be off by default. To encourage the user to turn certain settings on, a dialog should be displayed during the setup process or the first-run experience for each user. Privacy settings should be placed on a separate privacy tab under the application's properties dialog to make them easy to find.

Developers should give IT administrators a way to manage the privacy settings for each of their desktops. In Windows, IT administrators can use Group Policy Editor to manage Registry-based settings. For other operating systems, administrators can deploy startup scripts to each user's desktop to be run when his or her machine is restarted or the next time the user logs in. Read Chapter 10 for examples on how to implement some of these suggestions within an application.

Onward Transfer

Onward transfer is the act of sharing a user's data with a third party. This could happen by an application sending data to the third party over the Internet. It could also happen when an application or Web service stores data collected from the user in a corporate database and then later shares it with a third party. Whenever data is to be shared with a third party, the user must always be informed and permission obtained before the transfer occurs. Even if the data is not sensitive, the user must be informed in advance, before transmitting it, to avoid any circumstances where the user is surprised or annoyed by the activity.

Access

Any time data is collected from the user, there must be a way for the user to access the data in order to verify, modify, or even delete it if they need to. In general, there must be an easy-to-find and easy-to-use user interface available to access the data. Making users access the Registry directly to modify their data is not an acceptable solution.

Security

When an application stores data on a user's computer or transmits data from the user's computer, other users should protect it from access. Consider the fact that more than one person may be using a computer. The user should be able to protect his or her data from other family members or colleagues using a form of access protection or encryption. When data is transmitted from the user's computer, it should be protected using encryption. If your application, after being installed by a user, sends data to your company for storage, ensure that there is adequate physical security to prevent unwanted access to the user's data.

Data Integrity

If your application collects data from the user, make sure that it is complete, accurate, and up-to-date before using it. Only collect data that is needed by the application. For example, if you only need the user's Zip code, don't ask for the street address. Add audit capabilities to your application to permit users to track any unwanted changes to their data. Provide a means for users to clear their data or have a retention policy for data stored at your company.

Enforcement

Give users a means to contact your company to resolve privacy issues that they may have. You can do this through e-mail, a Web form, or a phone number. A Web form is the best approach, because you will be able to capture users' complaints in their own words. You can also guide the user to providing a full set of information by providing the appropriate fields on the form with defaults and multiple-choice responses. The form will prevent your company from receiving spam, which can occur if you provide an e-mail address for filing privacy complaints. Signing up for a privacy seal program is another means for providing the user a means to obtain resolution to privacy issues. More information about privacy seals can be found later in this chapter.

Children's Online Privacy Protection Act (COPPA)

COPPA prohibits companies, Web sites, or software from collecting or transmitting data from children under the age of 13 without explicit permission from their parents.[10] If your software or Web site is targeted at children 12 years of age or younger, you need to obtain explicit consent from their parents. You can obtain a parent's permission via e-mail, fax, or

---

10. http://www.ftc.gov/ogc/coppa1.htm

by insisting on a credit card number to gain access to your site or software. When trying to determine a child's age, ask for the child's birth date rather than just his or her age.

Amazon recently had 11 organizations file a complaint with the FTC[11] over their practice of accepting toy reviews from children 12 and under. Even though Amazon's privacy statement[12] clearly states it does not provide products for sale to children, the fact that they sell items targeted to children and ask for reviews on toys without verifying the writer's age encouraged the group to file the complaint.

Computer Fraud and Abuse Act (CFAA)

CFAA prohibits anyone from accessing someone else's computer without permission from the owner.[13] This includes placing data on, sending data from, or modifying or deleting data on a user's computer. Your data handling practices should be mentioned in the product's EULA. Applications with features that send a user's data over the Internet must inform the user in the product's EULA or other disclosure mechanism. Better yet, have a separate privacy statement that is presented to the user when your application is first run. This will cover you in the cases where one computer is used by multiple people who may run your program from their individual computer account.

Gramm-Leach-Bliley Act (GLBA)

GLBA covers the handling of financial information.[14] If your solution handles a user's financial information, make sure that you have someone who is an expert with GLBA to review your product. By following the Safe Harbor Privacy Principles, you will be ahead of the game. Creating a set of privacy guidelines for product development that use the Safe Harbor Privacy Principles as a foundation will place an application far along the path toward compliance with GLBA.

---

11. Declan McCullagh and Alorie Gilbert, "Is Amazon.com No Place For Kids?", CNET News.com April 22, 2003

12. Amazon's privacy statement can be found at http://www.amazon.com/exec/obidos/tg/browse/-/468496/002-7536629-3530444

13. http://www4.law.cornell.edu/uscode/18/1030.html

14. http://www.ftc.gov/privacy/glbact/

Health Insurance Portability and Accountability Act (HIPAA)

This act is similar to GLBA except it covers medical information instead of financial information.[15] If you are creating solutions that collect medical information or are targeted at the medical industry, make sure that someone who has a thorough understanding of the HIPAA provisions reviews the solution. Once again, using the Safe Harbor Privacy Principles as a framework for your product development will help you with your HIPAA compliance. Auditing is also one feature, not specifically mentioned in Safe Harbor, that you should invest in. Robust auditing can be a deterrent to the theft of data by insiders.

Privacy-Certification Programs

When browsing the World Wide Web, users make mental notes about each Web site visit, which collectively helps them determine whether a site should be trusted. One of these notes may be whether a site displays a seal from a privacy-certification program. Subscribing to a certification program is one way to get potential customers to feel better about buying products from a Web site. So even if the seals do not apply to a specific set of products per se, they can help a site sell more products.

Subscribing to one of these programs tells visitors to a site that a company has passed certain criteria to achieve the seal. It also tells them that they have an alternative place to go to resolve issues they may have with a company's privacy practices.

The following table shows some of the most popular programs. The BBBOnline, TRUSTe, and WebTrust seals indicate businesses in good standing. Businesses with this seal have agreed to meet certain standards with the way they do business and have had some level of verification performed by the company providing the certification.

The ESRB seal is from the Entertainment Software Rating Board. The company focuses mostly on the online gaming industry. They sponsor a standard privacy program as well as a children's privacy program.

The BizRate site collects information from customers on their experiences with companies and their products. This is not a seal program, but it performs worthwhile monitoring to help ensure a company that it is being viewed positively by its customers.

---

15. http://www.cms.hhs.gov/hipaa/default.asp

BBBOnLine[16]

http://www.bbbonline.org/business

BizRate[17]

http://merchant.bizrate.com/oa/customer_satisfaction/index.xpml

ESRB

http://www.esrb.org/privacy_wp_register.asp

TRUSTe

http://www.truste.org/business/seal_programs_overview.php

WebTrust

http://www.cpawebtrust.org/onlstart.htm

Conclusion

No matter where you do business, there is probably a piece of privacy legislation that governs the way that you collect, use, and disclose of personal data. Understand what your obligations are for handling personal data and to the data subject to which the privacy legislation applies. If you are an international company, your data handling practices will probably come under the jurisdiction of privacy legislation from multiple countries.

Don't make assumptions about what may be permissible in other countries based on your experiences in your native country. For example, in America monitoring employees is okay, whereas it is forbidden in other countries without a warrant. Consider this when creating features that may send tracking information from a client machine to a central server.

For companies with a Web presence, investigate participating in a privacy-certification program that could assist you with the proper way to design your Web site, with regard to privacy compliance, and improve your trust quotient with visitors to your site.

---

16. Reprinted with permission of the Council of Better Business Bureaus, Inc., Copyright 2003. Council of Better Business Bureaus, Inc., 4200 Wilson Blvd., Arlington VA 22203. World Wide Web: http: www.bbb.org.

17. BizRate.com collects customer satisfaction information from actual customers regarding their experiences with online merchants. This is not a seal program but it helps merchants understand how their customers view their company and it also helps other online buyers know what to expect from a particular merchant. Every year the "best of the best" e-tailers are recognized with a Circle Of Excellence award from BizRate.com

4 Managing Windows Privacy

Considering the amount of information and the Internet-based Web services available on the Internet, it is easy to see why application developers would want to take advantage of the Internet. The downside, of course, is that applications could inadvertently transmit sensitive information over the Internet, making it susceptible to interception by untrustworthy individuals. Some enterprises even want no automatic communication with the Internet whatsoever. For example, government agencies involved in secret research are wary of any information leaving the confines of their research facility.

This chapter looks at various Windows components and applications that communicate with the Internet. The chapter discusses how these communications can be managed by users at their workstations and by IT administrators through Group Policy. Although the examples given here are based on Windows Server 2003, many of the examples will also apply to Windows XP and Windows 2000. For specific information about a particular operating system, view the appropriate white paper indicated in the "Resources" section of this chapter.

Privacy Disclosure Documents for Microsoft Windows

When creating applications, developers often aren't aware of the importance of creating a privacy deployment guide. A privacy deployment guide helps IT personnel, and even consumers, understand the features in an application that might affect an individual's privacy and how to safely deploy the application. While deploying an enterprise application, one of the things that IT administrators want to know is how to manage any features that might communicate with the Internet. With complex applications, several Internet-enabled features may need to be managed.

When Windows XP shipped, it was difficult to determine how to manage its Internet-enabled features. Not only was it difficult to know how to manage the Internet-enabled features, it was also difficult to know what features were Internet-enabled in the first place. In response to requests from enterprises, Microsoft came out with a series of privacy disclosure documents described in the following sections.

Management Papers

Soon after the release of Windows XP, Microsoft released a white paper that described how to manage the Windows XP features that communicate with the Internet. The information in the white paper was designed to provide IT administrators with supplementary information that is not part of the standard documentation that ships with the operating system. The white paper provided details on the following items where appropriate:

- The purpose of the feature
- The user benefit from the feature
- The data sent over the Internet
- How to manage the feature via user settings and Group Policy

After the creation of the white paper for Windows XP, subsequent white papers were written to cover the features in Windows 2000 and Windows Server 2003. The feature list and corresponding settings for each feature will vary, so refer to the white paper that corresponds to the operating system in which you are interested.

First Privacy Statement

When Service Pack 2 for Windows XP is released, Microsoft plans to have the first comprehensive privacy statement describing the components that communicate with the Internet. It will be accessible from the operating system. This privacy statement will take the place of the previous white papers. Future releases of the Windows operating system will have their own versions of a privacy statement that will be accessible from the desktop. Read this privacy statement to get an understanding of the Windows components that could be sending data to the Internet and how to manage them.

Using Group Policy for Centralized Setting Management

If you understand what Group Policy is, feel free to skip to the next section. Otherwise, if you want to know what Group Policy is and why you should care, let me go over it briefly for you. Many applications that you use on your computer have settings that you modify on occasion. The value for many of these settings is stored in your computer's Registry. For example, the Display Properties dialog enables you to change the image displayed on the desktop. The name of the image file that is selected to display is stored in the Registry in the value HKEY_CURRENT_USER\Software\Microsoft\Internet Explorer\Desktop\General\Wallpaper. Suppose that as an administrator you want to display the logo of your company on each desktop in the company. You could go around to every computer and manually do this, or you could use Group Policy, which is a component that ships with Windows 2000 and later servers. Group Policy enables IT administrators to manage the Registry-based settings of every computer in their company. To use Group Policy, you must deploy Active Directory and add each computer in the company to an Active Directory domain. Afterward, an IT administrator can manage all the desktops in her enterprise.

Some parents probably would like this same ability for their family's computers. However, deploying Group Policy is probably overkill for a house with only a few computers, especially if they are not networked.

The Group Policy Management Console

The Group Policy Management Console (GPMC) was designed to make it easier to manage Group Policy settings for multiple domains or even forests. It extends the MMC-based tool that comes with the Windows 2003 Server operating system. It includes a reporting mechanism to make it easier to document the settings that have been applied to a specific Group Policy object. Figure 4.1 provides an example of what the GPMC looks like. It suffices to say if you run an enterprise and use Group Policy, you will be delighted to be able to use the new GPMC. The GPMC is free for download from the Microsoft site. See the "Resources" section at the end of this chapter for the download address.

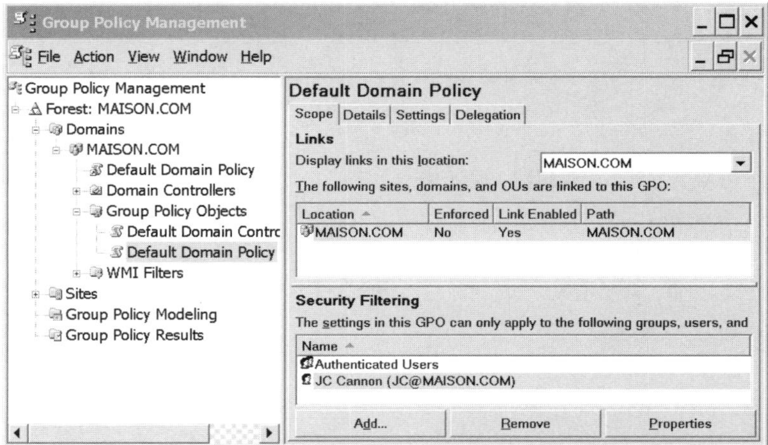

Figure 4.1 The Group Policy Management Console

Online Help and Top Issues

If you are connected to the Internet when you use the Help and Support command from the Start menu or press F1 to bring up the Help and Support Center, the Top Issues section automatically updates from the Internet and your search queries are automatically sent to the Microsoft Knowledge Base Web site. Because the majority of your queries will seek assistance with Microsoft products, there is little chance that sensitive information will be sent out. However, both of these features can cause an unwanted increase in network traffic. Users can disable the Top Issues feature by adding the DWORD value **headlines** to the Registry key indicated below and setting it to zero (0):

```
HKEY_LOCAL_MACHINE\SOFTWARE\Microsoft\PCHealth\HelpSvc\
```

Administrators can use Group Policy to disable the Top Issues feature. Just enable the Do not allow "Did you know" content to appear setting under the Administrative Templates > Windows Components > Help and Support Center folder under the User Configuration section of a Group Policy object (GPO).

Users can disable Online Search by bringing up the Help and Support Center window, selecting the Set search options link below the Search box, and then clearing the Microsoft Knowledge Base checkbox in the pane on the right. Figure 4.2 shows this checkbox.

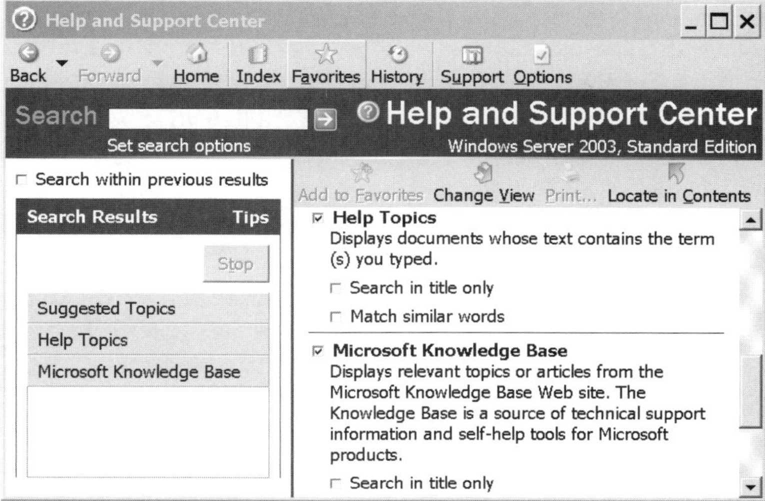

Figure 4.2 Help and Support window

Windows Error Reporting

The Windows Error Reporting (WER) mechanism provides Microsoft a means to obtain feedback on application and operating system crashes. Before any data is sent, the user is presented with the WER dialog and given a choice of whether the error-reporting data should be sent. The user can also select the *click here* link to see what data is to be sent. Figure 4.3 provides an example of a WER dialog.

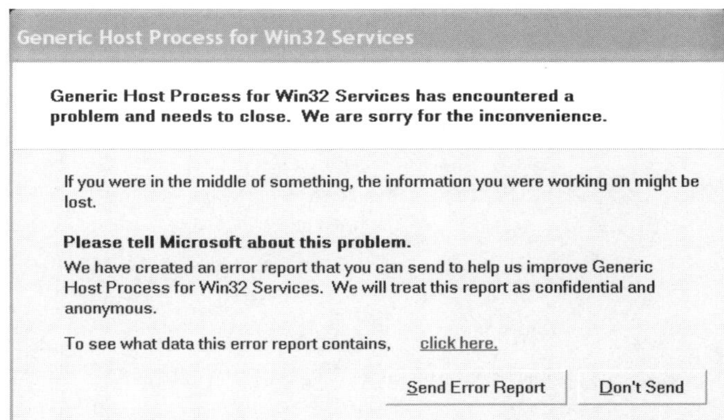

Figure 4.3 Windows Error Reporting dialog

When WER sends error information to Microsoft, there is a chance that sensitive data could be included. For this reason, users and administrators may want to manage which applications report errors using this feature.[1] For example, you may not want to report errors for Microsoft Money. It is important to note that the data is encrypted during transmission and protected during storage.

Using the Windows Error Reporting Dialog

Users can control error reporting by using the Windows Error Reporting dialog shown in Figure 4.4. To access this dialog, right-click the My Computer object, select Properties, select the Advanced tab, and then click the Error Reporting button. You can also access the Properties dialog by double-clicking the System icon in the Control Panel.

The other settings in the Error Reporting dialog enable the user to indicate the types of incidents that will cause an error report to occur. The dialog includes the following options:

Figure 4.4 Windows Error Reporting settings dialog

1. You may have expected to hear a stronger message about blocking any information being sent to Microsoft. The reality is that data sent to Microsoft is relatively safe because of the protections placed on access to the data, and the sheer volume of information makes it implausible to mine for sensitive information. Although the WER data has been instrumental in fixing problems, individuals and companies may feel more comfortable restricting what information is sent across the Internet.

Disable Error Reporting

Selecting this radio button will disable the error-reporting mechanism for your computer. You will not see the WER dialog when an error occurs, and no information will be sent from your computer by the WER mechanism.

But Notify Me When Critical Errors Occur

When the Disable Error Reporting radio button is selected and this checkbox is selected, the WER dialog will still display when critical errors occur, but no data will be sent to Microsoft. The Send Error Report and Don't Send buttons will not be available, but will have been replaced by a Close button.

Enable Error Reporting

This radio button is used to turn on the WER mechanism. The checkbox selections and programs selected in the Choose Programs dialog determine which applications generate error reports that can be sent to Microsoft.

Windows Operating System

When this checkbox is selected, crashes in the operating system will generate an error report. If this checkbox is not selected, when an operating system crash occurs and that crash causes a running application to crash, the application may still generate an error report that can be sent to Microsoft.

Unplanned Machine Shutdowns

When this checkbox is selected, an unplanned shutdown of the computer will cause an error report to be generated. Unplanned shutdowns can include a critical error that causes a system restart or the power cord being unplugged. By default it is unchecked.

Programs

When this checkbox is selected, programs running on the computer will cause an error report to be generated based on the values selected on the Choose Programs dialog.

Choose Programs

This button is used to display the Choose Programs dialog, which is shown in Figure 4.5. It enables the user to select a category of programs or specific programs that will or will not generate error reports. The Choose Programs dialog includes the following fields:

- **All programs**—When this radio button is selected, all programs that are not in the Do not report list will be able to generate error reports.
- **All programs in this list**—When this radio button is selected, the program types or individual programs specified in the accompanying list will generate error reports.
- **Programs from Microsoft**—When this checkbox is selected, all programs that are products of Microsoft will be able to generate error reports. This includes programs that were shipped with the operating system, such as Notepad, and programs that may be installed separately, such as Visual Studio. This setting will also cause errors to be generated for Windows components overriding the value of the Windows components checkbox.

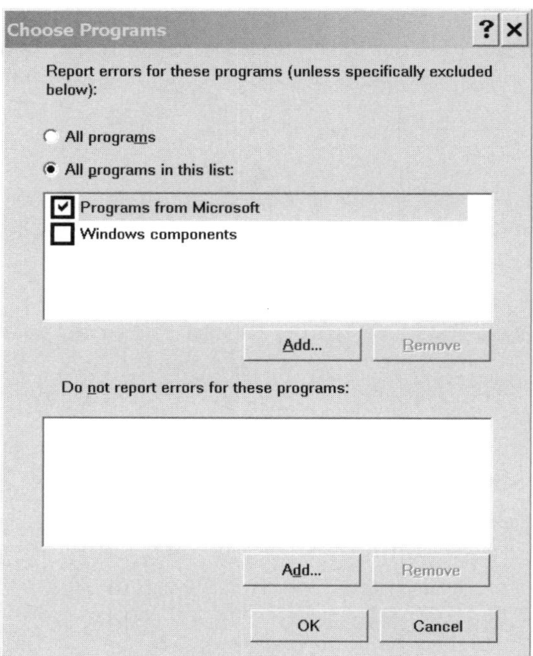

Figure 4.5 Choose Programs dialog

- **Windows components**—When this checkbox is selected, all programs that are products of Microsoft that ship with the operating system will be able to generate error reports. This includes programs such as Notepad. This setting is ignored when the Programs from Microsoft checkbox is selected.
- **Add**—This button displays the Add Program dialog, which enables the user to add the name of a program or select one from the file system to be added to the list of programs that are permitted to generate an error report. Only the name of the program and not the entire path for the application need be entered.
- **Remove**—This button is used to remove a program name from the list of programs that can generate an error report.
- **Do not report errors for these programs**—This list contains the names of programs that are not permitted to create an error report when a crash occurs. The programs in this list will override any selections made in the previous list that displays programs that are permitted to generate error reports.
- **Add**—This button displays a dialog that enables the user to add the name of a program or select one from the file system to be added to the list of programs that are not permitted to generate an error report. Only the name of the program need be entered and not the entire path for the application.
- **Remove**—This button is used to remove a program name from the list of programs that are not permitted to generate an error report.

Force Queue Mode for Program Errors

When this checkbox is selected, error reports will be placed into a queue instead of being presented to the currently logged-on user. The next time an administrator logs on to the computer system, he or she will be presented with the errors that occurred.

Using Group Policy to Manage Windows Error Reporting

IT administrators can use Group Policy to manage WER settings for all of their desktops and to control WER at a more granular level. Two of the WER settings can be found under the Computer Configuration section of a GPO under the Administrative Templates > System > Error Reporting folder. Advanced settings are located in the subfolder labeled Advanced

Error Reporting settings. By opening the object for any of the settings and selecting the Explain tab, you can obtain a full description of the setting and how it should be used. Each WER Group Policy setting is described below.

Display Error Notification

This setting determines whether the user is shown the WER dialog when an error occurs. Disabling it will suppress the display of the WER dialog and an error will be sent based on the value of the Group Policy Report Errors setting. Disabling this setting is useful for servers that usually operate without a user.

Report Errors

This setting has several values that can be modified. The ones that affect Internet communications are as follows:

- **Do not provide links to any Microsoft 'more information' web sites**—When checked, links to Microsoft sites that have more information about the error message will not display.
- **Do not collect additional files**—When checked, it prevents additional files from being sent with the error report.
- **Do not collect additional machine data**—When checked, it prevents additional machine data from being sent with the error report.
- **Force queue mode for application errors**—When checked, users are not shown errors. Instead errors are queued up until the next time an administrator logs in, at which time the administrator can choose whether to send the error.
- **Corporate upload file path**—This edit box permits the administrator to enter a file share where error data should be sent instead of sending it to Microsoft.

The remaining WER settings are found in a subfolder named Advanced Error Reporting settings. These settings are ignored if the Report Errors setting is disabled or not configured. The folder includes the following settings:

Default Application Reporting Settings

This setting enables the user to determine the category of applications that should have errors reported on or ignored. This setting has the following values:

- **Default**—Indicates whether all application errors should be reported or no application errors should be reported.
- **Report all errors in Microsoft applications**—When checked, errors in Microsoft applications are reported whether they were shipped with the operating system or not. Selecting this option will include Windows components. Microsoft applications are defined as those that do not ship with the operating system. When this checkbox is checked, the value in the Default drop-down list is ignored.
- **Report all errors in Windows components**—When checked, errors in Microsoft Windows components are reported. When this checkbox is checked, the value in the Default drop-down list is ignored.

List of Applications to Always Report Errors For

This setting is used to indicate a list of applications that should cause an error report to be generated. Enter the simple name of the executable file and not the full path. This setting overrides any values set in the Default Application Reporting Settings setting.

List of Applications to Never Report Errors For

This setting is used to indicate a list of applications that should not cause an error report to be generated. This setting overrides any values set in the Default Application Reporting Settings setting. This setting also overrides values set in the List of Applications to Always Report Errors For setting.

Report Operating System Errors

This setting is used to indicate whether operating system errors should be reported. This setting overrides any values set in the Default Application Reporting Settings setting.

Report Unplanned Shutdown Events

This setting is used to indicate if unplanned events, such as a power outage, should be reported. This setting overrides any values set in the Default Application Reporting Settings setting.

Automatic Updates

By default, Windows downloads new operating system updates when you are connected to the Internet. To do this, the operating system first sends an inventory of your Windows components along with your operating system version to the Windows update site to determine which updates should be downloaded. Updates are not actually installed until the user chooses to do so. Users can use the Automatic Updates dialog shown in Figure 4.6 to modify these settings. To access this dialog, right-click the My Computer object, select Properties, and then select the Automatic Updates tab.

Administrators can manage automatic update settings for their enterprise through Group Policy. Under the User Configuration section in the Administrative Templates >Windows Components > Windows Update folder is the Remove access to use all Windows Update features setting, which permits the removal of all Windows update features. This controls access to the following functionality:

- The Windows Update link on the Start menu
- The Windows Update link on the Internet Explorer Tools menu

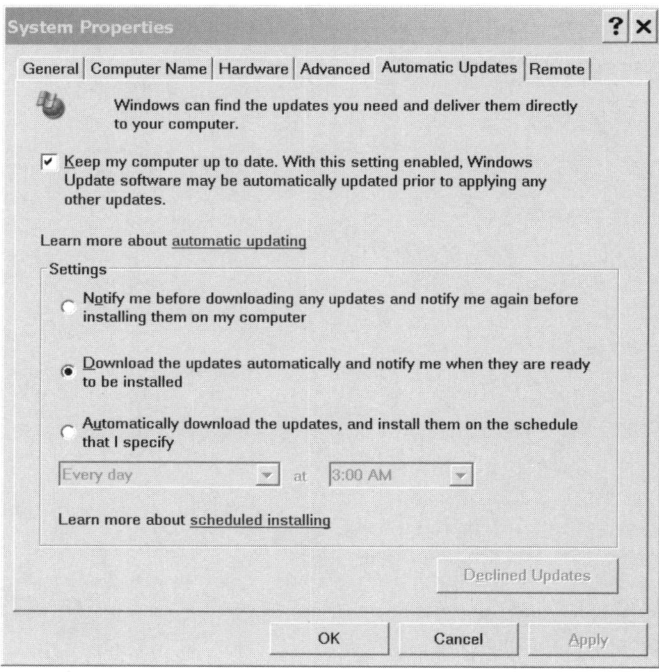

Figure 4.6 Automatic Updates dialog

- Automatic updates
- Device Manager Driver updates

Under the Computer Configuration section in the Administrative Templates > Windows Components > Windows Update folder are four settings for Windows Update. These settings are valid only if the Remove access to use all Windows Update features setting is not enabled. They are described below.

Configure Automatic Updates

This setting indicates the type of automatic update that should occur, which can be one of the following:

- Notify for download and notify for install
- Auto download and notify for install
- Auto download and schedule the install

For scheduled installs, the schedule can be specified and the computer will be automatically restarted if necessary as long as a user is not logged on.

Specify Intranet Microsoft Update Service Location

This setting enables the administrator to indicate an internal enterprise server that contains the Microsoft Update service for its desktops. The server that is to receive the update statistics from enterprise desktops is also indicated here.

Reschedule Automatic Updates Scheduled Installations

This setting enables the administrator to indicate the number of minutes that scheduled installation should occur after a computer is rebooted. This setting is for scheduled updates that did not take place earlier for some reason.

No Auto-Restart for Scheduled Automatic Updates Installations

If this setting is enabled, it will prevent a computer from being automatically restarted during a scheduled installation if a user is logged in to the computer. Instead, the user will be notified to restart the computer to complete the installation.

My Recent Documents

When a computer is shared with other users at home or at work, there could be a concern that subsequent users of the computer could see the files that the current user has been viewing. This can happen when the computer is configured to have one user account for all users or a user looks at another user's Recent Document folder.

To avoid this, the user can clear the List my most recently opened documents checkbox under the Advanced tab of the Customize Start Menu dialog shown in Figure 4.7. To display this dialog, right-click the taskbar, select Properties, select the Start Menu tab, and then click the Customize button.

Administrators who want to manage this setting for all of their desktops can use Group Policy to modify the Clear history of recently opened documents on exit setting located in the User Configuration section of a GPO in the Administrative Templates > Start Menu and Taskbar folder.

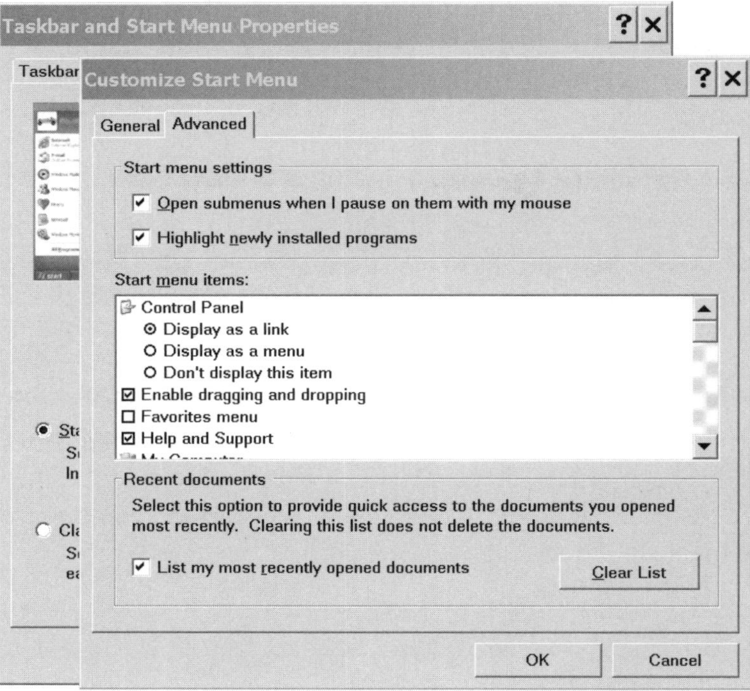

Figure 4.7 The Customize Start Menu dialog

Windows Media Player 9

Windows Media Player 9 (WMP9) is a rich multimedia utility that can play CDs, DVDs, and permit users to listen to online radio stations. Many of the features of WMP9 are implemented by downloading information from the Internet to enrich the media playback experience. To provide this enriched experience, information about what you are watching or listening to must be sent to the WindowsMedia.com site. The Customer Experience Improvement Program can send information about how you use the media player to Microsoft to help them improve future versions of the media player.

The WMP9 Privacy dialog shown in Figure 4.8 enables users to manage information about them that is collected by the media player. This dialog has two kinds of privacy settings. One set manages information that could be sent across the Internet. The other set, in the History section at the bottom of the dialog, has settings that enable users to clear the history of the media they have accessed to prevent other users on the same computer from viewing it.

The dialog appears when the user selects the Options item from the WMP9 Tools menu. Following is an example is what is sent across the wire when a music CD is placed in the CD player with WMP9 running:


```
<?xml version="1.0" encoding="UTF-8" ?>
   <METADATA xmlns:sql="urn:schemas-microsoft-com:xml-sql">
  <version>4.0</version>
  <WMCollectionID>7A5AF1A4-7DE2-4E3D-AA7C-202EF5D80AD5
  ➥</WMCollectionID>
  <WMCollectionGroupID>7A5AF1A4-7DE2-4E3D-AA7C-202EF5D80AD5
  ➥</WMCollectionGroupID>
  <uniqueFileID>AMGa_id=R...180690</uniqueFileID>
  <albumTitle>Greatest Hits [Pro Arte]</albumTitle>
  <albumArtist>Duke Ellington</albumArtist>
  <releaseDate>1989-01-01</releaseDate>
  <label>RCA</label>
  <genre>Jazz</genre>
  <providerStyle>Jazz</providerStyle>
  <publisherRating>5</publisherRating>

<largeCoverParams>200/drd600/d619/d6192157pj2.jpg
  ➥</largeCoverParams>

<smallCoverParams>075/drd600/d619/d6192157pj2.jpg
  ➥</smallCoverParams>
  <moreInfoParams>a_id=R 180690</moreInfoParams>
  <dataProvider>AMG</dataProvider>
```

```
  <dataProviderParams>Provider=AMG</dataProviderParams>
  <dataProviderLogo>Provider=AMG</dataProviderLogo>
</METADATA>
```

I captured the preceding data using the Microsoft Network Monitor tool. Can you guess what I was listening to?

IT administrators, especially in research or military organizations, may be concerned that media titles are being sent across the Internet. Group Policy can be used to manage each of the privacy settings located on the WMP9 Privacy dialog. When Group Policy is used to manage the WMP privacy settings, the dialog settings are disabled to prevent the user from modifying them. Following is a description of the Group Policy settings for WMP9 that could impact a user's or enterprise's privacy or network bandwidth.

Under the Computer Configuration section in the Administrative Templates > Windows Components > Windows Media Digital Rights Management folder is the Prevent Windows Media DRM Internet Access setting. When this setting is enabled, the Windows Media Player DRM component is prevented from accessing the Internet or intranet for license acquisition and security upgrades. This can prevent some media from being played.

Under the Computer Configuration section in the Administrative Templates > Windows Components > Windows Media Player folder is the Prevent Automatic Updates setting. When this setting is enabled, the Internet is not checked for updates and the user is not able to check for updates to WMP9. This feature is different from Windows Update.

Under the User Configuration section in the Administrative Templates > Windows Components > Windows Media Player folder are the Prevent CD and DVD Media Information Retrieval and Prevent Music File Media Information Retrieval settings. These settings match the two checkboxes on the WMP9 Privacy tab in the Enhanced Playback Experience section. By enabling these settings the administrator will prevent information about CDs, DVDs, and music files, respectively, that have been accessed by users from being sent over the Internet.

In the Playback subfolder is the Prevent Codec Download setting. Enabling this setting will prevent missing codecs from automatically being downloaded to the user's computer when attempting to play music. (A codec is a piece of software used to compress or decompress a specific format of music.)

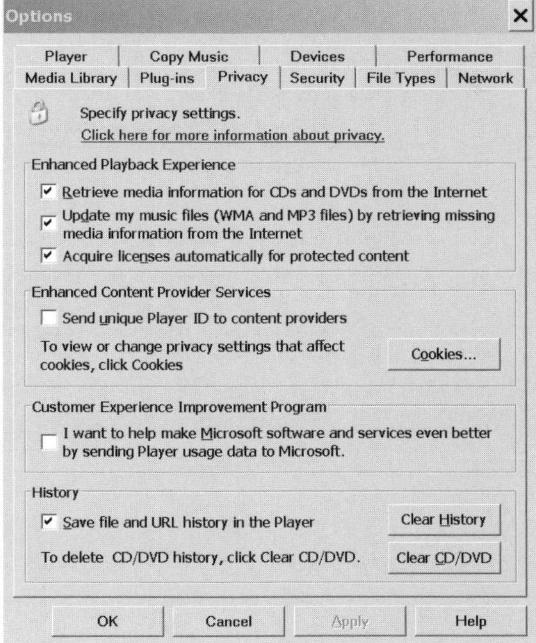

Figure 4.8 Windows Media Player 9 Privacy dialog

Microsoft Office 2003

Microsoft Office 2003 has two types of privacy settings that affect users. One set affects Internet-enabled features such as online help and clip-art insertion. Another set affects the metadata and tracking features such as versioning and comments.

Microsoft Office 2003 Online Settings

The settings to control the Internet-enabled or Online features can be found on the Customer Feedback Options dialog, which can be accessed under the Help menu. Select the Online Content category in the left pane to access the settings. The settings are shown in the dialog in Figure 4.9.

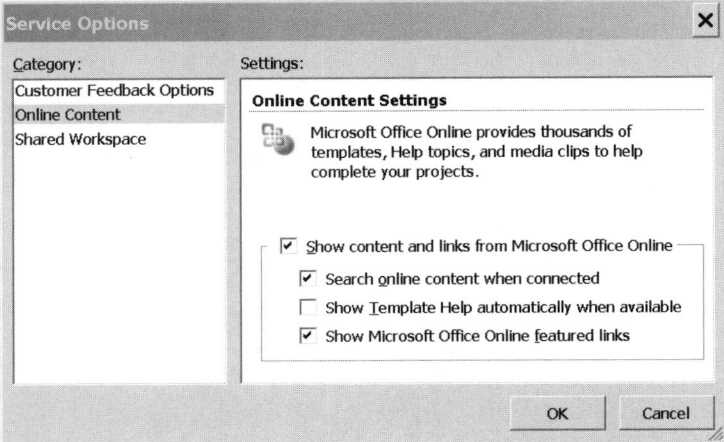

Figure 4.9 Online settings for Microsoft Office 2003

The online settings apply to all Microsoft Office 2003 applications. For example, when the settings are modified in Microsoft Word, they are applied to Microsoft Excel the next time it opens. The application in which you change the setting has to be closed and reopened before the change takes affect. The settings in this dialog are as follows:

- **Show content and links from Microsoft Office Online**—When checked, it enables the other checkboxes to be selected. When unchecked, it prevents all online features from communicating with the Internet. All of these features will continue to work with local information except for the Templates feature.
- **Search online content when connected**—When checked, it permits online features to communicate with the Internet when there is an Internet connection. When unchecked, the Internet-enabled features will use local data.
- **Show Template Help automatically when available**—When checked, it permits templates to be downloaded from the Internet. When unchecked, the Templates features are disabled.
- **Show Microsoft Office Online featured links**—When checked, it enables the Office Spotlight feature. This feature displays Web links in the task pane, which is located on the right side of a document when it displays. Figure 4.10 has an example of the task pane.

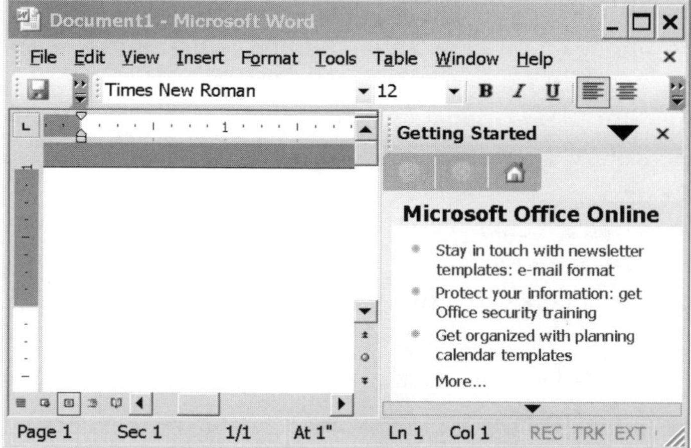

Figure 4.10 Task pane with spotlight links displayed

These settings can also be managed through Group Policy. To access them in Group Policy, you must load the administrative template file Office11.adm. This file is part of the Microsoft Office 2003 Resource Kit, which can be purchased from Microsoft Press. After loading the Office11.adm file, you will find the Online content options setting under the User Configuration section in the Administrative Templates > Microsoft Office 2003 > Tools | Options | General | Service Options > Online Content folder. After enabling this setting, you can select between one of the three values:

1. Never show online content or entry points
2. Search only offline content whenever available
3. Search online content whenever available

When these values are set using Group Policy, they will override the settings that a user may have selected in Office applications. In Office, although the settings may still be active, changes to them are ignored as long as Group Policy overrides them.

Microsoft Word 2003 Metadata Settings

Although some of the other Microsoft Office applications have metadata settings, the majority of them are located in the Word application, and this is the application whose metadata causes problems for users. The most important metadata settings are located in the Privacy section of the

Security tab on the Options dialog, which is displayed in Figure 4.11. To display the Options dialog, select the Options command beneath the Tools menu.

Removing metadata from a document is a five-step process:

1. Set the Remove personal information from file properties on save checkbox.
2. Remove tracked changes.
3. Remove comments.
4. Delete all versions from the document.
5. Clear any comments with your information from any macros you may have created.

Setting the Remove personal information from file properties on save checkbox will clear the personal information from the Properties dialog and anonymize the personal information in the Word document and all versions. To remove tracked changes, use the Reviewing toolbar shown in

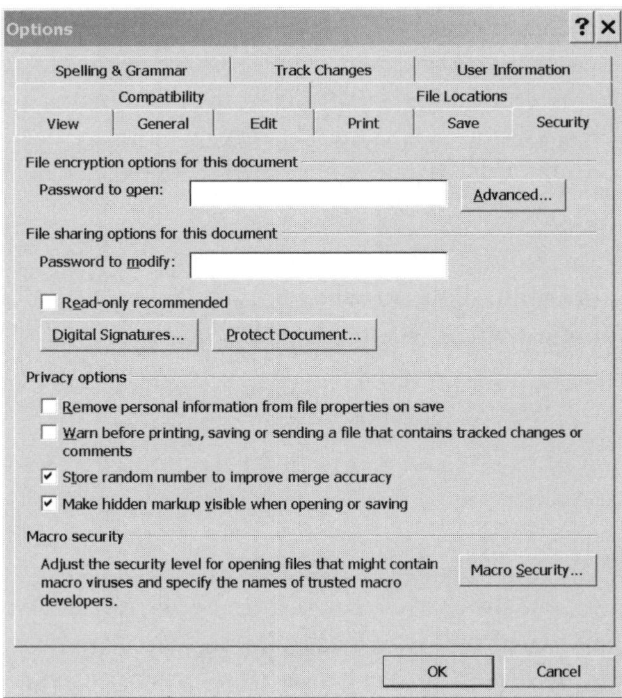

Figure 4.11 Microsoft Office 2003 privacy settings

Figure 4.12. Select the Accept Change button on the Reviewing toolbar (the one with the blue check), and select Accept All Changes in Document. To remove all comments, click the Delete Comment button (the one with the red *X*) and select Delete All Comments in Document. To remove any versions of the document that you may have created, go to the File menu and select the Versions command. On the Versions dialog, select each version and click the Delete button. This will not affect any data in your document.

If you are using Information Rights Management to protect your document, your e-mail address will be embedded in your document in clear text. This is necessary to identify the document to the Rights Management Server and cannot be removed.

These settings cannot be applied using Group Policy. One workaround is to set the Remove personal information from file properties on save checkbox in the Normal.dot file, the global template used by Word. Then whenever you create a new document the checkbox will be pre-selected. However, this will break collaboration and merge features.

Microsoft Office Remove Hidden Data Tool

In January 2004, the Microsoft Office team released the Remove Hidden Data Tool, which enables the user to remove all hidden data from Word, Excel, or PowerPoint files. Although the program has to be installed on a computer with Office 2003 installed, it can run against documents created with previous versions of Office. Once installed, it adds a menu item beneath the Office application's File menu, to provide access from the file to be cleansed. The tool can be used on multiple files when run from the command line. By default, the tool copies a cleansed version of the current file to a separate file. The tool can be installed on computers running Windows XP and later operating systems.[2]

Figure 4.12 Microsoft Office 2003 Reviewing toolbar

2. The *Removed Hidden Data Tool* can be downloaded for free from http://www.microsoft.com/downloads/details.aspx?FamilyID=144e54ed-d43e-42ca-bc7b-5446d34e5360&displaylang=en. A freeware product that can report on and remove the metadata from Microsoft Word 97, 2000, and XP files can be found at http://www.docscrubber.com/.

Note

You can overwrite the current file, but doing so will remove metadata that would be necessary for collaboration in case you ever want to update the file. Cleansing a file also prevents Information Rights Management[3] from being used.

Creating a Custom ADM File

The file association Web service enables users to go to the Internet to search for a program that can be used to read files with an extension that is unknown to the user's system. When a user attempts to open such a file, Windows XP will launch a dialog whose default selection is to go to the Internet to identify the file type and present a list of applications to the user that can be used to open the file (see Figure 4.13). Users often just press Enter before they realize what they are doing and are sent to the Internet when all they wanted to do was use Notepad to open the file.

This behavior can be modified by creating the Registry key shown below and adding the DWORD value **NoInternetOpenWith** to it. After the value is

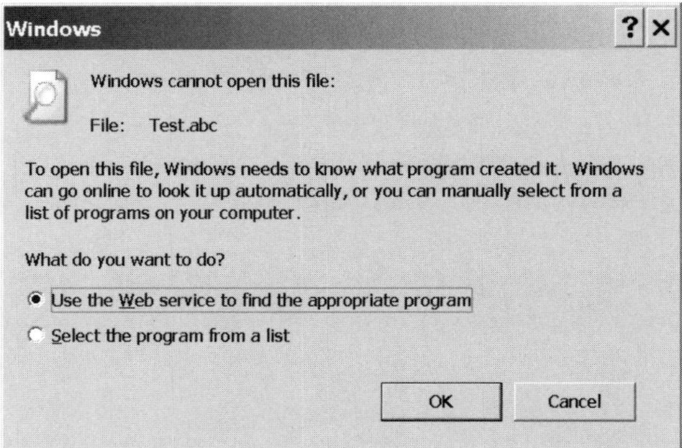

Figure 4.13 Dialog for unknown file type

3. This is a rights management feature that was added in Office XP. It is discussed in Chapter 15.

added, set it to a one (1) to activate the new behavior. When this is done, attempting to open a file of an unknown type will display the Open With dialog shown in Figure 4.14 that used to display in older versions of Windows. Modifying the Registry may be reasonable for some people, but not for an untrained user or for an IT administrator who wants to manage 10,000 desktops.

```
HKLM\Software\Microsoft\Windows\CurrentVersion\Policies\System\
```

Registry settings such as the one above can be managed with Group Policy by creating a custom administrative template (.adm) file and loading it into a GPO for use. The following is the code needed to create the administrative template file with the above Registry setting:

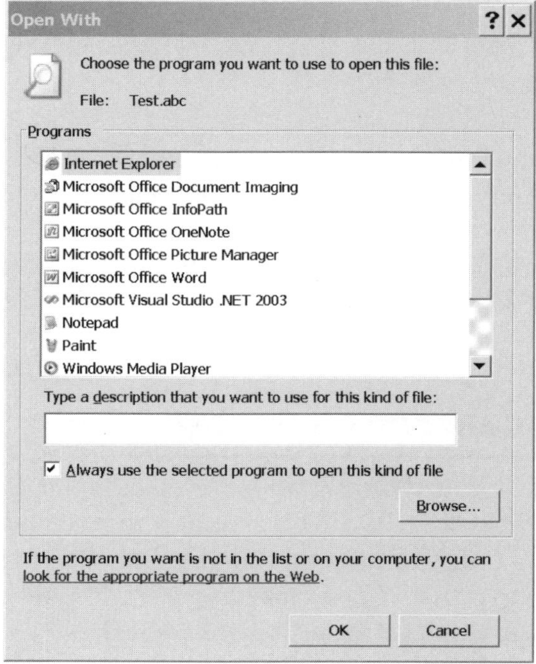

Figure 4.14 Open With dialog for selecting an application

```
CLASS MACHINE

CATEGORY "File Association"
KEYNAME "SOFTWARE\Microsoft\Windows\CurrentVersion\policies\system"

POLICY "Restrict File Association"
EXPLAIN "This policy is used to control the file association
feature's access to the file association Web service on the
Internet.

If the setting is enabled then the user will not be prompted to
access the file association Web service to resolve an unknown file
extension.

If this setting is disabled or not configured then the user will
be prompted to access the file association Web service to resolve
an unknown file extension."

    PART "Prevent connection to file association Web service" CHECKBOX
        VALUENAME "NoInternetOpenWith"
        VALUEON NUMERIC 1
        VALUEOFF NUMERIC 0
    END PART
END POLICY
END CATEGORY
```

To load the template, select one of the Administrative Templates folders in Group Policy, and then select Add/Remove Templates option from Group Policy's Action menu. You then click the Add button and select the file in the Policy Templates dialog. Group Policy will then include a new Administrative Templates > File Association folder in the Computer Configuration section.

Creating a Custom GPO for Privacy

To test some of the Group Policy settings for this chapter, I created a custom Group Policy object (GPO). A GPO is an object that is used to store a collection of group policy settings that can be applied to users and computers in Active Directory. Active Directory has two GPOs defined: the Default Domain GPO and Default Domain Controller GPO.

By creating a custom GPO, I am able to isolate the settings that I made from other settings that had been previously made in another GPO. This

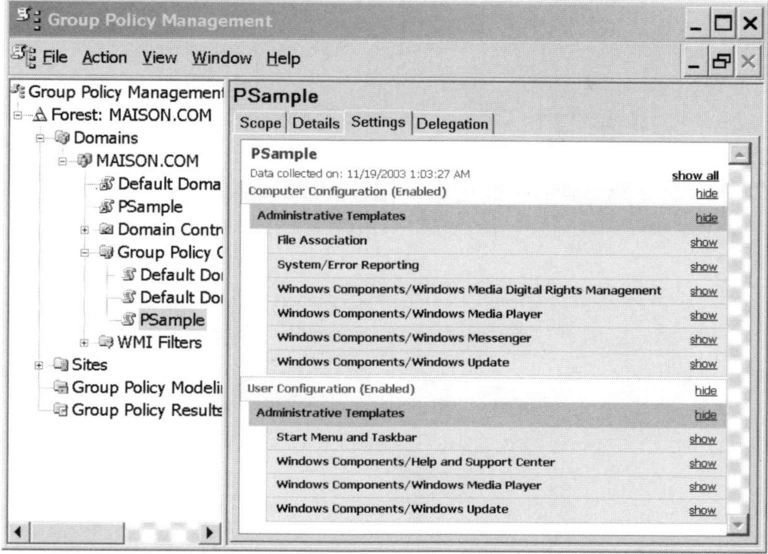

Figure 4.15 Sample report from the Group Policy Management Console

enables me to create a report on the settings that I created that I can use to verify my settings before deploying them across the enterprise. Figure 4.15 shows the report that was made.

If you are an IT administrator and would like to reuse privacy-specific Group Policy in multiple domains, you can use the GPMC to back up your settings from a GPO and then later load them into a new GPO in another domain using the Import Settings command that can be found by right-clicking a GPO. During the backup process, a folder is created, which is named using a GUID. A manifest.xml file is also created. These files are included on the CD-ROM that accompanies this book.

Conclusion

Several options are available to consumers and IT administrators who are using Windows-based systems and are concerned about managing data leaving their computer or enterprise for the Internet. Many of the Windows components provide settings for managing these Internet communications on the desktop and through Group Policy. Many of the new Microsoft applications and applications designed by other companies are including privacy settings in their applications and providing administrative template files for management of these same settings using Group Policy.

As a developer, when creating applications that interface with the Internet, be sure to include settings to enable users to control the Internet communications if they need to. Also permit these settings to be managed by Group Policy or some other centralized mechanism to make it easier for IT administrators to control communications with the Internet and minimize network traffic.

This chapter focused on Microsoft applications and the Windows operating system, but you should also examine applications written by other companies and the components delivered with other operating systems to understand how they communicate with the Internet and protect yourself and your company from exposing sensitive information on the Internet.

Resources

Using Windows XP in a Managed Environment
http://www.microsoft.com/technet/prodtechnol/winxppro/maintain/xpmanaged/00_abstr.mspx

Using Windows 2000 in a Managed Environment
http://www.microsoft.com/technet/prodtechnol/windows2000pro/maintain/w2kmngd/00_abstr.mspx

Using Windows Server 2003 in a Managed Environment
http://www.microsoft.com/technet/prodtechnol/windowsserver2003/maintain/security/ws03mngd/00_abstr.asp

Using Windows Group Policy Management Console
http://www.microsoft.com/windowsserver2003/gpmc/gpmcwp.mspx

Implementing Registry-Based Group Policy
http://msdn.microsoft.com/library/en-us/policy/policy/extending_registry_based_policy.asp

Internet Explorer Administration Kit
http://www.microsoft.com/windows/ieak/

Microsoft Office 2003 Editions Resource Kit
http://www.microsoft.com/office/ork/2003

5 Managing Spam

Most people consider spam to be any unsolicited e-mail that they might receive that attempts to sell them something[1]. It can also include e-mails with chain letters, political statements, or messages from people who just need some attention. Although some people might think that the e-mail version of spam was named after the food SPAM,[2] because both are considered tasteless and a waste of time (at least to some people), nothing could be further from the truth. (As an aside, SPAM is served during breakfast at McDonald's in Hawaii, where it has the highest consumption rate per capita in the United States.[2])

The origin of the use of the term *spam* for unsolicited e-mail appears to come from the Monty Python skit about SPAM[3]. The Vikings in the skit annoyed a waitress by repeating the word *spam* over and over again. In much the same way, unsolicited e-mail can elicit the feeling of annoyance in people who receive it. The way in which the Monty Python skit was connected to the act of unsolicited communication came from the Multi-User Dungeon (MUD)[4] community. One member of that community, after becoming upset with his treatment by some of the other members, created a macro to repeat the word *spam* several times in the MUD environment during a sacred hatching. Later on, MUD members would refer to the event as the time they got "spammed."

---

1. What is spam? Visit http://spam.abuse.net/overview/whatisspam.shtml and http://www.templetons.com/brad/spamterm.html for their answers.

2. http://www.bizjournals.com/pacific/stories/2002/06/10/daily22.html

3. http://www.ironworks.com/comedy/python/spam.htm

4. http://www.british-legends.com/

Spam As a Privacy Issue

In 1928, Justice Louis D. Brandeis wrote, "They conferred, as against the government, the right to be left alone—the most comprehensive of rights and the right most valued by civilized men."[5] *The right to be left alone* became the battle cry of many privacy advocates. Spam is considered an invasion of a right that is categorized as communication privacy.[6] Just as you would not want a stranger knocking on your door, calling you on the phone, or following you down the street, receiving unsolicited mail is an infringement of your right to be left alone. The receipt of spam can also be considered a violation of your right to determine for yourself when, how, and to what extent information about you is used.[7]

Users should always be in charge of how and when they are contacted. Even after agreeing to be contacted, users should be able to opt out of future contacts. Continuing to contact someone after he or she has opted out of contact, or not providing a way to opt out of contact, is akin to electronic stalking. Respecting your customers' privacy is a good way to earn their trust and their loyalty. As a consumer, demand that online services respect your privacy. This chapter provides several ways for you to fight back against spammers and discusses how to send commercial e-mail without becoming a bane of society.

The Cost of Spam

The processing of spam has become a major issue for most companies and consumers. The time it takes to process spam is not only a distraction, it is also a source of lost productivity that is affecting bottom lines. According to a recent survey, the effort being applied to managing spam will cost companies $8.9 billion yearly, with $650 million being spent on antispam and content-filtering products alone in 2003.[8] Even if you are simply

5. This was written during the case *Olmstead v. United States*, http://caselaw.lp.findlaw.com/scripts/getcase.pl?court=US&navby=case&vol=277&invol=438&friend=oyez

6. Many organizations have defined unwanted e-mail as a type of communication privacy (http://www.caslon.com.au/privacyguide1.htm, http://www.privacyinternational.org/survey/Overview.html).

7. Stefan Brands, PET Workshop, Brussels, Belgium, July 2003

8. IETF Anti-Spam Research Group

reading the subject line and the sender's name of an e-mail, it takes time to determine whether an e-mail is a legitimate message to you. Often a cursory scan of the subject line is not enough, and you are forced to open some e-mails to determine their validity. This converts to lost man hours processing unsolicited and unwanted e-mail. There is also a cost associated with processing each e-mail where it enters a company or an Internet service provider (ISP). For example, if it takes four servers to process one million e-mails per hour and half of the e-mail being received is spam, then half of your equipment costs are basically going to process e-mails that rarely benefit anyone. You also have to consider the electrical power, maintenance, administration, and storage costs for the extra equipment you have to purchase just to keep up with the additional e-mail traffic that you have to process.

Consider some numbers: Nortel Networks indicates that 70 percent to 80 percent of the e-mail that they receive each day is spam, and the rate of spam doubles every 4 to 6 weeks. This costs them about $1,000 to $5,000 per day. Aristotle Inc., a small ISP in Little Rock, Arkansas, indicated that spam costs the company $5 per customer per year. The annual cost to pay for new technology and manpower to manage the spam problem comes to $112,000 a year just for that ISP.[9]

A report by London-based security firm mi2G shows that spam caused more economic damage than hackers and viruses in October 2003. The report goes on to say that spam caused $10.4 billion in economic losses worldwide, whereas viruses and worms caused $8.4 billion in losses, and hackers $1 billion in losses. Not only have spammers been filling the inboxes of corporations, they have also started attacking operators of spam block lists, which are providers that assist companies with detecting unsolicited e-mail. Spammers are flooding servers of the block list operators with spam attacks, forcing them to shut down. This is leading to increased costs to acquire more bandwidth and protection, costs that will probably have to be passed along to customers.[10]

9. Kris Oser, "Live from FTC Forum: What Spam Costs," *Direct Newsline*, May 1, 2003.

10. Tim Lemke, "Spam Harmed Economy More Than Hackers, Viruses," *The Washington Times*, November 10, 2003.

Spam Litigation

Many states and even foreign governments are passing antispam laws. Virginia went so far as to make sending unsolicited e-mail a felony for egregious offenses. A conviction can lead to a prison term of one to five years, a hefty fine, and a seizure of profits and income from the sale of spam advertising.

Companies have also successfully used legal action to extract damages from spammers. EarthLink was awarded $16.4 million from Howard Carmack for using EarthLink services to send 825 million pieces of spam. EarthLink was also awarded $25 million in damages in a suit against Kahn C. Smith. Both individuals have been banned from sending future spam.” America Online has won 25 spam-related lawsuits against more than 100 companies and individuals, including one resulting in an award of $6.9 million from a Virginia-based spammer.

Not only does processing spam negatively affect productivity and increase IT costs, it often contains obscene images, financial scams, and malicious software that can damage a user's computer or an enterprise's network. A practice known as *phishing* is used by criminals to fake solicitations from online companies such as eBay and Citibank. These solicitations are sent as e-mails that are dressed up with logos and other formatting to look like an e-mail that could have been sent by the company that they are attempting to impersonate. The e-mails request personal information such as a credit card number or social security number. Brightmail, an e-mail protection vendor, indicated that 27 percent of the e-mails that they filtered in October 2003 were phishing e-mails.[12]

Malicious e-mails cause consumers to lose confidence in doing business online, which can affect every company with an online presence. It behooves all of us to support the antispam movement. Developers and researchers are working on solutions to the spam problem. As the perpetrators of spam become cleverer in their techniques for circumventing standard antispam solutions, software developers have become cleverer in their approach to antispam solutions. Several of these antispam solutions are discussed later in this chapter.

11. "EarthLink Wins Antispam Injunction," Associated Press, May 7, 2003.

12. David Strom, "'Phishing' Identity Theft Is Gaining Popularity," *Security Pipeline*, November 20, 2003.

What Can Be Done to Fight Spam

The previous sections describe various aspects of spam and how it affects individuals, companies, and developers. Based on the enormous negative impact that spam has on our lives, we all bear a responsibility to do what we can to stop spam. The following sections look at ways in which each of us can help to fight spam.

Individuals

Individuals have the biggest opportunity to affect spam.[13] It's individuals who are running the companies, marketing departments, and data centers that send out spam. Individuals are also the terminus for spam; meaning collectively we could use tools that can make spam a bad memory. The suggestions that I am providing here for individuals applies to consumers, employees, students, and other direct users of computers:

- **Use antispam software**—ISPs often provide antispam tools as part of their service. Most e-mail applications come with antispam features. You can also obtain free tools from advocacy groups on the Internet. Turn on the antispam features of your applications. Use these features as part of your decision-making process for companies and products that you are researching. Client-side antispam software is discussed in the "Antispam Approaches" section.
- **Discourage spam**—We all face situations where we could send on a chain e-mail, pass on e-mail-based ads, or choose a company that has a less-than-reputable reputation for delivering bulk e-mail. To quote Nancy Reagan, "Just say no!" It may seem cute, or harmless, or a way to make more money, but in the end it costs us all money in lost productivity and even lost jobs due to lower profit margins.
- **Validate attachments**—Some spam can carry a piece of devious software that can cause spam and the software itself to be propagated to everyone on your contact list. Be certain of attachments before you open them, even if they come from someone you know. I even call my wife before opening an attachment from her, just in case!
- **Don't buy from spammers**—Spammers who send advertisements only continue to do it because it's profitable. Whatever they are selling, you can get from someone else. Use Google.com to find alternative suppliers of anything you might find interesting in spam.

---

13. The Sarasota PC User's Group also has a great list of 2004 New Year's resolutions, http://www.davebytes.com/db010504.htm.

Companies

Companies can be seen as bearing the greatest burden when it comes to spam. Spam causes them to lose money and productivity. Spam clogs their networks. But their advertising campaigns are also the originators of spam, either directly or indirectly. Here are some suggestions for corporations to nip spam in the bud:

- Use antispam software—Ensure that your e-mail servers use antispam software. Work with organizations such as Brightmail[14] to deploy a spam-prevention solution for your company. Insist that your employees use antispam software on their desktops and at home. As an ISP, provide free antispam software to subscribers of your service. Both server-side and client-side antispam software is discussed in the "Antispam Approaches" section.
- **Have an anti-spam policy**—Each company should have a policy that discourages sending spam as a marketing tool or doing business with distributors of spam. All of your customers and potential customers should have a way to opt out of e-mails from your company. These opt-out preferences should be honored by all of your employees and agents.
  - As an ISP, don't permit your members to use your resources to send spam. Use a challenge-response system to avoid the automatic creation of accounts for sending spam and other devious software.
- **Join the organized fight against spam**—Join organizations to fight spam and to pass appropriate legislation for going after spammers.[15] Be a visible advocate of spam prevention. It will show your employees that you are serious about your antispam stance and enhance your corporate brand with consumers.

Developers

Developers build applications, Web services, and line-of-business applications that could potentially send e-mails to the general public. Your software could also collect contact information from consumers that could later be

14. Brightmail, Inc. is the award-winning creator of enterprise-level antispam software, http://www.brightmail.com/.

15. "Yahoo, Microsoft, AOL Sue Under New Anti-Spam Law," Bloomberg News, March 10, 2004.

used to send spam to them. You have a choice to protect people like yourself and your family who are recipients of spam by doing the following:

- **Discourage bad behavior**—Many developers, including myself, run across people who are a bit extreme in their views about what constitutes fun. We are in a unique position to be part of the community of people who can create many of the applications that are reported in the news. As part of this community, we should discourage the creation of spam tools or devious software and their proliferation.
- **Write privacy-aware applications**—When creating applications that can send or collect e-mail, we should add features that permit adherence to a user's privacy preferences. When creating Web sites that send e-mail to users, provide a means for users to opt out of any e-mails that your Web site might send.
- **Expand antispam research**[16]—Several organizations are conducting antispam research. Typically, the work performed by researchers is rarely developed into products. It is important that product developers recognize the value in the research and incorporate it into their products. Work with research groups to see whether there is a new approach from which your product or service could benefit.

Antispam Approaches

This section looks at several approaches that have been taken to combat spam. Most of these are techniques that have been incorporated into tools and larger applications. The last two are approaches with which many of us could become more involved:

- **Accept list**—This is a list of e-mail addresses or domains that are determined to be trusted. This list is built over time as the user determines which e-mails are spam and which ones are legitimate. The drawback to the approach is that spammers often use fake e-mail addresses to evade being identified by these lists. For example, I often get e-mails that have my e-mail address as the sender. This approach also requires constant interaction from the user.

16. The Anti-Spam Research Group is the best place to get connected with researchers, http://asrg.sp.am/.

- **Block list**[17]—This is a list of e-mail addresses or domains that are determined to be responsible for sending spam. This list is built over time as the user determines which e-mails are spam and which ones are legitimate. The drawback to the approach is that spammers usually use fake e-mail addresses and domain names and often change them to evade being identified by these lists. This approach also requires constant interaction from the user.
- **Challenge-response**—This technique sends an e-mail to the originator of an e-mail asking the originator to validate the e-mail by answering a question or typing in a sequence of numbers and letters displayed in an image that cannot be easily read by a computer. This method easily catches spam sent by automated systems where no one is monitoring received e-mails. Unfortunately, this can include legitimate automated response systems from which you may receive an e-mail as the result of an online purchase or a subscription to an online newsletter. This technique can also be an annoyance because e-mails are delayed by a request being sent to the originator asking for validation.
- **Keyword-search**—This approach looks for certain words or a combination of words in the subject line or body of an e-mail. For example, an e-mail that promotes organ enlargements or Viagra would be considered spam. Using a keyword search to validate e-mails for children may be fine. However, many of the words in a keyword search could be part of legitimate e-mails. Moreover, many spammers use clever misspellings to get around these types of filters. Search rules are not case sensitive (so SEX, Sex, and sex as subject words would all be detected). Misspelling and punctuation in the middle of a spam word defeats keyword search spam detectors. Spammers also add additional white space or invisible characters between letters in a word to avoid these filters.
- **Hashing**—With hashing, the contents of a known piece of spam is hashed and stored. Each received e-mail is then hashed and if the hash matches any of the stored hash values for spam, it is rejected. Although this technique is quite accurate at rejecting known spam, it requires additional computing power to process each e-mail, and it is not very effective against most spammers. Many spammers modify their e-mails by adding a random phrase at the beginning or end of an e-mail, which renders hashing useless.

---

17. A directory of sites that provide block lists can be found at http://www.spam-blockers.com/SPAM-blacklists.htm. Although the terms *whitelist* and *blacklist* are used to discuss lists used in spam control, many people find the terms inappropriate, so I don't use them. For Carla.

- **Header analysis**—Each e-mail that is sent across the Internet has a header associated with it that contains routing information. This routing information can be analyzed to determine whether it has the wrong format, because many spammers try to hide their tracks by placing invalid information in the header. For example, the from-host field of one line may not match the by-host field of a previous line. Although this may indicate spam, it could also indicate a misconfigured e-mail server. Equally, a well-formed header doesn't necessarily mean that an e-mail is not from a spammer.
- **Reverse DNS lookup**—This approach validates the domain name of the originator of an e-mail by performing a Domain Name System (DNS) lookup using the IP address of the originator. The domain name that is returned from the lookup request is compared against the domain of the sender to see whether they match. If there is no match, this e-mail is considered spam. Although this can be effective in many cases, some companies do not have their DNS information set up properly, causing their e-mail to be interpreted as spam. This happens often enough to be a problem. That, combined with the performance hit for doing this, makes this solution less than optimum. To perform your own DNS lookup, go to http://remote.12dt.com/rns/.
- **Image processing**—Many advertising e-mails contain images of products or pornographic material. These images usually have a link associated with them so the recipient of the e-mail can click it to obtain more information about the product or service being advertised. Images can also contain a Web bug used to validate an e-mail address. Blocking these images can protect children from harmful images. Some spam tools flag e-mails with images, especially if they are associated with a link, and block them from the inbox. Some sophisticated tools can perform a keyword search of images and reject an e-mail based on the results.
- **Heuristics**—This technique looks at various properties of an e-mail to determine whether collectively enough evidence exists to suggest that a piece of e-mail is spam. Using this approach, several of the techniques previously mentioned, such as header analysis and reverse DNS lookup, are combined and a judgment made based on the results. Although this approach is more accurate than any of the approaches used individually, it is still not foolproof and requires a lot of tweaking to compensate for new evasion techniques that spammers deploy.

- **Bayesian filter**[18]—This filtering technique is one of the cleverest and most effective means for combating spam.[19] It is a self-learning mechanism that can continue to outwit spammers during its lifetime. It works by taking the top tokens from legitimate e-mails and spam e-mails and placing them in a weighted list. Tokens are words, numbers, and other data that might be found in an e-mail. Fifteen tokens are considered to be the optimum number of tokens to use. Too few tokens and you get false hits because the few tokens will exist in good and bad e-mail. Selecting too many tokens results in more tokens appearing in good and bad e-mail. [20]
  - Suppose, for example, that you are a doctor. It may be common for you to receive e-mail with the words *breast* and *Viagra* in them. However, the words *examination*, *patient*, *x-ray*, and *results* should be more common for your legitimate e-mails than spam. These words would become tokens for the legitimate list, and spam-related tokens would go in the other list.
  - You can see how this technique would be more effective on the client than at the server. Deploying this at the server will result in a more generic set of tokens than tokens that are customized for the type of e-mail that each individual would receive. Looking at the previous example, the tokens for the doctor would probably not appear in the legitimate e-mail list because the majority of the e-mails being received by the e-mail server probably won't be for a doctor, or certainly not for the same type of doctor.
- **Payment at risk**—This is an idea that was presented at the World Economic Forum in Davos.[21] It would charge the sender of e-mail a small amount of money each time one of the sender's e-mails was rejected as spam. Although this may be worrisome for senders of legitimate bulk e-mail, it should not be a problem if they are using an opt-in model for determining who is sent e-mails.

---

18. CRM114, the Controllable Regex Mutilator, is considered one of the best Bayesian filter algorithms, http://crm114.sourceforge.net/.

19. One researcher found a way to defeat this type of filter. However, the effort involved is basically cost-prohibitive, http://news.bbc.co.uk/1/hi/technology/3458457.stm.

20. K9 is a software filter that works with POP3 mail servers that implement a Bayesian filter and it is absolutely free, http://www.keir.net/k9.html.

21. http://news.bbc.co.uk/1/hi/business/3426367.stm

- **Honeypots**[22]—Some spammers use open relays on the Internet to send their spam on to its final destination, thus hiding their own identity. A honeypot is a service that simulates the services of an open relay to attract spammers and detect their identity. Deploying these can help fight spam, but could also make you a target. There have been cases where companies that deployed honeypots suffered denial-of-service attacks from spammers attempting to seek retribution. Operators of honeypots can also risk litigation by interfering with Internet communications.[23] Funding one may be better.[24]
- **Legislation**—Legislation such as the Controlling the Assault of Non-Solicited Pornography and Marketing (CAN-SPAM) Act[25] has made great strides in stopping U.S.-based spammers from sending out spam. The European Union's E-Privacy Directive Proposal also seeks to stop spammers.[26] Support of these types of legislation can do a lot for national spam control and will hopefully encourage other nations to pass similar laws.

Challenge-Response for Account Creation

Several ISPs, such as MSN, AOL, and Yahoo, have implemented challenge-response systems for the creation of new accounts to thwart spammers who use automated programs to create new e-mail accounts from which to send new spam. In typical challenge-response systems, the user is presented with a blurred image and asked to enter the characters displayed in it using the keyboard to complete the creation of a new account. This represents a major barrier to spammers who use automated account-creation systems. EarthLink has even extended this feature to force e-mail senders to respond to a challenge e-mail before their initial e-mail is delivered to the addressee.[27]

---

22. http://www.honeypots.com/about.html

23. Kevin Poulsen, "Use a Honeypot, Go to Prison?," SecurityFocus, April 16, 2003, http://www.securityfocus.com/news/4004.

24. Steven J. Vaughan-Nichols, "Stopping Spam Before the Gateway: Honeypots," eSecurityPlanet.com, November 13, 2003, http://www.esecurityplanet.com/trends/article.php/11164_3108311_2.

25. http://www.spamlaws.com/federal/108s877enrolled.pdf

26. The European Coalition Against Unsolicited Commercial Email, http://www.euro.cauce.org/en/index.html.

27. Jonathan Krim, "EarthLink to Offer Anti-Spam E-Mail System," *Washington Post*, May 7, 2003.

A variation of this idea proposes to send a response to each sender of an e-mail to force the sender to perform a simple operation that will use up the resources of the originating e-mail server. Although this is not of any consequence to a sender of a few e-mails, this would heavily impact a company that sends millions of e-mails.

Client-Side Antispam Solutions

Client-side e-mail solutions are features that come with an e-mail client such as Outlook, Netscape, or Eudora. ISPs such as MSN, Yahoo, and AOL also provide antispam features for their client software. These features usually consist of filters that check incoming e-mail and block it based on various criteria. Many of these filtering techniques were described in the previous section.

E-mails that are filtered may be placed into a spam folder, deleted-items folder, a specified folder, or just deleted. One of the problems with these filters is they can inadvertently filter out valid e-mails. Suppose, for example, that you have a filter that routes e-mails to a spam folder based on obscene words. After setting up the e-mail filter, you may receive an e-mail from your doctor about breast cancer. This e-mail could be filtered out of your inbox as spam. For this reason, some e-mail clients permit the user to flag e-mails that have been routed to a spam folder as legitimate e-mails. This flagging tells the filter utility to accept e-mails from specific e-mail addresses or domains. The utility remembers the user's selection and uses the information to filter successive e-mails that arrive at the client. However, this can be a bit tedious. Some more advanced filters automatically place the e-mail addresses of contacts and sent e-mails on the list of acceptable e-mails, relieving users of this burden.

Microsoft Outlook 2003 and MSN software both block images by default. Images that are embedded in e-mails may contain Web beacons that can be used by spammers to validate e-mail addresses. For users who have enabled the preview feature of their e-mail client, these Web beacons can be activated without reading the e-mail.

Peer-to-peer software such as Cloudmark permits users to mark e-mail as spam. Information about the marked e-mails goes to the other members in the peer-to-peer network to block the e-mails from other members' inboxes. This permits everyone in the peer-to-peer network to benefit from spam detection by any of the members.

The company Cobion[28] makes Windows, Linux, and Solaris-based e-mail filtering software. Their Web filter software controls which Web sites employees can visit based on the employee's role, the Web site's address, and the Web site's content. Their e-mail filter can control e-mail entering or leaving an enterprise. The e-mail filter makes use of acceptance and rejection lists. They also filter on domain name, subject, body content, and the content of attachments. The software is also able to scan an image file to determine whether it contains restricted text.

Spam and Infected Attachments

Undesired attachments that often accompany e-mail are not considered spam. However, when they contain viruses, they can be more harmful than the spam that delivered it. One thing that makes malicious attachments insidious is the fact that they can come from people you know who were previously infected by the same software virus. Using an antivirus application such as the ones that are made by McAfee, Symantec, or Computer Associates can help protect your computer and data from harm. Following are some guidelines that can help protect you against viruses:

- Don't open attachments from unknown e-mail addresses.
- Validate that attachments sent by friends were actually sent by them.
- Use antivirus software to scan e-mail attachments.

Server-Side Antispam Solutions

For enterprises and ISPs, the client-side filter does nothing to relieve the network traffic or reduce the resources needed to process e-mail. To positively impact a company's infrastructure costs, an antispam solution needs to stop spam before it enters the enterprise. This section looks at various types of solutions to help do this.

Block List Companies[29]

A block list is a list used to indicate e-mail addresses or domains from which you want to block e-mail. Companies have used their own lists for years to help determine which e-mails are spam. Block list companies such as

28. Cobion was recently acquired by Internet Security Systems, http://www.iss.net/.

29. A selection of block list companies is at http://www.spam-blockers.com/SPAM-blacklists.htm.

Brightmail, Spews.com, and SpamCop make the process more efficient by combining lists from multiple companies. This is one of the easiest ways for companies to protect themselves from unwanted e-mails. The savings made from not having to process spam can easily compensate for the fee charged by these companies.

Antispam Server Software

Some companies sell software that is run on a server between the Internet and the company's e-mail server. The purpose of this software is to remove the burden of filtering e-mail from the e-mail server. This type of software can relieve companies of the expense of having to create and manage their own solution. In an effort to benefit from their investment in antispam software, for example, Boeing is commercializing its internal solution, which it is calling MessageGate Security Edition.[30]

IronPort not only creates systems to permit companies to send bulk e-mail, they also sell servers that enable companies to filter spam.

In addition, two solutions—Spam Sleuth and SpamSquelcher—take a slightly different approach to the way that they protect companies from spam.

Enterprise from Blue Squirrel provides a solution that blocks spam from reaching a company's e-mail server. This product enables administrators to configure the many filtering options while enabling users to personalize their settings through a client application. The following list identifies some of the product's many features:

- Works with any e-mail server
- Challenge-response to force senders to validate their e-mail at a Web site
- Permits domain-level rejection or acceptance lists
- Replies to spam transmissions as undeliverable
- Validates senders by using the following criteria:
    - Checks for missing reply address
    - Validates that from address is equivalent to reply address
    - Compares the IP and DNS data against rejection lists
    - Checks subject and body text against blocked words

The product SpamSquelcher is marketed by ePrivacy Group. This product is unique in that it does not block any e-mails from reaching your company.

30. Matt Hines, "Boeing's Antispam Spinoff Takes Flight," CNET News.com, August 21, 2003.

What it does is increase the processing time for delivering spam for companies sending spam. In this manner, legitimate e-mail is not accidentally lost because of an overly sensitive filter. Decreasing the delivery bandwidth for spam has the effect of increasing the bandwidth for legitimate e-mail while increasing the costs of spammers who send e-mail to companies that deploy this technology.

Developing E-Mail-Friendly Solutions

Many companies and developers are building solutions that include a feature for sending newsletters, service updates, or marketing literature. When doing so, only collect the minimum amount of information needed to provide this service. Provide a way for your customers to opt out of these mailings. If you are bothered by the volume of e-mail that you receive on a daily basis, you can understand that customers want an easy way to manage their own e-mail. Your solution should include a way for users to manage their e-mail settings during the install process, while using the solution, and by going to your Web site.

If you provide a purely online service to customers, you should permit visitors to your site to decide whether they want to receive e-mails, including confirmation e-mails. Don't assume that your customers want to receive these e-mails. Enabling customers to look up a confirmation to an online transaction is a better long-term approach. Provide a means for customers to easily modify their e-mail settings in case they want to remove themselves from an e-mail list. Look at providing options that control how frequently customers receive e-mails. For example, consumers may only want to know about travel specials around holidays instead of every week.

Make sure that your policies on bulk e-mail are followed by agents to whom you outsource the distribution of e-mail. In addition, when you share e-mail lists with partners (with the consent of your customers only), be sure that they follow your e-mail policies.

If your company sends out bulk e-mails, be sure to register with block list companies to avoid having your e-mails flagged as spam. Although you may have a legitimate reason to send out thousands of e-mails at a time, there is no easy way for a recipient to distinguish these e-mails from spam unless you make an effort to inform the intended recipients ahead of time. Any cost associated with doing this should be offset by an increased delivery rate of your e-mails.

Protecting Legitimate Bulk E-Mail

Often companies send newsletters, monthly statements, airline specials, and security alerts using bulk e-mail to consumers who have subscribed to receive these mailings. Unfortunately, many of these mailings are blocked by spam filters and rejection lists. This has led to lost revenue, litigation, and the inconvenience of consumers who rely on the mailings.

Companies such as ePrivacy Group are creating solutions that block spam while permitting legitimate bulk e-mails to make it to their destination. ePrivacy's Trusted Sender Program requires that bulk e-mail companies register with them and adhere to certain practices in order to be accepted into the program. Subscribers to the service are able to add a trust stamp to their e-mail, informing users and e-mail servers that the e-mail can be trusted.

Bonded Sender is a similar program that is run by IronPort. Their program requires participants to pay a bond and agree to send e-mail only to users who have requested e-mail. Participants are added to an e-mail acceptance list. Companies that violate the agreement are placed on an e-mail rejection list and forfeit their bond.

Project Lumos, which is run by the E-mail Service Provider Coalition (ESPC), is an e-mail registry and authentication system that will help distinguish between valid and rogue bulk mailers. The 30 members of the ESPC represent more than 200,000 commercial marketing clients. Its success requires participation from ISPs.[31]

Participating in programs such as these will help lower costs and ensure the delivery of legitimate e-mail.

The SpamCon Foundation has gone a step further than simple participation; they are helping to fund companies running e-mail validation lists that are defendants in lawsuits. Spews.com, which was being sued by a group of spammers, was SpamCon's first client. A Florida judge eventually vindicated Spews.com's antispam tactics and dismissed the suit.[32]

31. Stefanie Olsen, "Marketers Unite to Cook Spam's Goose," CNET News.com, April 23, 2003.

32. Daniel Tynan, "Antispam Activists Win (and Lose) in Court," PCWorld.com, October 14, 2003.

Conclusion

For many companies and individuals, spam is an annoyance and undesired expense. Many products and services are available to help avoid spam. Only by using these tools can we help to stem the tide of the ever-increasing unsolicited e-mails that reach our inboxes every day. If companies with which you do business send you spam, make them stop. Support programs such as the Trusted Sender Program and efforts from companies such as the SpamCon Foundation to assist antispammers.

If you are a solution provider or developer, create e-mail-friendly solutions. Make sure you give customers an easy way to manage e-mails from you. Register with companies that may mistakenly tag your e-mails as spam.

References

Spam.abuse.net is the best site on the Internet dedicated to fighting spam. It contains a wealth of content, tips, and links to help you and your organization fight spam. Help for consumers can be found at http://spam.abuse.net/userhelp/. Help for IT administrators can be found at http://spam.abuse.net/adminhelp/.

Stopspam.org is another site dedicated to stopping spam and other abuses of the Internet. They provide similar tools and content to help consumers and companies fight spam. This site provides information in other languages, such as Hungarian, and they are always looking for volunteers to translate their content into other languages.

Spamresearchcenter.com is a Web site that is dedicated to creating free antispam software for the general public.

6 Privacy-Invasive Devices

In my line of work, I get to see new gadgets and technology all the time. I get excited thinking about all the scenarios in which a new piece of technology could be applied. Part of my job is also to look at the possible privacy issues that might exist with a new technology. I would like to think that people wouldn't misuse technology for personal gain or kicks, but it happens far too often. Expecting technology to always be used properly is not realistic. However, I'm hoping that by now when people are pushing the envelope with the capabilities of a new gadget, they are also thinking about the possible negative uses of the technology and providing protection mechanisms. A case in point: General Motors provided a feature in their OnStar system that permits conversations in the car to be heard in case the car is stolen. The FBI found out about this and decided it would be great to use the feature for listening in on passengers in a car. Fortunately, a federal appeals court did not approve of this use of the technology.[1]

The ruling was not based on a privacy invasion, but because it would interrupt the OnStar system. General Motors was able to avoid a possible privacy issue because of the design of the system. One way this could be looked at is to avoid the possibility of invading someone's privacy by not collecting his or her data or by making it difficult to identify the owner of any data that you do collect. For example, all identifying information should be removed from logs, and the length of time that logs are stored should be limited.

1. Declan McCullagh, "Court to FBI: No Spying on In-Car Computers," CNET News.com, November 19, 2003.

This chapter looks at some cool devices whose features on the surface may look rather innocuous. However, further investigation will show how these devices could be used to invade a person's privacy. The knee-jerk reaction might be to resist the use of new technology altogether (although you probably use a cell phone and wireless phone in your home, which are both susceptible to eavesdropping). A healthy level of paranoia is a good thing. It can encourage you to investigate a new technology before using it and not just dismiss it due to unsubstantiated fears.

With the right implementation, these devices can provide great convenience while protecting a person's privacy. The challenge to developers is to provide devices with great utility while at the same time including adequate privacy protections.

As you read about these devices, understand the risks as well as the opportunities that are afforded by a device. The things that you don't want to give up with these new devices are choice and control. Don't let others take away your right to choose.

Radio Frequency Identification (RFID) Tags

The RFID tag, also known as the smart tag or the RFID chip, is a small electronic device that contains a microchip. When activated by a signal from a scanning device, it emits a unique 64-bit or 32-bit code that can be used to not only tell the operator the type of object being scanned, but also the specific one being scanned, where and when it was manufactured, and the route it took to arrive at the store. Of course this requires support from a distributed back end that first registers the device and then tracks its movements from creation to purchase (and maybe on to destruction).

The technology behind these tags is not a new one. The technology was first used during World War II to identify friendly ships and planes. As microprocessors became smaller and cheaper, the technology was used in chips to track livestock such as cattle. If you live in Dallas or other cities with tollways, you are probably familiar with the tags that have been used on cars for years to provide drivers a quick way to get through tollbooths. RFID tags are also used to track shipping containers, pallets, and expensive items. Not until recently have they been considered viable for tracking less-expensive individual items.

Think of the time that could be saved over doing inventories manually. Instead of a person having to manually count each item to perform an inventory or make frequent walks down retail store aisles to determine whether shelves need restocking, RFID systems will do all of that automatically. They can even check the warehouse to see how many items are left and automatically place a new order. A receiver in the store could monitor shelves on a continuous basis. The data it collects could be correlated against the warehouse computer to not only tell the stockers when to restock store shelves, but also to tell the purchasers when some items need to be reordered.

Store customers could save an incredible amount of time when going through the checkout counter. Customers could just wheel their carts up to the cashier and the entire contents of their cart could be scanned simultaneously. Of course, produce and some other items may still have to be individually weighed at grocery stores.

Antitheft systems could be integrated into the RFID detection system to prevent theft by customers as well as employees. This would remove the need for additional theft-protection systems that are not integrated into inventory tracking. That would eliminate the need for bulky devices attached to garments, especially the ones with ink in them that can accidentally damage merchandise. Even if a person were able to run out of the store with an item, the store would be able to determine everything that was stolen and possibly track the person as he or she runs through a mall or shopping center. This would permit security personnel to more easily apprehend would-be thieves.

Blocking RFID Tags

Retail outlets that sell items that carry RFID tags could use erasure or reprogram devices to help protect consumers' privacy. However, this could increase costs, which are passed on to consumers, and prevent after-sale scenarios. Consumers concerned about their privacy with RFID tags can protect themselves through various means, including an RFID reader-jamming device or a blocker tag.[2]

An RFID jamming device can block a reader's capability to read tags. Although this is an effective approach to prevent RFID tags from being read, it can also be overkill. Not only is using a jamming device more expensive than other approaches, it can also inadvertently disable nearby systems being used in a legitimate fashion. This could expose the wearer to litigation.

---

2. Ari Juels, Ronald L. Rivest, and Michael Szydlo, "The Blocker Tag: Selective Blocking of RFID Tags for Consumer Privacy," RSA Laboratories and Laboratory for Computer Science, MIT, May 16, 2003

A consumer could use a foil or metal mesh to avert radio signals from RFID tag readers. This approach is simple and relatively inexpensive. However, this approach is impractical for large devices. When shopping, consumers could use a foil-lined bag or a metallic tarp to protect items when they are stored in a car.

Blocker tags can be used to deflect a reader from accessing the serial numbers of real tags. A blocker tag simulates a valid range of tags, thus obscuring real tags from a reader. These tags can be used to block a specific range or multiple ranges of tags that may be of concern to consumers.

Whereas these tags may be important to consumers, thieves could also use these mechanisms to circumvent shoplifting-detection devices. This is just another example of how technology can be used for good or bad purposes. The challenge is to stay one step ahead of people looking to exploit technology for illegal gain. Try to anticipate scenarios in which these could be misused and look for ways to protect yourself or to build technologies to help others to protect themselves.

Subdermal RFID Devices

Applied Digital Solutions makes an RFID chip called a VeriChip that can be placed under the skin to identify wearers at ATM machines or places that take credit cards.[3] This version of the device is called VeriPay and is about the size of a grain of rice. When the wearer is in the proximity of the reader (about 4 feet away), it is automatically activated for the wearer. At $200 to insert the device, it's not terribly expensive. There is also an additional $50 yearly maintenance fee. It costs around $1,200 if you need to purchase the handheld reader. Although this device provides some convenience, it does not provide a great deal of flexibility in cases where the owner needs to replace a compromised number or just wants to get rid of it.

The VeriKid version of the VeriChip is marketed as an antikidnapping device.[4] Although the reports state that it can aid in retrieving a kidnap victim, it will work only if the victim happens to be within 4 feet of a detection system that has been activated with the victim's ID. Of course, at this point the victim has already been kidnapped. Because the victim can't

---

3. Applied Digital Solutions' CEO Announces "VeriPay" Secure, Subdermal Solution for Payment and Credit Transactions at ID World 2003 in Paris, http://www.adsx.com/news/2003/112103.html.

4. Julia Scheeres, "Tracking Junior with a Microchip," Wired News, October 10, 2003, http://www.wired.com/news/technology/0,1282,60771,00.html.

be tracked, the VeriKid device isn't a very good deterrent against kidnapping. Advertising the use of the devices would merely encourage would-be kidnappers to attempt to remove them and to stay away from any places that might be monitoring for kidnap victims.

Deployment of the chip is meeting a great deal of resistance from several groups. Privacy advocacy groups such as the American Civil Liberties Union (ACLU), the Electronic Frontier Foundation (EFF), and the Electronic Privacy Information Center (EPIC) have sponsored a petition calling for a moratorium on RFID tagging until further investigation can be done on possible privacy implications.[5] The subdermal RFID devices are a concern of the FDA because of the possible effect they may have after being inserted into the human body.[6] However, further investigation has to be done by the FDA to determine whether VeriChips can be considered a regulated device. If that is not enough resistance to the technology, religious groups are calling it an electronic "Mark of the Beast."[7]

Other RFID Tag Uses

RFID tags are being used for many and various purposes. Here are some suggestions that may help you to come up with your own unique application of RFID technology.

Telltale Golf Balls

World Golf Systems LLC embeds RFID tags in golf balls that are used by TopGolf Game Centers to track the balls hit by customers.[8] At most driving ranges, you have to guess where your balls land, and there's no record of how well you are progressing over time. With this system, you can know exactly where your balls land and have a record that you can take with you when you leave. Multiple players can even compete against each other; gaining points based on the distance and accuracy of shots.

---

5. Sherrie Gossett, "Bio-chip Implant Arrives for Cashless Transactions," WorldNetDaily.com, November 21,2003, http://www.worldnetdaily.com/news/article.asp?ARTICLE_ID=35766.

6. Julia Scheeres, "No Cyborg Nation Without FDA's OK," *Wired News*, October 8, 2002, http://www.wired.com/news/technology/0,1282,55626,00.html.

7. "Bio-Chip Implant 'VeriPay' Arrives for Cashless Checkless Society," These Last Days Ministries, Inc, December 23, 2003, http://www.tldm.org/News4/MarkoftheBeast.htm.

8. http://worldgolfsystems.yuccamedia.com/index.asp

Counterfeit-Proof Casino Chips

Soon casinos will be using RFID tags to identify their chips. The embedded chips will help prevent counterfeiting and employee theft. Tracking chips as they move from one gambling table to the next may even help casinos understand the gambling habits of their patrons. This idea led the European Central Bank to consider placing RFID tags in money to foil counterfeiters.[9]

Express Credit Cards

American Express and Texas Instruments teamed up to produce the first RFID-activated credit card service, called ExpressPay.[10] This service is implemented via a small device that can be attached to your key chain. Although some people may have security concerns about this device, an encrypted signal, a $150 daily spending limit, and online transaction verification for customers make the device relatively safe. The device is held near a reader at the checkout to initiate payment; no signature is required. The device's ease of use has encouraged consumers to spend up to 30 percent more money while reducing checkout times by as much as 40 percent.

Intelligent Car Keys

One of the coolest uses of an RFID tag is the ability to automatically open a car door and trunk, and even to start the car, without using a key or having to pull out the clicker. A random code is used when communications occur between the car and the device to prevent a snooper from making a copy of the device.[11]

Market Acceptance of RFID Tags

Even at their current cost, the Gillette Company ordered 500 million RFID tags to track their shaving-related products. Their plan is to embed the chips in the packaging for their razors. Proctor & Gamble is attaching the chips to some of its cosmetic products.[12] Benetton ordered 15 million RFID chips,

---

9. Jeff Hecht, "Casino Chips to Carry RFID Tags," NewScientist.com, January 9, 2004, http://www.newscientist.com/news/news.jsp?id=ns99994542

10. Learn more about ExpressPay at https://www65.americanexpress.com/expresspay/.

11. The Intelligent Key from Infiniti is an RFID device, http://www.infiniti.com/content/0,,cid-31266_sctid-32005,00.html.

12. Alorie Gilbert, "Major Retailers to Test 'Smart Shelves'," CNET news.com, January 8, 2003.

which they plan to attach to their garments, from Phillips.[13] The Department of Defense has ordered all of its suppliers to apply RFID tags to its pallets and cases by January 2005. Although Wal-Mart has also demanded that its suppliers attach RFID tags to its merchandise by January 2005, they have also asked that pharmaceutical companies have their containers of prescription drugs tagged by March 2004.

Problems with RFID Tags

Although the shoplifting problem might be solved, a bigger theft-related problem could emerge. Consider a would-be thief armed with a reading device in the parking lot of a mall. He would easily be able to determine the newly purchased items that are locked away in a car. This would be especially alarming around Christmas time, when shoppers often carry gifts in their cars as they go shopping from place to place. This could be avoided, of course, if the devices were deactivated after an item was purchased. Unfortunately, there is no easy way to do that today. Placing the devices in a microwave oven for five seconds on the high setting will destroy the devices. Unfortunately, this is not practical for many items.

One problem with deactivating RFID tags at the point of sale is the loss of opportunities after a device is purchased. For instance, RFID tags greatly improve the return process. Because each device is serialized, you shouldn't even need a receipt because a store would know which items were sold by its store. If tags were left intact after the sale, at-home inventories for insurance purposes could be automated. An intelligent security system could even sound an alarm when particular articles are moved near a door or window. This would be extremely useful during parties, when there could be a lot of guests moving in and out of your house. And more importantly, you would no longer have to argue with your spouse about who really bought a CD.

The deactivation problem and the cost of the devices are current barriers to their acceptance. The devices can cost from 5 cents to 30 cents depending on size and volume. Even at these prices, the RFID tags are too expensive for most items in a grocery store. However, research groups, such as the Department of Engineering at the Massachusetts Institute of Technology, are looking for ways to lower the cost of these tags. Decreasing the size of the tags is also a priority for research groups.

---

13. Michael Kanellos, "Intel, SAP Shop 'Store of the Future,'" CNET news.com, April 23, 2003.

RFID Tags and Privacy Concerns

Up to now, we've looked at how RFID tags can lower inventory costs, help prevent theft, and make shopping easier for consumers. However, we haven't thoroughly covered the privacy aspects of these devices, which have many privacy advocates considerably worried. If every article of clothing that you purchase in the future has one of these tags sewn into it, anyone with a scanning device will be able to tell what you are wearing. Anyone equipped with a reading device could tell what type of underwear someone was wearing, including sizes. Imagine going to a dinner party where the hostess was able to determine that you are wearing a fake Versace.

Using RFID Tags to Enable Stalking

There's been a lot of talk about using RFID tags to stalk people. Although a well-placed RFID sensor might be able to detect an RFID tag in a person's coat or shoes, it's just not practical to try to track an individual using this mechanism. Considering the limited range of the devices, it would be easier to just use a camera or follow the person around.

Suppose you are in a large department store and you have placed a couple of items in a shopping cart. Would you feel comfortable as you walked through the store if an automated display gave you suggestions about accessories that you could purchase along with the current items in your cart? What if you could save money in the process? For example, a voice in the lingerie department might say, "If you purchase another pair of silk panties, you can get a third pair for free. Or maybe you would like to purchase a matching bra, which is on sale for half price." This type of assistance can be helpful, but could be considered disturbing and invasive. Maybe you don't want other shoppers to know what you have in your cart. Or maybe you don't even have a cart, but are wearing the underwear. This leads us to another set of services that you may or may not find beneficial.

If you saw the movie *Minority Report*, perhaps you remember a scene where a shopper is given a personal greeting upon entering a clothing store. That is not at all impossible with this technology. By wearing an RFID tag that uniquely identifies you, you would be able to get personalized service or access to a members-only establishment without being interrogated. Imagine walking into a restaurant that you frequent and getting a specialized vegetarian or nondairy menu and having your favorite drink ordered as you are being seated. At your house, you and your spouse could have personalized settings for lighting, radio, and the television when you are in the workout room.

Think of the many things you could do with a set of RFID tags and some sensors around your house if you could purchase and program them yourself. You would always know where you left your keys or wallet in the house. You would be able to detect when your dog or cat leaves the yard. If your neighborhood had detectors on each corner, you could track the movement of anything you tagged. You could more easily track stolen goods, find your pet when it disappears, or more importantly, more easily find a lost child.

The ability to retrieve something precious can be invaluable, but not necessarily at the risk of always exposing your identity or the identity of your family to the outside world. A big problem with the technology today is that there is no way to easily activate and deactivate the device. As the device becomes smaller, it will become almost impossible to detect it, and possibly destroy it, without a special device. Think of how easy it would be to put one on your car or attach one to the bottom of your shoe. Then every time you go to a location that has receivers installed, the receivers can track you. The challenge with RFID tags is to be able to permit consumers to know when they are carrying them and to be able to easily deactivate or control access to them.

Neighborhood tracking systems should be able to track IDs only upon request. The retention time for logs that track tag movement should be programmable by the owner of the tags. Providing informed choice to consumers should be the number-one requirement of all tracking systems.

Obtaining RFID Tags

If you are interested in deploying RFID tags for tracking inventory or automating purchases, you can obtain them from many companies, such as Infineon, Intel, Matrics, Phillips Semiconductor, ST Microelectronics, TagSys, and Alien Technology. Exypnotech, a German company, sells readers that work with most of these devices. If you are interested in building your own RFID tag-based system, you can purchase an RFID starter kit from Exypnotech that provides everything you need to get started with RFID tag research and development.[14]

14. http://www.exypnotech.com/draft/data/produkte/development_kits_e.html

Radar-Based Through-the-Wall Surveillance System

The Radar-Based Through-the-Wall Surveillance System is being funded by the National Institute of Justice.[15] This system is to be used by the law enforcement community to track the movement of suspects in the interior of a building. This device will track an individual through an 8-inch wall up to a distance of 75 feet from the device. That would permit a police officer to track someone through most homes without the officer having to move. The fact that this device fits into a suitcase would make it easy for operators to move it around as they use it. According to a June 2001, Supreme Court ruling, however, this device cannot be used without a warrant.

Because the device uses ambient energy, it can be impossible to detect. The only protection against it is lead-lined walls or for the individual being tracked to remain motionless. Those solutions aren't very reasonable. However, privacy laws can limit the abusive use of these devices. One can only hope that as technologies such as this are developed, that someone is designing protective screens to permit individuals to protect themselves from these devices.

Spotme Conferencing Device

Spotme is a handheld device made by the Swiss company Shockfish SA.[16] It's a UNIX-based device that provides attendees of a conference with access to conference information. Did you ever want to get up-to-date information on schedule changes and special events? This embedded Linux device provides those features and many more. You can access product information, read speaker bios, retrieve personal messages, and fill out surveys all online with this device.

I'm sure you're saying that any Web-enabled PDA can do all those things. However, these devices have some personal networking features such as the ability to exchange electronic business cards with other attendees whom you meet. You can point the device at anyone else carrying a device within 30 meters and get his or her picture and contact information. You can also program the device to alert you when a specific person or a person with certain attributes, such as loves basketball, gets within range of your device.

---

15. http://www.raven1.net/nij_p26.htm

16. http://www.spotme.ch/spotmeinfo.html

A friend of mine used one of these devices at a conference and told me how great it was. He wasn't concerned about any privacy implications because the information it provides is normally available on an attendee's badge. However, he was astonished when he was walking to his room at the hotel and the device identified another attendee within another hotel room (who had left the device on). Of course, the device can always be turned off for privacy.

When using devices like these, think about the possible privacy implications and how to enjoy the cool features while protecting yourself from possible abuses by outsiders.

nTAG Smart ID Badges

The nTAG device is a smart badge that is worn by attendees at a conference or workshop. They use RFID technology to communicate with each other and a central server. They are manufactured by nTAG Interactive, LLC.[17] These intelligent devices permit conference administrators to accurately track the number of users who attend each session, restrict access to certain areas, deliver messages to attendees, and survey an audience electronically.

On a personal level, the badge enables attendees to exchange information with each other. It can even help connect people with common interests. During the registration process, attendees enter some of their major work-related or recreational interests. When the attendee comes within five feet of someone and is facing the person's badge, the attendee's badge indicates the shared interests of the two of them. This information can be used as a professional or social icebreaker.

The device is pretty simple, consisting of only three control buttons and an LCD display. However, it doesn't provide an easy way for a person to be selective about the people with whom she shares her interest. As long as it is being worn and is active, people walking by can gather information about the wearer. So don't forget to turn it off when you are ready for some privacy.

17. http://www.ntag.com

Smart Dust

Smart dust devices are basically small integrated circuits that sit on top of a battery. They are bidirectional communication devices smaller than 12mm^3. As small as they are, researchers are working to get the size of these devices down to the size of a grain of sand. As Robert Heinlein wrote many years ago, "The only things privacy laws accomplish is to make cameras smaller."[18] The only protection from abuse by these types of devices is possible if everyone can detect them. Although this may sound radical, protecting yourself from gangsters and government is more important than any benefit that could be derived by law enforcement.

Smart dust can communicate at a distance of more than 600 feet. Using a laser, this range could be increased to 13 miles (about 21 kilometers). However, the beam needs to be directed in order to be practical to use. These devices act as sensors with the capability of monitoring temperature, light, humidity, vibration, and location. Currently these devices are a research project of Professor Kristofer Pister at the University of California, Berkeley.[19]

This is a fascinating technology that could bring many benefits to mankind. Think of a central computer being able to monitor the environmental characteristics of dozens of machines on a manufacturing floor. The ability for a computer to maintain the settings of a manufacturing machine within optimum operating range would be greatly improved. The climate conditions of a tropical rainforest could be monitored at a granular level, which could provide for better weather forecasting.

The device also has numerous military applications. The ability to track enemy movements and recover captured personnel, equipment, and landmines are just a few. Considering their size, they would be easy to distribute and conceal. The major limitations to the technology right now are its power requirements and cost. The device can last only one week, or two years with a 1 percent duty cycle, which may be sufficient for some applications. The current cost is between $50 and $100, which is cost-prohibitive for most applications.

Although the possible applications are endless, the opportunity for abuse is also vast. As small as these devices are, it would be extremely easy

18. Robert A. Heinlein, *Stranger in a Strange Land*, Ace Books, 1961

19. http://www-bsac.eecs.berkeley.edu/~pister/SmartDust/

to deploy smart dust in a building or home for malicious purposes. It is important that the release of these devices be combined with the ability to detect and deactivate them. This is the challenge for solution developers who want to avoid criticism from consumer advocacy groups. This can also be an opportunity for companies that want to fill the market niche of building sensors to help consumers protect themselves from these types of privacy-invasive devices.

Devices That Look Under Clothing

So far, we have looked at devices that can be used to track people and objects. Although these types of devices may be considered privacy-invasive, at least they leave your modesty intact. This section covers two technologies that can take a vivid look beneath your clothes. Of course, it's all in the name of security.

Passive Millimeter Wave Scanners

Passive Millimeter Wave (PMMW) devices provide a means to detect metallic and nonmetallic weapons hidden under clothing. Current weapons-scanning systems depend on the ability to detect the metal in a weapon. Weapons made of plastics or other manmade materials can go undetected by standard airport scanners. John C. Smith University is currently the only educational institution that is studying these devices.[20]

PMMW devices use the radiant heat from a person's body to detect hidden objects. These devices can even work on moving objects, which makes them more practical for scanning large groups of people. Because they are passive devices, it is not possible to detect that they are in use. The unsettling part of this technology is the fact that it can provide an image of what a person looks like under his or her clothing. The November 2003 edition of *National Geographic* has an article with samples of what one of these images might look like.

If the PMMW device could provide 100 percent safety to passengers, would you feel comfortable standing in front of one? Even if it were used randomly or only on individuals that fit a certain profile or didn't pass a background check, would you be okay with its use?

---

20. http://www.photonics.com/XQ/ASP/url.readarticle/artid.179/QX/readart.htm

Backscatter X-Ray Devices

Backscatter x-ray devices provide a means to examine beneath a person's clothing using x-rays without causing harm to people.[21] The dosage of x-ray radiation consumed by an individual with this device is equivalent to the typical exposure to the sun. Forget the fact that some scientists think that sunshine can cause skin cancer. Like the PMMW technology, it provides a pretty vivid black-and-white image of a person's body under his or her clothing. Although the devices are not currently being used in airports, they have been used for years to scan South African miners on their way home.

In addition to the problem with radiation exposure, these devices are pretty large, which would make them difficult to deploy in most airports. Both devices need a feature that can hide a person's sensitive areas on the image or extract dangerous-looking devices from a scan for presentation to a screener before these devices will be acceptable for general use. It's hard to say whether people will be allowed to wear protective underwear to shield their modesty if it could also block a dangerous device.

A Legal View of New Technology

As advances in technology occur, there will be a greater likelihood that new technology will be used to spy on individuals, even if that is not the purpose of the technology. When creating technology, put in safeguards to prevent it from being used for illegal purposes. For the most part, the Fourth Amendment protects us from illegal searches with new technology where there is an expectation of privacy.

The advent of new technology does not give the government any additional flexibility when it comes to monitoring someone. It was determined in the Supreme Court case *Kyllo v. United States* that using a thermal-imaging device to measure the amount of heat emanating from someone's home to determine whether marijuana is being grown on the premises constitutes an illegal search. Citing *Katz v. United States*, the Court stated that a search has occurred when a reasonable expectation of privacy is expected and violated, even when one is in public. Furthermore, according to *Silverman v. United States*, using sense-enhancing technology, which

21. http://www.cbsnews.com/stories/2003/07/17/eveningnews/main563797.shtml

is not in general public use, to gather information regarding a home's interior that could not otherwise have been obtained without physical intrusion constitutes a search. The government contended that it had not invaded the privacy of the home, because no intimate details were uncovered. But according to the Court, the fact that "intimate details" were not uncovered is no defense, because all details in the sanctity of the home are considered intimate details. According to *United States v. Karo*, even a minuscule intrusion is considered an invasion of privacy interests.[22]

Conclusion

Technology is advancing at such a rapid rate that it is outpacing our ability to restrict its possible abuses. The devices described in this chapter provide examples of the many ways that people and items can be tracked and exposed. Far too often individuals are unable to protect themselves from exposure to these devices. As shown in the preceding section, *A Legal View of New Technology*, the government is willing to use new technology against its citizens until they are constrained by the court system. The problem is that the courts are typically silent unless someone is smart enough and brave enough to challenge the government.

Even with the many abuses that have occurred in the past due to these new technologies, we shouldn't turn into Luddites.[23] With the right protections, and with the proper amount of transparency, these devices can be of great benefit to mankind. No one wants to go back to the horse and buggy or give up his or her privacy to feel more secure. We should be able to enjoy both new technology and privacy. Technology should add value and protection to citizens while enabling them to avoid abuse.

---

22. *Kyllo v. United States*, http://caselaw.lp.findlaw.com/scripts/getcase.pl?court=US&vol=533&invol=27, *Katz v. United States*, http://caselaw.lp.findlaw.com/scripts/getcase.pl?court=US&vol=389&invol=347, *Silverman v. United States*, http://caselaw.lp.findlaw.com/scripts/getcase.pl?court=US&vol=365&invol=505, *United States v. Karo*, http://caselaw.lp.findlaw.com/scripts/getcase.pl?court=US&vol=468&invol=705

23. Audrey Hudson, "Orwellian eyes," *The Washington Times*, November 27, 2003, http://washingtontimes.com/national/20031126-113641-3955r.htm.

A lot of effort is put into equipping the home and car of the future with many timesaving conveniences, but very little effort is spent creating a selection of privacy-protection devices. The challenge for technologists and others who want to benefit from consumers looking to protect their privacy is to create devices that will counteract the privacy evasiveness of the many devices that will soon be on the market. For example, the market for RFID devices and supporting systems is estimated to be in the billions of dollars over the next few years. This doesn't take into account the market in devices to protect people from RFID systems. To keep up with the progress of RFID technologies, view the online RFID Journal at http://www.rfidjournal.com/.

II Privacy and the Organization

7 Building a Privacy Organizational Infrastructure

Let's consider two examples of the way in which some people attempt to be successful at an endeavor without first laying the proper foundation. Benjamin and Victoria each want to start a successful home-building business. Benjamin has worked on a couple of houses and determines that he could probably do it faster, better, and cheaper than the people for whom he is working. So he hires a few of his smart friends and decides to buy some land and put up some houses. However, his lack of experience didn't prepare him for the challenges he would soon face. Some of those challenges include the following:

- Zoning requirements based on the type of house to be built must be met.
- Permits are required for much of the work involved in building a house.
- Licensed professionals are required for some tasks.
- Building on a slope requires a special building technique.
- Some housing sites don't have access to city sewers, and percolation tests need to be run to determine whether the ground is suitable for septic.
- Some important selling points such as high-speed Internet access and cable TV are not available in all areas.

Benjamin was out of money before he completed the first house due to delays and fines for not having the appropriate permits in place. This is an example of bad planning and wishful thinking that didn't work out.

Victoria, in contrast, not only worked with a contractor to build several homes, she also got a degree in building construction. When she decided to start building her first house, she partnered with some people who had long experience in housing construction. She worked with a property specialist to find the right site for her homes and had all her permits in place before having the first piece of lumber delivered. Her preparation gave her the foundation she needed to be successful.

In another example, a very successful French wine producer decided that he wanted to start exporting his wine to the expanding market in China. The president of the company hired a native Chinese wine merchant as a consultant. The consultant would travel with the company's salespeople on meetings with store and restaurant owners to negotiate contracts to distribute the company's wine. After a few successes, the salespeople started to branch out on their own without the consultant to cover more area. Even though they could speak Chinese, the salespeople did not understand Chinese customs very well and made mistakes that caused them to lose important contracts. For example, they would sometimes offer a clock as a gift to a storeowner during an initial meeting. This would be like offering someone in the United States a miniature coffin as a gift. Needless to say, it did not go over very well.

A couple of things can be learned from these examples. First, just because you have done something a few times doesn't mean you can go out and be successful on your own without the right preparation. Second, just because you have one expert in your company doesn't mean that everyone in the company is going to become an expert just by being around her in a few meetings.

Developing your company into one that is well-versed in privacy best practices takes strong investments in your people, processes, and organization. The people will take responsibility for getting the job done, the processes form the road map for how they will get the job done, and the organization indicates how the many departments across your company will work together to be accountable for building a successful privacy infrastructure.

The Absence of a Privacy Infrastructure Can Be Costly

A simple search of the Internet of privacy incidents in the news will provide several examples where companies have been fined or embarrassed because of privacy issues. The cost of not formalizing and enforcing a set of privacy policies can be pretty high. One of the most famous legal cases concerning online privacy occurred when DoubleClick was accused of tracking the browsing habits of millions of people without their knowledge or consent.

DoubleClick was fined nearly $2 million dollars and suffered additional costs fighting the class-action suits and revamping their online service to comply with the final judgment.[1]

Ziff Davis Media, a magazine publisher, had to pay a settlement totaling $125,000 to three states and magazine subscribers for permitting the credit card numbers of magazine subscribers to be exposed on the Internet. These credit card numbers were visible on the Internet for more than a month.[2]

Prime Minister Tony Blair's staff created a document on Iraq's security and intelligence organizations. This is the same document that Secretary of State Colin Powell praised and cited during an address to the United Nations. Because of metadata that was left in the Word document, it was found that the information came from sources other than Mr. Blair's staff. It appears that much of the content was actually written by an American researcher on Iraq.[3]

Having a set of privacy policies in place that are enforced and complied with is a good way to avoid these types of costly entanglements. This chapter looks at how the corporate privacy policy should be disseminated to the departments within a company and used as a basis for departmental policy. Understand that policies without mechanisms to measure and enforce compliance, without penalties for failure to comply, are in fact not policies at all; they are just wishful thinking. Consider how to incorporate metrics and consequences into every policy element to ensure compliance. Auditing is also important to ensure that employees comply with corporate policies and sometimes to comply with regulatory compliance. It's unfortunate that companies have to invade their employees' privacy to protect their customers' privacy.

Understanding Your Company's Data Handling Practices

A company should have policies in place to govern the collection, storage, sharing, and retention of data being collected by its employees. All employees should understand these policies. A company should think about all the ways in which it collects data:

1. Stefanie Olsen, "DoubleClick to Settle Privacy Suits," March 29, 2002, ZDNet.

2. Seanna Adcox, "Ziff Davis Agrees to $125,000 Settlement with Three States," Associated Press, August 28, 2002.

3. Richard M. Smith, "Microsoft Word Bytes Tony Blair in the Butt," ComputerBytesMan.com, June 30, 2003.

- From Web site visitors or online commerce
- Product registration and magazine subscriptions
- Business cards left at conferences and workshops
- Notes from customer meetings
- Mailing lists purchased from other companies

Is this collection being tracked in a way that can be audited from a corporate group? Is this collection being done in a consistent fashion across the company? Is the company even aware of all the places where data is being collected? If an irate customer threatens the company with a lawsuit if it doesn't stop sending an e-mail to him or her, how confident is the management that it can comply with the request?

These are the types of questions that should be resolvable by employees upon reviewing their corporate policies or departmental privacy practices. The company's privacy department should go over these topics to make sure they are being covered by corporate policies. If not, the best way to prepare a set of policies that govern your data handling practices is to first understand what data your company is collecting. Then determine the dataflow and lifecycle for the data. Document where data comes into your company, where does it flow, where is it stored, who accesses it and for what purpose, how long is it kept, and where is data sent outside of the company. Chapter 11 describes the use of dataflow diagrams and will assist you in building your own dataflow diagrams.

Companies should also investigate purchasing software that can help them better manage and track the flow of data through their company. Companies such as IBM[4] and Zero-Knowledge Systems[5] sell enterprise privacy management software. Watchfire[6] and COAST[7] sell privacy compliance software for Web sites. Vontu[8] and Lumigent[9] build solutions that help to track the flow of enterprise data.

---

4. http://www-306.ibm.com/software/tivoli/products/privacy-mgr-e-bus/

5. http://zeroknowledge.com/en/eps.php

6. http://www.watchfire.com/

7. http://www.coast.com/index.html

8. http://vontu.com/solutions/

9. http://lumigent.com/solutions/

The Chief Privacy Officer

The Chief Privacy Officer (CPO) should be the person in charge of privacy for an entire company. For large companies, this should be the person's full-time job. The policies created by the CPO help to mitigate litigation, lower barriers to sales, improve employee retention, and improve the corporate image. Considering the importance of this job, it should be at a high enough level to give the CPO the authority necessary to enforce the adoption of the company's privacy policies. The CPO should report to a senior executive. The senior executive provides visibility and validity for the CPO. Without this reporting structure, the CPO will not be able to influence adoption of the company's privacy policies. The CPO should be part of an organization that will help him or her to be successful. For example, the executive, policy, legal, and operations departments all provide environments that can contribute to the success of the CPO. Placing the CPO in the sales or marketing departments would put the person at odds with goals of the department and limit the influence of the position.

The CPO should be an experienced privacy professional. He should be a member of privacy organizations such as the Privacy Council[10] and the International Association of Privacy Professionals (IAPP).[11] These organizations provide training, online content, and host conferences where privacy professionals can meet and learn from each other. Being a lawyer can be beneficial for a CPO, but it could also be a hindrance. Some lawyers like to limit their decision making around policies to simply following the letter of the law instead of providing employees and customers with the appropriate level of transparency to feel comfortable about the company.

There will be times when the CPO will weigh business practices against privacy norms and choose to continue a business practice that goes against corporate policy. Suppose, for example, a group at a company comes out with a brand new product and builds a new Web site to accompany the product launch. A day before the launch, it is determined that none of the Web pages for the site has a privacy statement. Should the launch be delayed, risking losing millions of dollars because the window for Christmas deliveries will be missed? In this case, it may be better to continue with the launch and let the public know in advance of the launch that the privacy statements are forthcoming.

---

10. http://www.privacycouncil.com

11. http://www.privacyassociation.org

The Corporate Privacy Group

Each company should organize a corporate privacy group (CPG) to manage privacy and its privacy initiatives. The CPG is responsible for creating the corporate privacy policies for a company. After this policy is created, it should be disseminated to each group in the company, expressed to customers, and its compliance should be ensured. The CPG should consist of the senior privacy people for an organization. A company's CPO should lead it. The CPG should work with the legal, marketing, and public relations departments to make sure that the CPG develops policies that do not conflict with current legislation or consumer opinion. The internal and external messaging for these policies is also important. Employees must understand the business reasons for complying with these policies. Consumers should understand the customer value that is obtained because the company has adopted these policies. Figure 7.1 provides an example of how a corporate privacy group can be organized.

Creating a Corporate Privacy Policy

When determining the content of the corporate privacy policy, the current principles defined by the Federal Trade Commission, Department of Commerce, Organization of Economic Cooperation and Development, and European Commission should be reviewed. For example, users should be

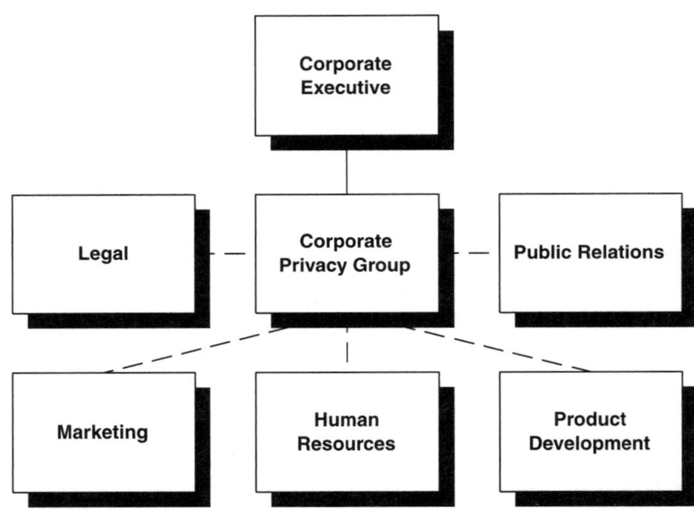

Figure 7.1 Organizational chart for a corporate privacy group

provided with informed consent before their data is collected. It should always be a goal to put users in control of their data. The entire lifecycle of data as it is collected, stored, used, shared, and eventually destroyed should be part of the privacy policy. There should be a policy that describes how employees, products, and services treat customer and partner data. Relationships should be built with privacy groups such as the Electronic Privacy Information Center (EPIC) to help create and validate the company's privacy policy.[12] Privacy advocacy groups can provide companies with expertise based on years of experience with working in the realm of privacy.

Legal, public relations, and senior management should review the corporate privacy policy. The following things should be taken into consideration during the review:

- Current privacy legislation
  - Including legislation in each region where the company does business
- The types of data collected
  - Employee, partner, customer, or data from children
- Data category, such as medical, financial, or legal
- Data transferred to third parties
- Customer requests regarding privacy

It's also a good idea for a company to have a privacy impact assessment performed early on and whenever major changes are made to data handling practices. Consulting companies such as PricewaterhouseCoopers[13] and Deloitte and Touche[14] offer a suite of privacy services that can assist with privacy impact assessments.

Each corporate privacy policy is going to govern the data lifecycle practices of the entire company, so its review should be taken seriously. After the final review is complete, it should be posted on the internal Web site for the CPG. An announcement should be made by the company's

---

12. More information can be found at http://www.truste.org/bus/pub_resourceguide.html.

13. http://www.pwcglobal.com/Extweb/service.nsf/docid/5452EF6E7B7ED061CA256B7200091A49

14. http://www.deloitte.com/dtt/section_node/0%2C2332%2Csid%25253D3489%2C00.html

president or CEO for all departments to comply with the company's privacy policy.

Creating a set of privacy policies for product development will be a challenge for most companies because the issues are completely different from those experienced by most groups within the company. Chapter 10 provides an in-depth look at developing policies for product development. For other groups, privacy policies need to look at how the groups collect and use data. For product groups, privacy policies will be more concerned with how the group's products collect and transmit data when they are used by end users. Having a person with product development experience involved in the creation of the policies will help to avoid issues that may become barriers to product sales.

Providing Privacy Training

After the privacy policy has been defined, training should be developed to help educate employees about the company's privacy policy. Multiple levels of privacy training may be required. One high-level training program can serve as a primer on privacy for employees. This level of training can often be obtained from privacy organizations or companies that provide privacy training, such as Deloitte and Touche, Ernst and Young, and MediaPro.[15]

Beyond the high-level privacy training, a more focused privacy training should be provided that reflects the privacy policy that applies to roles within a company that apply to only a small group of people. For example, there may be a policy that only applies to executives or lawyers. Major departments within a company may also want to provide privacy training that describes the privacy practices that will affect the day-to-day tasks of employees within the department.

The Flow of Privacy Policy to Departments

Each department should be engaged by the CPG to make sure that they are signed up for complying with the company's privacy policy. The task for each department will be to create a standard that will map the company's privacy policy to a set of practices that will guide the way they do business. For example, the privacy policy may talk about how data should be protected during storage. There may be a requirement for encrypting the storage of certain types of data being collected from customers. This may

15. http://www.mediapro.com/privacy

require that a department augment its storage practices to comply with the new policies. This is basically the role that the department leads are supposed to take. Each department should analyze how each privacy policy affects their data handling practices. Based on this analysis, a set of standards should be created that instructs the department how they will perform their duties in order to remain compliant with the company's privacy policy.

To show how the translation from a corporate policy to a departmental standard might work, I will pick a hypothetical policy and see how it might apply to two different departments. Suppose, for example, that a policy states, "All customers must agree to secondary use of their data." The operations department can create a standard that states, "All Web sites that collect data must provide a checkbox to permit customers to select whether they want to participate in secondary usage of their data, such as receiving a newsletter. The default for the checkbox must be off to indicate that the customer does not want to receive a newsletter." By itself the practice would not be useful unless the marketing department was honoring each customer's preferences. So the marketing department could create a standard such as, "All customer mailings that are not part of the Terms of Use for a program require consent from the customer. Consent should be implemented as a Boolean flag stored in a database that maps to the specific mailing. This flag must mirror the checkbox value on any Web page that advertises the mailing."

After the department has completed the creation of its privacy standard, it should be rolled out to each team in the department. The rollout should start with privacy training for each team member, which includes an understanding of the importance of privacy to his or her job. Each team should create a rollout plan that provides a task list with dates that describes how and when the new privacy standards will be implemented.

Each department should be held accountable for compliance with the corporate privacy policy. An audit should be performed periodically against each department to ensure compliance. There should be a direct correlation between the number of privacy incidents that occurred against a department and how well the department rolled out their privacy standards. Only by careful planning and monitoring will compliance happen. Departments are often short of resources. A request to comply with a set of privacy policies is certain to be ignored or deferred. This is where executives can assist with reassigning priorities or increasing resources to support the privacy compliance effort.

Building a Privacy Hierarchy for Developing Solutions

Product groups normally have a formal organizational structure for the efficient development of products. In this structure, rarely is anyone assigned to ensure privacy compliance. Faced with the new task of privacy compliance, what is the best way to assign resources to this task without disrupting the current development process? When security became an important issue in the product development process, there was probably no one person assigned to security. It is everyone's responsibility to understand how security affects his or her job.

Privacy should have the same level of importance as security. Every component team member should have a general understanding of privacy and how it impacts his or her job. Testers, developers, program managers, and writers all have a part to play in privacy compliance. A privacy lead should be assigned to each component team. Their specific guidance should be provided by a group such as a privacy council to ensure consistent adoption by each component team in the product group. The diagram in Figure 7.2 provides an example of how component teams work with a privacy council.

Creating a Privacy Council

A privacy council can act as the governing body for developing, delivering, and validating privacy practices across product groups. A privacy council is typically made up of a group of stakeholders who are responsible for

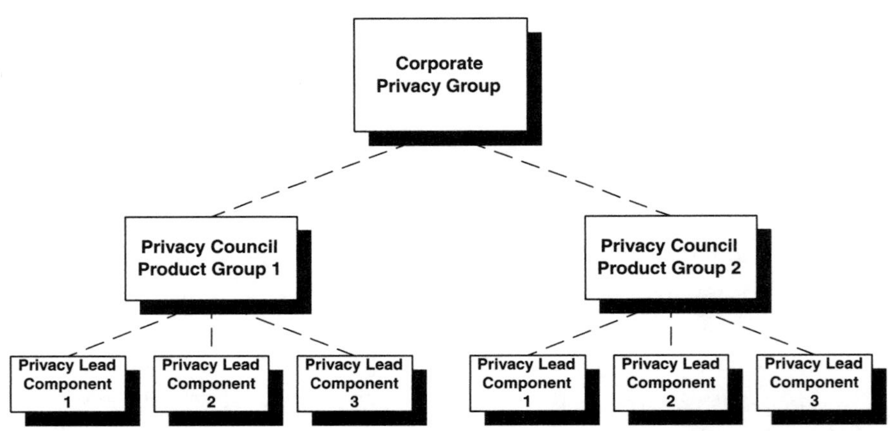

Figure 7.2 Organizational chart for a privacy council and component teams

defining what privacy means for the organization, such as how corporate policy applies to the way the organization operates. The privacy council acquires its authority through executive sponsorship. Because decisions made by the privacy council are going to affect the features, content, and schedule for all of the company's products, it is imperative that it has the backing of the executive in charge of product development. The privacy council should

- Consist of members from the CPG, legal, marketing, and product development departments.
- Have an understanding of the company's products.
- Complete corporate privacy training.
- Review the corporate privacy policy.
- Have sponsorship from executive management.
- Be a project management group that actively engages the teams in product development organization. To track its success it should be held accountable for producing the following specific deliverables:
  - Create a privacy standard based on corporate privacy policy that is applied to the product development process
  - Create a privacy training program that applies to the products that they build
  - Deliver a privacy project plan from each product group team to senior management
  - Be responsible for driving the product group's privacy program
  - Conduct a privacy review for each product team based on an agreed-upon schedule

One major responsibility of the privacy council is to create a set of privacy standards based on corporate privacy policy that must be followed by everyone in the organization that the council represents. After this privacy standard has been developed, it should be delivered to each component team. A point person or privacy lead for each team should be appointed to be responsible for the team's compliance. The privacy council should interface with each privacy lead to track their progress towards compliance. The privacy council is also responsible for providing guidance during the initial phases of the rollout of the privacy standard. Specific guidance should be provided for each role on a product team.

Privacy Leads

Each component for a product team should have a privacy lead assigned to it. The privacy lead is responsible for ensuring privacy compliance for the component team. A program manager or project manager, who has a good understanding of the component's architecture (specifically the dataflow for the component), should hold this position. The privacy leads get training from the CPG and the privacy council for their product group. The privacy lead should then train each member of the component team for which he or she is responsible. The privacy lead should perform a privacy analysis of their component, recording anything that conflicts with the product group's privacy standard. A compliance plan should be developed based on discrepancies that were found. The plan should include milestones with resource requirements that should be aligned with the overall product plan. The final compliance plan should be vetted with the privacy council. When the plan is complete, the privacy lead is responsible for ensuring its execution.

Overall, the privacy lead is responsible for the following tasks:

- Formulate the privacy plan for the team based on direction from the privacy council
- Train the team on privacy best practices based on their role
- Drive the privacy analysis for each feature
- Assist the creation of privacy statements for his or her component
- Ensure privacy is part of each feature specification sign-off
- Head the privacy review for each of the team's components
- Be the point person for resolving any privacy issues that involves the team's components

Developing a Privacy Standard

The privacy standard is a set of rules and guidelines derived from the company's privacy policy. The privacy policy expresses a certain expected behavior based on the company's values. The privacy standard indicates how the privacy policy applies to a specific business practice such as marketing to consumers or building products. For example, if a policy states that customers must be in charge of their information, a rule in the marketing standard might state that all marketing e-mails can be sent only with consent from the consumer. Likewise, a rule in the product group standard might state that no data can be sent from the user's computer without consent.

Every company should have a privacy standard that can be used as a basis for the development of products. The privacy council, in conjunction with the CPG, should create this standard. For smaller companies that may not have the CPG or privacy council, the development team can create a privacy standard and have it reviewed by the company's legal counsel.

In the end, the privacy standard provides a consistent set of rules that guide each product team through compliance with the company's privacy policies for the collection, storage, transmission, and use of data by the company's products and product teams. This standard should answer questions such as the following:

- How will disclosures be made to users?
- Will privacy statements be online or offline?
- What will be the mechanism for accessing privacy features by the user?
- How will administrators and parents be able to manage the privacy of the computers for which they are responsible?
- Which method will be used to encrypt sensitive data during storage and transmission?

When determining the scope of the privacy standard, a thorough evaluation should be made of each software component being built and the data handling practices of each. For organizations in which there are a small number of similar components, one standard should suffice to cover them all. For larger companies with many disparate components, having a separate standard for a category of components may be more appropriate. For example, there could be a standard for components that do not collect, store, or share any data at all. A second standard could apply to components that store logging information for later viewing by a user or administrator. A third standard could apply to components that collect data from the user's computer and send it to the Internet. After the standards are in place, each privacy lead should ensure that his or her component complies with the standard to which it applies.

Developing a privacy standard is one of the more important things that an organization can do with regard to privacy. It is the road map that every team is to follow for building privacy-aware components. It will also serve as a mechanism for ensuring consistent compliance with the company's privacy practices. Appendix F provides an example of a privacy standard.

Conclusion

Being successful at privacy starts with selecting the right people who can build a strong privacy foundation for the company. Then a corporate privacy policy should be created that can be applied to every process and each department in the company. Each employee should be provided with training to help that employee understand the basics of privacy and the importance of following the company's privacy policy. Set up a compliance program to ensure that the company's privacy policies are being adopted.

Failure to develop a solid privacy infrastructure can increase a company's risk of exposure to a privacy incident that could shed negative light on a company. Review the section *The Absence of a Privacy Infrastructure Can Be Costly* earlier in this chapter to get an idea of what happened to other companies that did not have a strong privacy infrastructure. Of course, investing in privacy is not a silver bullet. Think of it as more of a soccer team. As long as everyone is doing his job, nothing unexpected will get through. If someone is not vigilant, however, it could lead to a negative news article in the morning paper.

A company privacy program embraced by employees will improve a company's image as trustworthy with customers, which will in turn increase employee pride in the company. These improvements in how people view a company are bound to affect the company's bottom line in a positive way.

For small companies with minimum resources, participating in privacy conferences is a cost-effective way to obtain a wealth of knowledge from industry privacy experts, legislators, consultants, and solution developers.

8 The Privacy Response Center

I'm going to share a scenario that I often describe to people during a presentation. Suppose you visit a restaurant for lunch near your job on occasion and you find the food and service just so-so. But it's convenient and inexpensive, so you go anyway. One day upon entering the restaurant, you notice a sign that says, "We will start serving good food and providing good service!" Maybe at this point you would feel a little cheated from all those other times, but you sit down for lunch just the same. Afterward, you still find the food and service just so-so. Do you feel better or worse about the place? Would you ever go back?

Think about the above scenario in the context of customer service. Companies shouldn't advertise that their customer service will improve; just make it better. Customers should be treated with respect and connected with someone who can solve their problems. Maybe after the initial conversation, a customer-support center may need to pass someone to a specialist. That's understandable. But don't send customers a Porsche mechanic when they are having a problem getting a BMW started. And don't use new hires to solve difficult problems.

Providing Customer Service for Privacy Issues

When I call a company about a privacy issue, not only do I want to speak to someone who understands the sensitivities of a privacy issue, but someone who can help me resolve it. The last thing I want is to be passed around to a bunch of people and have to repeat my privacy problem to them. It's like being at the desk of a doctor's office and having to repeat through a window, "I have a *rash* I want the doctor to look at!" It doesn't matter where the rash is, you may be too embarrassed to stay and prefer to keep the rash than have to suffer the humiliation of publicizing your condition to everyone.

Companies that collect personal information or create software probably have a customer service center. Part of the responsibilities of the service center should include the ability to handle privacy issues. Many companies spend a great deal of time and money planning for and creating a customer-support department, but don't consider that privacy issues may arise and that it would be inappropriate for standard customer-support personnel to handle them. Most product support and customer service people will not have the background or legal expertise needed to handle privacy issues. Companies that collect information from users directly or indirectly through their products should seriously consider forming a privacy response center. Of course this may not be practical for many small businesses. Companies with limited resources should train their customer service personnel on how to handle privacy issues.

Privacy issues require a special understanding of current privacy regulations and sensitivity to people's need for privacy. The types of privacy issues about which customers may complain include the following:

- The reception of unsolicited e-mail or letters
- Inappropriate contact by phone
- Improper collection or use of personal information
- Identity theft
- Leakage of personal information

One of the things that customer service people do during the course of a call is type everything that a caller says into an incident tracking system. Some of this information may be of a sensitive nature, whose storage may be covered by regulatory requirements. Customer-support departments routinely store the credit card number or social security number of callers in the standard incident description area in an incident-tracking system for anyone who can access the system to read. This practice could be unknowingly contributing to identity theft.

Handling Privacy Issues

In a company that handles personal information, the department handling privacy issues needs to be familiar with the lifecycle of data usage by all of the company's applications—that is, what data is being collected, stored, and shared by the company or its applications. If the company builds solutions that send data to the company's Web site, what happens to the data after it is received? How is it stored, who has access to it, how is it used, and with whom is the data shared? Having this knowledge will permit a company's customer service department to better understand a consumer's complaint and which department in the company should handle the complaint. The prompt and accurate handling of privacy issues can help avoid litigation and inflammatory articles that could negatively affect sales.

All privacy issues should be stored in a database when they are received. Sensitive information should be placed in protected fields or placed in a separate document that has limited access. This document can be then be attached to the original issue. For software development companies, there should be a way to link customer issues to product error-tracking databases. The customer-tracking database should include the following fields:

- A flag to indicate the customer complaint is privacy related
- The type of privacy issue[1]
- The group responsible for resolving the issue
- Links to any fixes in a product database

When Microsoft started having security problems, they set up a separate security response center to handle security issues for the entire company.[2] This department proved to be invaluable when it came to effectively handling security issues. Based on the success of the security response center, Microsoft is creating a privacy response center to handle privacy issues.

Having a formalized system for handling privacy issues will greatly improve a company's ability to successfully avoid damaging the reputation of its products and the company itself due to privacy issues. Consider the possibility of an article in the *Wall Street Journal* or a news report on CNN lambasting a company for mishandling personal information. It could tarnish the image of a company and affect its sales. Investors would also be negatively affected by such news. Effectively managing privacy is a way to avoid costly entanglements. Or put another way, how much money would a company lose in a day, week, month, whatever, if a privacy incident causes

---

1. You can use the OECD Fair Information Practices described in Chapter 3 as a basis for these values.

2. An online form was deployed for sending security issues to the Microsoft Security Response Center. It can be found at https://s.microsoft.com/technet/security/bulletin/alertus.mspx.

customers to stop buying the company's widgets for a while? See Chapter 2 for more information on the impact privacy can have on a company's revenues.

The mishandling of privacy issues can exacerbate the original problem. Suppose that a company's product support department tries to handle the accidental disclosure of contact information without involving privacy experts. They could easily respond in a manner that leaves the company open to litigation. A privacy expert could determine whether the accidental disclosure occurred because of a poorly written privacy policy or a policy that was not followed. She could also determine whether the incident occurred because of differences in regional privacy legislation. Based on the results of the investigation, the proper response could be made and a change in practices deployed to help prevent future occurrences.

The Importance of a Privacy Response Center

Based on the size of a company, a privacy issue could originate from many sources within the company. Multiple groups could pick up the same issue and provide multiple conflicting responses to the same issue. Handling privacy issues using a centralized and formalized department, such as a privacy response center (PRC), improves consistency and knowledge transfer across teams within a company.

A PRC should act as the first line of defense for all privacy issues for a company. It should be staffed by personnel who are familiar with the company's products and who are versed in privacy. The PRC should work closely with the public relations, legal, and privacy departments, as well as representatives from all the major groups in an organization. A PRC can provide the following benefits:

- Centralized processing of privacy issues
- Consistent responses to privacy issues presented to a company
- Reduction in the duplicate processing of issues
- Ensuring that all appropriate stakeholders are involved in each issue
- Faster processing of repeat issues
- Easier reporting and trend-analysis capabilities

After a company has established a PRC, it will be able to quickly see the benefits. Companies that take customer surveys should be able to track the increase in trust of the company against the decrease in privacy issues as they are resolved. Just announcing the establishment of a PRC will do a lot to improve the trust that customers have in a company.

Organizing a Privacy Response Center

The PRC should be organized by the corporate privacy group (CPG) in conjunction with the legal and public relations departments. As long as it is adequately staffed, a different department can handle the administration of a PRC. A customer care or product support department is a likely choice for running a PRC, because it generally has the experience and systems to handle customer issues. The organizational placement of a PRC is not as important as the people who staff it and the processes you put in place to run it. A PRC should be staffed by personnel who are not only experienced with handling customer complaints, but who are also familiar with current privacy legislation, the data collection features of the company's products and services, and who are sensitive to the importance of handling personal data. See Chapter 3 for a sample of current privacy legislation.

The PRC should work closely with the legal, public relations, privacy, and product groups. The PRC should also have executive sponsorship in order to be successful. The executive sponsor for the PRC ensures that the needs of the company are met during issue resolution and ensures the legitimacy of the organization whenever the PRC requires a timely response from other groups in the company.

Integrating the PRC with Product Groups

Part of the release requirements for any new product should be the development of a privacy response process. The process should be used to pinpoint an individual who is the contact person for all privacy inquiries related to the product. The product's privacy contact should be familiar with the product's privacy deployment plan and overall architecture. The privacy response process should be vetted with the PRC by the privacy contact. Upon product deployment, all privacy complaints against the product should be logged by the PRC and assigned to the product's privacy contact. Any product issue reported by a customer that turns out to be a privacy issue should be logged in the PRC database and linked to the product issue for tracking purposes. More about the workflow for handling privacy issues is described later in this chapter.

Figure 8.1 provides an example of how a PRC can be organized. The PRC will be most effective when it includes a team of key people from all groups across the company.

Working with Foreign Subsidiaries

Branch offices and subsidiaries in foreign countries can have their own special challenges. In these cases, there should be a privacy specialist who is familiar with the foreign country's privacy legislation working with the product group to resolve issues initiated by local consumers and companies. These issues should still be logged with the corporate PRC located at the company's headquarters; however, the corporate PRC should not attempt to apply domestic privacy practices to resolve issues originating in foreign countries.

To help subsidiaries stay abreast of privacy issues that are handled at a corporate level and to enable a company to track privacy issues that may happen across a company, each privacy database should be linked with all

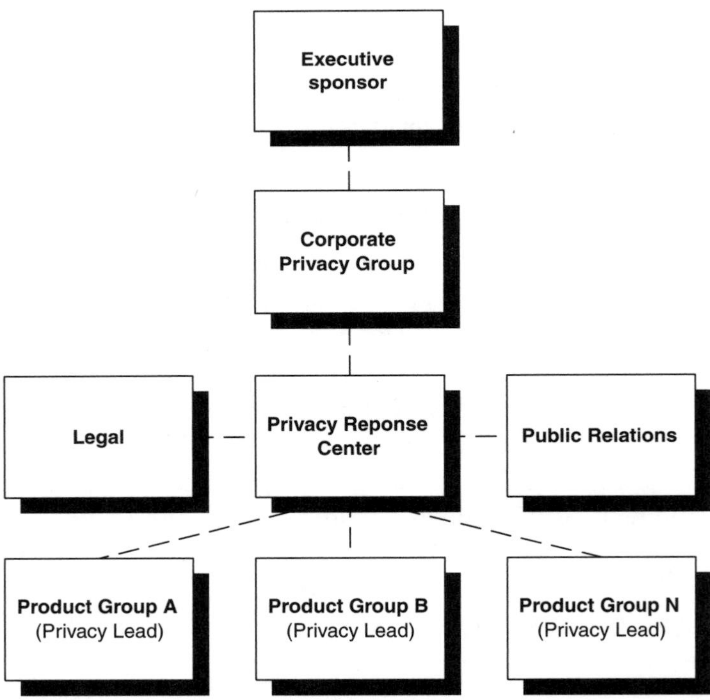

Figure 8.1 Organizational chart for a privacy response center

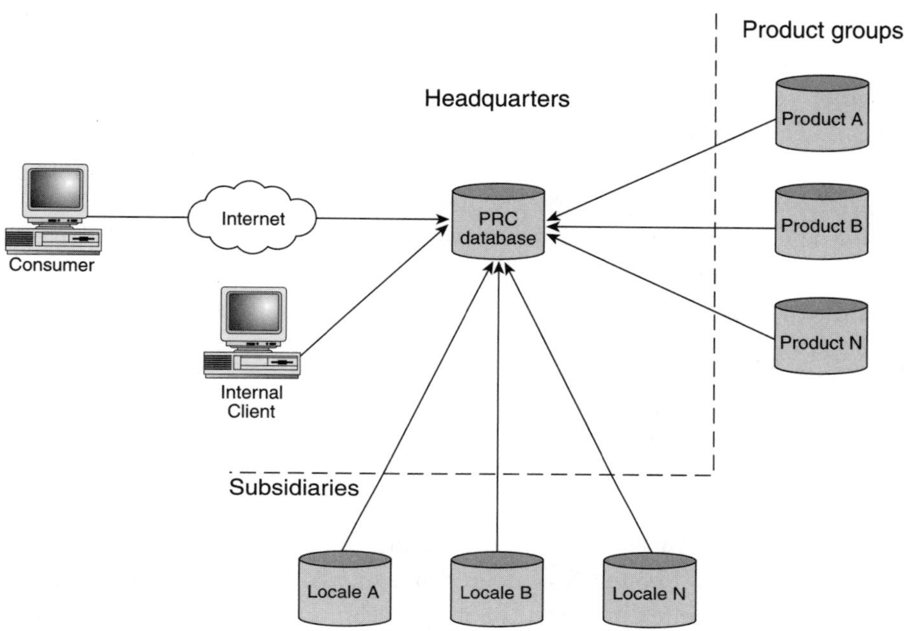

Figure 8.2 Linking databases from subsidiaries

the others. Figure 8.2 provides an example of various databases that can be linked for tracking purposes. In the diagram, not only are subsidiary databases attached to the database for the PRC, product group databases are connected as well. Thus, similar issues across the company can be linked to each other. In addition, any issue that occurs in a subsidiary can be linked to the product with which the issue is associated.

PRC Workflow

Privacy issues can originate from many places. A consumer may call a company, send an e-mail, fill out an online form, or contact a regulatory agency such as the Federal Trade Commission to complain about a privacy infraction against the company. A PRC member may even enter a new privacy issue as the result of a news article from a newspaper or news report that was heard on radio or television. In general, a privacy issue can be reported to anyone or by anyone in a company. No matter what the origin of an issue is, the privacy concern should be placed in the PRC's database for tracking.

Some product groups may resist reporting their issues with the PRC because they are sensitive about airing their dirty laundry to the rest of the company. This kind of shortsightedness will only hurt the company in the long run. The lessons learned from each issue resolution should be shared across the company to assist with the mitigation and quick resolution of similar issues that may occur with other products.

Figure 8.3 shows an example workflow to resolve privacy issues that may be reported regarding one of a company's products or services.

The workflow, as shown in this diagram, is as follows:

- A—The PRC member receives a new privacy issue from an internal or external source. The privacy issue may even be recorded based on a news report that was observed by a PRC member. The report is added to the privacy response database and assigned to the appropriate product group, if known.
- B—The PRC member informs the initiator of the issue that the issue was received and will be processed as soon as possible. A tracking number is assigned to permit the initiator to follow up on the issue. Avoid using autoresponders; they are not as comforting as a personal contact. The issue should then be routed to the product team responsible for the issue.

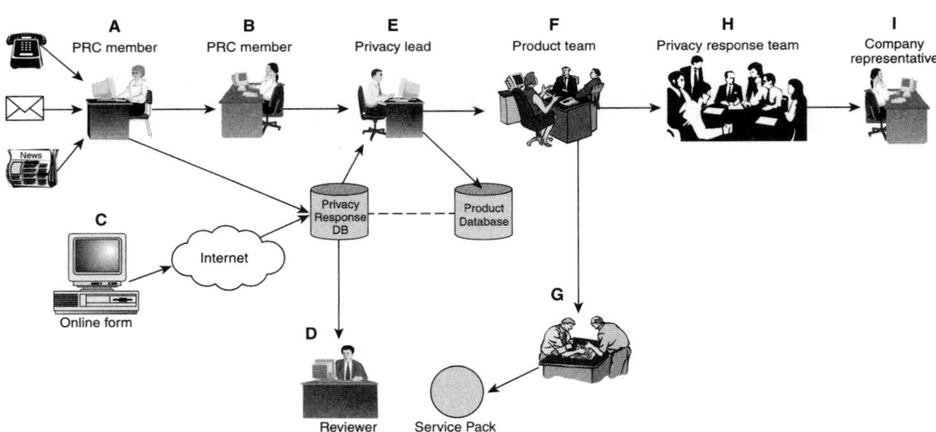

Figure 8.3 Workflow for the privacy response center[3]

3. Incorporate any image(s) into your own original work and publish, display, and distribute your work in any media—provided you include a copyright ownership of both you and Corel, as follows, "Copyright© 19_[your name] and its licensors. All rights reserved."

- C—A company should consider a Web form to provide people with an online method of submitting a privacy issue. Avoid using an e-mail address to submit privacy issues; it can encourage spam and e-mail requests that are not privacy related. See Figure 8.4 for an example of a Web form.
- D—Someone should review the new online form submissions and remove any submissions that are not privacy related. To maintain goodwill with customers, erroneous submissions should be rerouted to the appropriate department. Valid privacy submissions should be routed to the appropriate product or operations group for resolution.
- E—The privacy lead for each product group should review each new privacy issue that is assigned to his group. A new bug report should be filed against the affected product, and the bug should be linked to the original privacy issue. For repeat issues, the previously prepared response should be sent to the initiator of the issue, and the issue should be referred back to the PRC for closure. The PRC should not make the decision for the disposition of a privacy issue without involving the product group responsible for its closure. This is done to avoid missing out on any new discoveries regarding a privacy issue.
- F—The privacy lead should meet with team members in the product group that can assist with resolving the issue. They should decide on the best resolution for the problem.
- G—Some privacy issues may require that a fix for the product be prepared and made available to customers.
- H—After the resolution has been decided, the product group should meet with the privacy response team, which should include CPG, legal, and PR, to decide on the way to respond to the issue, including whether other external parties besides the initiator should be made aware of the privacy issue.
- I—To complete the issue resolution, the product group and PRC databases should be updated to reflect the resolution and indicate the parties that were contacted. If a document or press release was created as part of the resolution, it should be attached to the issue in the PRC database. A company representative should contact the initiator of the privacy issue to deliver the resolution. At this point, a company may also want to contact a privacy analyst or journalist to update any important issues.

Privacy Submission Form - Microsoft Internet Explorer

File Edit View Favorites Tools Help

Privacy Submission Form

This form is used to submit a privacy issue to our company's Privacy Response Center. Please fill in as much information about the issue as possible. Feel free to leave some fields with their default value if you are not sure what to enter in the field. The completed form will be placed into our PRC database. If you provided your contact information you should receive a response from us within 24 hours of your submission.

If you have an issue other than a privacy issue with which you need assistance please visit our support site at http://support.psample.com.

Issue title:

Your name:

Email address:

Product or web site:

Issue type: Other

Description of issue:

Severity:

- 1 - Issue causes loss or exposure of personal data
- 2 - Issue infringes on my privacy
- 3 - Issue makes me feel uncomfortable

Priority:

- 1 - Must fix as soon as possible
- 2 - Must fix in next service release
- 3 - Should fix in next product release

Steps required to reproduce the problem:

Create Issue Clear

Figure 8.4 Sample online privacy form

Technology Description

Having a manual process in place for resolving privacy issues is key to developing an effective privacy response center. This is done by perfecting the workflow between teams through validation, modification, and reevaluation. After the manual process has been perfected, methods should be examined to make the process more efficient with technology. Companies may already have an application that is being used to track customer-support issues and that just needs to be customized to handle privacy issues.

Store information for all privacy issues in a tracking system accessible only by members of the PRC. Access may also be granted to individuals from other teams who work with the PRC for privacy-issue resolution. With some slight modifications, a customer-support system would work well for this purpose. The tracking system should have the following minimum capabilities:

- To attach various types of documents to the issue definition
- To store links to Web pages or file shares
- To link to issues in other databases
- To track the transfer of ownership during the life of the issue
- To create reports based on various privacy-issue categories

At Microsoft, an application called Product Studio (PS) has been developed for internal use only and is used for the creation and storage of privacy-issue data. This is the same product used to track security issues and bugs. This product enables Microsoft to link issues across multiple teams and products. It has a robust reporting engine that can be used to perform trend analysis. This system can also link privacy issues to customer-support issues that are reported to the product support department.

Recording Privacy Issues

The form used by a PRC to record a privacy issue should have enough fields to not only record the issue, but also to permit proper tracking, review, and later trend analysis. Figure 8.5 shows a sample privacy form that can be used to record privacy issues. Companies that are a member of TRUSTe, a privacy-advocacy organization, may want to add a Watchdog field to the form to track issues that originate with the TRUSTe organization.

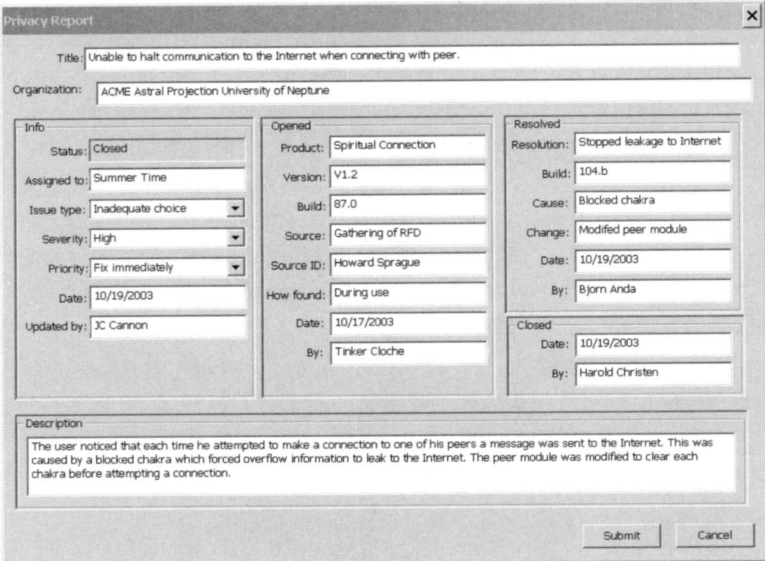
Privacy Report

Title: Unable to halt communication to the Internet when connecting with peer.

Organization: ACME Astral Projection University of Neptune

Info
Status: Closed
Assigned to: Summer Time
Issue type: Inadequate choice
Severity: High
Priority: Fix immediately
Date: 10/19/2003
Updated by: JC Cannon

Opened
Product: Spiritual Connection
Version: V1.2
Build: 87.0
Source: Gathering of RFD
Source ID: Howard Sprague
How found: During use
Date: 10/17/2003
By: Tinker Cloche

Resolved
Resolution: Stopped leakage to Internet
Build: 104.b
Cause: Blocked chakra
Change: Modifed peer module
Date: 10/19/2003
By: Bjorn Anda

Closed
Date: 10/19/2003
By: Harold Christen

Description
The user noticed that each time he attempted to make a connection to one of his peers a message was sent to the Internet. This was caused by a blocked chakra which forced overflow information to leak to the Internet. The peer module was modified to clear each chakra before attempting a connection.

Submit Cancel

Figure 8.5 Privacy-issue form

The form contains the following fields:

- **Title**—Enter the title of the issue.
- **Organization**—The organization that was assigned the issue. This may change.
- **Info**
  - **Status**—The status for the application, which indicates whether the issue has been assigned to someone, resolved, or closed.
  - **Assigned to**—The name of the person assigned to the issue.
  - **Issue type**—The type of privacy issue, possibly using the categories defined by the FTC's Fair Information Practices or Safe Harbor.
  - **Severity**—The severity of the issue. The criteria that the PRC uses for the evaluation of the severity and prioritization of privacy issues should be based on the company's privacy policies as defined by the CPG.
  - **Priority**—The priority for resolving the issue.
  - **Date**—This field should be filled by the application to indicate the date the issue was last updated.
  - **Updated by**—This field should indicate the last person updating the issue.

- Opened
  - **Product**—The name of the product, service, or group for the issue, if known.
  - **Version**—The product's version number.
  - **Build**—The build number for the product when this issue occurred, where appropriate.
  - **Source**—Indicate where the issue originated.
  - **Source ID**—Enter the name of the person or source for the issue.
  - **How found**—A short description of how the issue was found.
  - **Date**—The date the issue was opened.
  - **By**—The person who opened the issue.
- Resolved
  - **Resolution**—Select the resolution for this issue. Be brief and leave the details for the Description field.
  - **Build**—The product build number when this issue is to be resolved.
  - **Cause**—The final cause for the issue.
  - **Change**—The change that was made to resolve the issue.
  - **Date**—The date the issue was resolved.
  - **By**—The person who resolved the issue.
- Closed
  - **Date**—The date the issue was closed.
  - **By**—The person who closed the issue.
- **Description**—A detailed description of the issue, including any possible ramifications.

Online Privacy Form

Companies should enable their customers to submit privacy concerns online. This could be done through e-mail, but this would make it too easy for customers to send unrelated e-mails. It also provides an opportunity for spammers to send e-mails that may cause customer e-mails to get lost. An online form can make it easy for customers to submit their issues without confusion. For this reason, this form should be simple to fill out. Excessive validation of fields could frustrate customers, dissuading them from completing the form or encouraging them to seek resolution using more drastic means. Upon form completion, the customer should receive an issue ID or other issue-tracking means. This can be done interactively by displaying a Web page with the issue ID after the privacy issue is submitted, or via e-mail if the customer provides a valid e-mail address. Figure 8.4 shows a sample Web page that could be used to report a privacy issue.

Improving the Privacy Response Process

The privacy response process should not end with the recording, tracking, and resolution of an issue. How will a company know whether it is getting better with regard to privacy relations? How can a company determine whether a particular product group is "getting" (or not) the message about how to mitigate privacy problems or whether a particular group should be charged for an inordinate number of issues?

No privacy response process is complete without a reporting mechanism. On at least a monthly basis, each PRC report should be examined. These reports should include the following details:

- Type of customers submitting issues
  - Consumer
  - Enterprise, including industry
  - Partner
- Total issues by category
  - By type of privacy issue
  - By department
  - By product and version
  - By severity
- Number of repeat issues
- Average time to closure
- Total issues for the period

These numbers provide an idea of the privacy health of an organization for a specific month. To determine how well a company is doing over time and whether it is improving, however, each company should create reports that provide a trend analysis. By creating reports that look at quantitative aspects of the privacy response process as well as at qualitative aspects, companies will be able to improve the process *and* their products. After the closure of an issue, the initiators of the issues should be contacted to see how happy they are with the resolution. This process can be a big factor in improving customer satisfaction and improving sales.

Determining Resources

At this point, the establishment of a PRC should be an obvious conclusion. Although this chapter has covered various aspects of creating a PRC, the discussion hasn't touched on the resources necessary to start. How many people and how much equipment will be necessary? This will vary depending on the size of the company, the number of products, and how much data is collected. To assist in determining what resources will be needed, companies should consider the following:

- Someone will need to develop and maintain the PRC tracking system.
- The PRC team and product groups will need to be trained on the PRC process.
- Someone will need to assist with the processing of issues for the PRC.
- Someone will need to interface with product groups to ensure issue closure.
- The number of privacy issues currently being handled should be determined.
- Monthly reports will need to be generated and delivered to senior management.
- Issues need to be reviewed to avoid excessive aging.

Companies that already have a mature privacy department should receive very few privacy incidents.

Conclusion

Customer service is an important part of any business. Customers should always have a way to voice their complaints and obtain resolutions for issues they may have with a company.

For large companies or companies that handle a lot of personal data, a privacy response center is a better approach to handling the possible privacy issues that may come in. Handling privacy issues requires a special sensitivity. The improper handling of privacy issues can damage a company's reputation. What can be even worse is permitting trends in bad privacy behavior to persist. A special database for tracking privacy issues should be part of every PRC. To create a system that empowers employees through involvement, companies should involve every department in the privacy-resolution process.

The success of a PRC is determined by the decrease in the number of reported privacy issues, the decrease in the closure time for issues, and the high satisfaction level of the individuals reporting the issues. This means that reports should be created that track how well a company's PRC is doing against these metrics.

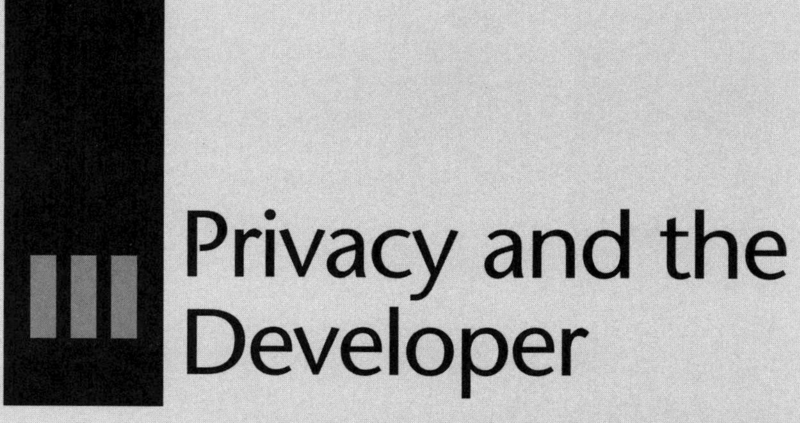

III Privacy and the Developer

9

Platform for Privacy Preferences Project (P3P)

Whether consumers are browsing or shopping online, there is a certain expectation that they will be giving up some aspect of their privacy when visiting Web sites. It's very much like shopping at a department store. There are probably surveillance cameras, undercover security guards, store personnel, and even other shoppers who are noticing you as you walk through the store. When you try on a dress or suit, other shoppers are interested in what captured your attention. I'm sure this does not surprise you. What you probably don't know is that every time you use your browser to access a Web site, behind the scenes a lot of information is being exchanged with the Web site in order to connect to it.

Data Captured by Web Sites

Data flows over the Internet using the Transport Control Protocol/Internet Protocol (TCP/IP). Browsers communicate with Web sites using the HyperText Transfer Protocol (HTTP). The fact that these protocols send information about you and your computer is inherent in the way they work. Here is a sample of the information that is provided to a Web site during a normal visit:[1]

- The language the browser is set to. For example, HTTP_ACCEPT_LANGUAGE: en-us.
- The protocol being used by the browser. For example, SERVER_PROTOCOL: HTTP/1.1.
- The Web page that referred the user agent to the current page. Usually the previous Web page. For example, HTTP_REFERER: http://snoop.cdt.org/.

continues

1. This information was collected from http://snoop.cdt.org/. Click You on the Web page to get an example of the information that can be collected on you.

- The name of the user agent or browser. For example, HTTP_USER_AGENT: Mozilla/4.0 (compatible; MSIE 6.0; Windows NT 5.1).
- The MIME types that the requestor will accept. For example, HTTP_ACCEPT: image/gif, image/x-xbitmap, image/jpeg, image/pjpeg, application/vnd.ms-excel, application/vnd.ms-powerpoint, application/msword, */*.
- The IP address of the user. For example, REMOTE_ADDR: 12.65.138.252.

Surveillance: Good or Bad?

Web sites normally log the IP address and other communication information from each visitor to their site for administrative and maintenance purposes. Web sites often use cookies to personalize a user's experience when browsing the site or to track the different stages of a transaction when the user is purchasing items online. These are some positive aspects of surfing the Web that can enhance a user's experience.

Cookies are also used, along with Web beacons,[2] to track user browsing habits. They enable potentially bothersome targeted ads and popup windows to be deployed on user desktops. With increasing frequency, consumers are asked to enter information about themselves, including their e-mail addresses, to get access to content at a Web site. This information is often sold, causing the users to receive unwanted spam. Many people see these experiences as annoying intrusions on their browsing. These annoyances are compounded when things like accepting cookies are required of the user to visit a site.

The fact that Web sites collect personal information may neither surprise nor disturb you. However, are you aware that many of the applications that are run from a user's computer are collecting a user's usage patterns? When an entertainment program such as RealOne Player is used to play a CD on a computer, the album art and song list for the CD magically appear. How do you think that happens? When a movie is being viewed from a DVD and information about the movie and its actors is supplied to the computer from the Internet, did you ever wonder how the mechanism to do that works?

---

2. Web beacons are also known as Web bugs or clear GIFs. They are typically an image that is only one pixel by one pixel in size. They are placed in e-mails or on Web sites to validate a user's e-mail address or track the user's browsing habits.

There are also financial and medical applications that take advantage of the Internet to embellish their research features. In each case, these applications have to send specifics about what is being requested to an Internet site to retrieve the information. The information that applications send to the Internet could be used to create a profile about the application's users. For example, if a consumer tends to watch certain types of movies and listen to related music, invalid assumptions about the consumer might be made.[3] If a user of a financial application often requests information about expensive investments, it could be inferred that the person is wealthy. Combining profile information with the registration data collected during the installation of an application provides a means to contact a consumer for the purposes of targeted marketing.

Often, the fact that an application is using the Internet to collect information about you is not at all obvious. For example, the Gator tool touts itself as a free tool to assist users with filling out Web forms. Although it does this very well, it also monitors the user's Web-browsing habits and displays targeted ads at the user. Gator is often installed as part of other downloads. The user is informed of these additional features during the install process for Gator. However, the notice is not very prominent. Several companies have labeled the tool spyware.[4] Their name was later cleared when a judge determined that their practices were perfectly legal.[5]

Web sites and applications should inform users about the information that they are transferring to the Internet and logging on their Web servers. Most of the time, transmitted data is used responsibly, and there is nothing to worry about. But it's still nice to be informed. Web sites inform users of their data handling practices through the use of a privacy statement. The Platform for Privacy Preferences Project (P3P) was introduced to provide a programmatic means to present a Web site's privacy policy to a browser. This makes it possible to read a Web site's policy and determine how it handles data.

---

3. Jeffrey Zaslow, "Oh no! My TiVo Thinks I'm Gay," December 04, 2002, *Wall Street Journal*.
4. http://news.com.com/2100-1024-5099601.html?tag=nl
5. http://news.com.com/2100-1024_3-1022791.html?tag=st_rn

Introducing P3P for Expressing Web Site Privacy

When using a browser to visit a Web site, there is no easy way to determine the privacy policy of the site or what you risk when you enter personal information at the site. In general, you are compelled to read the Web site's privacy statement (if it even has one), which can be long and perplexing. Wouldn't it be great if there were an easier way to determine whether it were safe to browse a Web site and leave data there without having to comprehend a complex privacy statement? The Platform for Privacy Preferences Project, or P3P, was designed to make understanding a Web site's privacy policy simpler. The World Wide Web Consortium (W3C) developed P3P. Its purpose is to permit Web sites to express their privacy statements in a machine-readable format. These formatted statements can then be read by P3P-aware user agents, which can provide users with visual and audible clues to the safety of a Web site with regard to privacy. Internet Explorer 6.0, Netscape Navigator 7.0, and the AT&T Privacy Bird are examples of user agents that can interpret the P3P content that has been deployed by a Web site. These user agents display icons and play sounds to warn a user against possible deceptive practices by a Web site.

If you are responsible for a Web site, look into deploying P3P for your Web site to make it easier for users to understand your privacy policy and avoid the negative indicators displayed by P3P-enabled user agents. In the future, there may be Web services and search engines that will select Web sites based on their P3P definition. Those without P3P deployed could be left out of the selection process. This chapter looks at what content makes up the P3P specification, the P3P integration of the most popular browsers, tools for deploying P3P for your Web site, and tips for creating your own code for reading a Web site's P3P content.

Deploying P3P at a Web Site

The integration of P3P for a Web site can be accomplished by creating three files and extending the HTTP response header. The first file is the P3P reference file. This file is used to define the location for a site's P3P policy file and the scope for the P3P policy. The second file is the P3P policy file, which is the eXtensible Markup Language (XML) version of the Web site's privacy policy. The third file is the full privacy statement, which most Web sites have already defined.

The P3P compact policy is the last piece of content that needs to be created to complete your P3P integration. This is a series of codes that are placed in the response header.

The complete definition for P3P can be found on the W3C Web site at http://www.w3.org/TR/P3P/.

The P3P Reference File

The P3P reference file is an XML file that is used to provide information about the P3P integration of a Web site. Among other things, it can indicate the following:

- The location of the site's P3P policy file(s)
- The scope of each P3P policy file
- The location and scope of other reference files
- The expiration date for the file
- Embedded P3P policy definitions

There are three ways to locate the P3P reference file for a Web site. The most common is to look for the file named p3p.xml in the well-known location of the W3C directory below the Web site's root node. For example, you can find the Microsoft P3P reference file at http://www.microsoft.com/W3C/p3p.xml. It is shown here:

```
<?xml version="1.0" ?>
<META xmlns="http://www.w3.org/2000/12/P3Pv1">
 <POLICY-REFERENCES>
    <POLICY-REF about="http://www.microsoft.com/w3c/p3policy.xml">
        <INCLUDE>/*</INCLUDE>
 </POLICY-REF>
</POLICY-REFERENCES>
</META>
```

The following list describes the major elements that can be found in a P3P reference file:

- The <POLICY-REF> element points to the location of the P3P policy file.
- The <INCLUDE> element indicates the domains to which this policy applies. The asterisk (*) indicates that it applies to all domains.
- The <COOKIE INCLUDE> element (not shown here) indicates the cookies to which this policy applies. The cookie can be identified by name, value, location, or domain.

The second way to find the P3P reference file for a Web site is to look at the policyref value in the P3P HTTP header. The following text shows the headers from expedia.com read using the W3C's P3P Validator tool, which is described later in this chapter. The P3P header is displayed in bold. This method can be used when there are multiple reference files for your site or for some reason you are unable to place a reference file in the well-known location.

```
Cache-Control: private
Connection: close
Date: Sat, 04 Oct 2003 22:13:33 GMT
Location: http://www.expedia.com/Default.asp?CCheck=1
Server: Microsoft-IIS/5.0
Content-Length: 121
Content-Type: text/html
Expires: Sat, 04 Oct 2003 22:12:33 GMT
Client-Date: Sat, 04 Oct 2003 22:13:34 GMT
Client-Response-Num: 1
P3P: policyref="/w3c/p3p.xml", CP="CAO DSP IND COR ADM CONo CUR
➥CUSi DEV PSA PSD DELi OUR COM NAV PHY ONL PUR UNI"
Set-Cookie: COOKIECHECK=1; domain=.expedia.com; path=/
```

You can also view the P3P header for a Web site using Internet Explorer 6.0 by first setting the Advanced privacy settings to prompt for cookies. When a Web site attempts to place a cookie on your computer, Internet Explorer will prompt you with a dialog. Click the More Info button to see the dialog in Figure 9.1, which has the P3P header at the bottom in the Compact Policy field.

The third way to locate a P3P reference file for a Web site is to read the link tag from the Web page being accessed from the Web site, if the tag is present. This method can be used when you are not able to place the reference file in the well-known location or point to it from an HTTP header. (This is common for Web sites that are hosted by an Internet service provider [ISP].) Although this mechanism provides a means for having multiple reference files, it is time-consuming to deploy and more difficult to maintain when changes need to be made. The link http://www.wellit-workedlasttime.com/ points to a page that uses the link tag, shown here, to point to the Web site's reference file:

```
<link rel="P3Pv1" href="/w3c/p3p.xml" type="text/xml" />
```

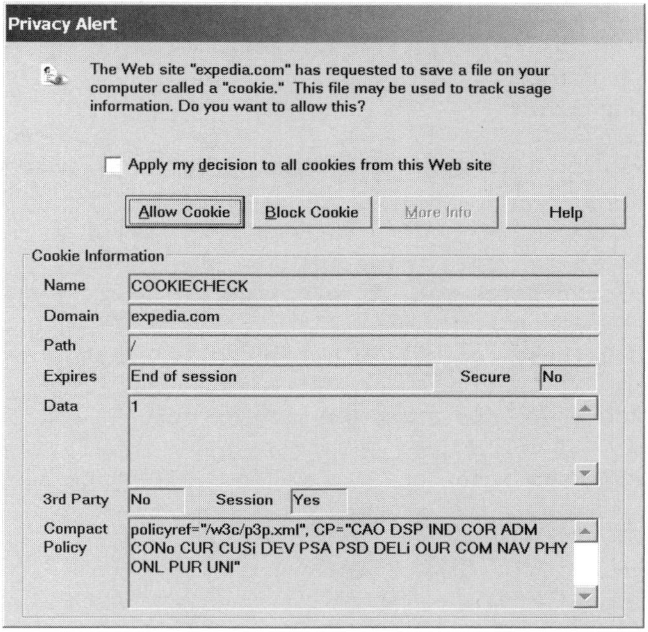

Figure 9.1 Viewing a P3P header with Internet Explorer 6.0

P3P Policy File

The P3P policy file is an XML file that is used to carry a Web site's privacy statement in P3P XML format. This file contains various elements and attributes that indicate the data collection practices for the Web site and other information. For example, the discuri attribute points to the full privacy statement for the Web site, and the opturi attribute points to the address where users can indicate their opt-in or opt-out preferences.

AT&T's P3P policy file can be found at http://www.att.com/privacy/p3p2.xml. An excerpt is shown here. You can find a description of the XML elements on the W3C Web site at http://www.w3.org/TR/P3P/.

```
<?xml version="1.0"?>
<POLICIES xmlns="http://www.w3.org/2002/01/P3Pv1">
    <!- Generated by IBM P3P Policy Editor version Beta 1.10.2
    ➥built 3/13/02 11:39 AM ->

    <!- Expiry information for this policy ->
    <EXPIRY max-age="86400"/>
```

```
<POLICY
    discuri="http://www.att.com/privacy/"
    opturi="http://www.att.com/privacy/consumer/"
    name="general">

    <!- Description of the entity making this policy statement. ->
    <ENTITY>
    <DATA-GROUP>
<DATA ref="#business.name">AT&T</DATA>
<DATA ref="#business.contact-info.online.uri">http://www.att.com/
➥</DATA>
<DATA ref="#business.contact-info.telecom.telephone.intcode">1
➥</DATA>
<DATA ref="#business.contact-info.telecom.telephone.loccode">888
➥</DATA>
<DATA ref="#business.contact-info.telecom.telephone.number">
➥928-8932</DATA>
    </DATA-GROUP>
    </ENTITY>

    <!- Disclosure ->
    <ACCESS><contact-and-other/></ACCESS>

    <!- Disputes ->
    <DISPUTES-GROUP>
        <DISPUTES resolution-type="independent" service="http://
        ➥www.bbbonline.org" short-description="BBBOnline">
            <LONG-DESCRIPTION>BBBOnline Privacy Program
            ➥</LONG-DESCRIPTION>
            <IMG src="http://www.att.com/privacy/images/
            ➥privacyseal3.gif" alt="BBBOnline Privacy Seal"/>
    <!- No remedies specified ->
        </DISPUTES>
    </DISPUTES-GROUP>

    <!- Statement for group "Clickstream" ->
    <STATEMENT>
        <EXTENSION optional="yes">
            <GROUP-INFO
xmlns="http://www.software.ibm.com/P3P/editor/extension-1.0.html"
➥name="Clickstream"/>
        </EXTENSION>

    <!- Consequence ->
    <CONSEQUENCE>
```

```
We want to make the content on our sites as relevant,interesting
and timely as possible and to do that we use information about
which pages you visit on our site. AT&T uses advertising companies
to deliver ads on some AT&T Web sites. The advertising companies
may also receive some anonymous information about ad viewing by
Internet users on AT&T Web sites. This information cannot be
associated with a name or email address without the customer's
permission.
</CONSEQUENCE>

    <!- Use (purpose) ->
    <PURPOSE><admin/><current/><develop/><pseudo-analysis/>
    ➥<pseudo-decision/><tailoring/></PURPOSE>

    <!- Recipients ->
    <RECIPIENT><ours/><other-recipient/></RECIPIENT>

    <!- Retention ->
    <RETENTION><indefinitely/></RETENTION>

    <!- Base dataschema elements. ->
    <DATA-GROUP>
    <DATA ref="#dynamic.clickstream"/>
    <DATA ref="#dynamic.http.useragent" optional="yes"/>
    <DATA ref="#dynamic.http.referer" optional="yes"/>
    <DATA ref="#dynamic.miscdata"><CATEGORIES><computer/>
    ➥</CATEGORIES></DATA>
    </DATA-GROUP>
</STATEMENT>
<!- End of policy ->
</POLICY>
</POLICIES>
```

The following list describes the major elements that appear in a P3P policy file:

- The <ENTITY> element provides the contact information for the entity collecting the data.
- The <ACCESS> element indicates that data category that can be accessed by individuals. The preceding sample indicates that there is access to contact and other identifying information.
- The <DISPUTES> element indicates how disputes can be handled. Here it indicates that BBB Online can be contacted to resolve disputes.

- The <CONSEQUENCE> element indicates the consequences that may result from not providing the requested information. In the sample, it indicates that relevant, interesting, and timely information may not be possible.
- The <PURPOSE> element indicates the purpose for which the data is being collected. In the sample, it indicates that data is being collected for administrative purposes, to process the current activity being requested by the user, research and development, pseudonymous analysis, pseudonymous decision making, and tailoring the Web site. Pseudonymous refers to using an identifier such as a GUID without including identifying information about the user.
- The <RECIPIENT> element indicates who the recipient is for the data that is collected. In the sample, it indicates that the collector of the data and a partner are the recipients of the data.
- The <RETENTION> element indicates the retention policy for the data. In the sample, it indicates that the data may be kept indefinitely.
- The <DATA> element indicates the data that is being collected. In the sample, it indicates that data from the browser and the computer is collected.

If you are building a user agent or Web service to programmatically determine the privacy policy for a Web site, read the P3P policy file. For performance reasons, most user agents read the compact policy—the series of codes placed in the response header—to determine whether a Web site is following a specific privacy policy. However, it is not as accurate as the P3P policy file. The following section discusses compact policies in more detail.

When a P3P-enabled browser displays a P3P policy file in a special display window, it first converts it to a human-readable format to make it easier to read. This display is also known as a privacy summary. Figure 9.2 shows how the Netscape browser displays the file. This display is accessed by selecting Page Info under the View menu. On the Page Info dialog, select the Privacy tab. At the bottom of the Privacy dialog, click the Summary button.

Figure 9.3 shows how the Internet Explorer browser displays the file. This display is accessed by selecting Privacy Report under the View menu. Although the two browsers are viewing the same file, the way they translate and display the contents of the file are somewhat different. In the end, the meaning should be the same. When creating a P3P policy file, test it against both the Internet Explorer and Netscape browsers to ensure that their translation looks accurate.

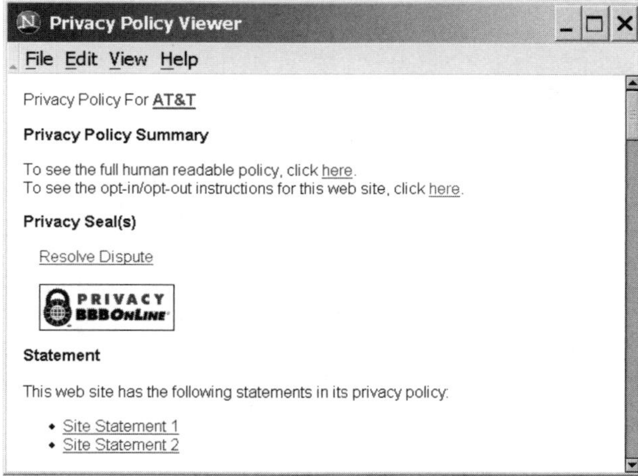

Figure 9.2 The AT&T policy file in the Netscape browser[6,7]

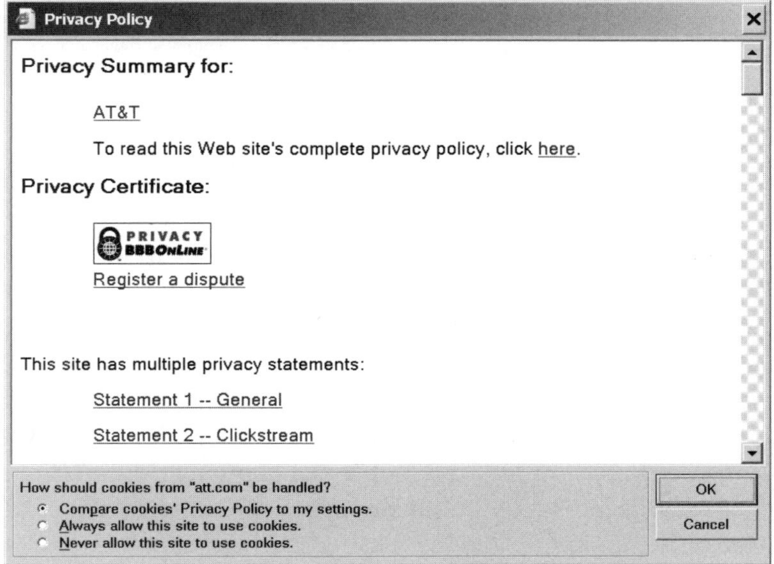

Figure 9.3 The AT&T policy file in the Internet Explorer browser[6,7]

6. Reprinted with permission of AT&T
7. Reprinted with permission of the Council of Better Business Bureaus, Inc., Copyright 2003. Council of Better Business Bureaus, Inc., 4200 Wilson Blvd., Arlington, VA, 22203. World Wide Web: http://www.bbb.org.

P3P Compact Policy

The P3P compact policy is a series of three-letter codes that are used to express the same information that is provided in the full P3P policy file, but in a simplified format. These codes may include an *i*, *o*, or *a* modifier that indicates that the code applies on an opt-in basis, opt-out basis, or always, respectively. For example, in the sample of AT&T's P3P policy, three elements describe their data collection purpose, data recipients, and retention policy. Here is a copy of those elements:

```
<!- Use (purpose) ->
<PURPOSE><admin/><current/><develop/><pseudo-analysis/>
➥<pseudo-decision/><tailoring/></PURPOSE>

<!- Recipients ->
<RECIPIENT><ours/><other-recipient/></RECIPIENT>

<!- Retention ->
<RETENTION><indefinitely/></RETENTION>
```

The equivalent compact policy would look like this:

```
P3P: "CP=ADM CUR DEV PSA PSD TAI OUR OTR IND"
```

You can see how using the compact policy would be more efficient, because it takes fewer bytes to transmit the same meaning than several lines of XML. The only problem is that it is sometimes possible to misinterpret a site's policy because of the lack of detail. For example, a Web site may collect anonymous information about how many people purchase a particular book and share this with third parties. It may also collect contact information that is shared only with the shipping department. However, it is not possible to indicate this distinction when there is only one compact policy. To avoid this confusion, use a different compact policy on pages that collect data to be specific about your privacy practices with regard to that data collection.

As an example of how to translate a compact policy, Microsoft's P3P compact policy is the following string:

```
P3P:CP='ALL IND DSP COR ADM CONo CUR IVAo IVDo PSA PSD TAI TELo
➥OUR SAMo CNT COM INT NAV ONL PHY PRE PUR UNI'
```

The following table describes the meaning of each token.

Token	Description
ALL	The user has access to all of his or her identifiable data.
IND	The user's data is kept indefinitely.
DSP	The site has a dispute mechanism to handle user privacy complaints.
COR	The site will remedy any errors or wrongful actions in connection with their privacy policy.
ADM	Data is collected for administrative purposes.
CONo	Data is used for contact purposes, but the user can opt out of this usage.
CUR	Data is collected for completion and support of activity for which it was provided.
IVAo	Data is used for analysis that can be related to individual users; the user can opt out of this usage.
IVDo	Data is used for decisions that can be related to individual users; the user can opt out of this usage.
PSA	Data is used for pseudonymous analysis.
PSD	Data is used for pseudonymous decision making.
TAI	Data is collected for one-time tailoring.
TELo	Data is used for telemarketing purposes; the user can opt out of this usage.
OUR	Data is collected for our purposes.
SAMo	Data is used by legal entities that follow site's practices; the user can opt out of this usage.
CNT	Content information about the user is collected.
COM	Computer information about the user is collected.
INT	Interactive information about the user is collected.
NAV	Navigation and clickstream information about the user is collected.
ONL	Online contact information about the user is collected.
PHY	Physical contact information about the user is collected.
PRE	User preference data is collected.
PUR	Purchasing information about the user is collected.
UNI	Unique identifiers that refer to the user are collected.

Browsers and P3P Integration

There are several Internet browsers out today. Some of them have P3P integration, whereas others don't. There is also a P3P-enabled user agent, called the AT&T Privacy Bird, which can be integrated into IE6. The integration of P3P into browsers for the most part assists users with the management of cookies. Cookies can be used to track your browsing habits, which may not be acceptable to you. These P3P-enabled browsers also can warn the user when a Web site's privacy policy conflicts with the user's privacy preferences. Unfortunately, Web sites have to deploy P3P for the browsers to accurately reflect a site's policy. Otherwise, the browser may provide a false reading.

When using a browser, you should know whether the browser has P3P integration and how to take advantage of the features that this integration makes possible. Some of the more widely used browsers are described in the following sections.

Internet Explorer

Version 6.0 of Internet Explorer[8] was the first browser to provide P3P integration. This integration enables users to manage cookies based on their privacy preferences. The user's preferences can be expressed as the types of cookies that are acceptable, the originating Web site for cookies that the user trusts or distrusts, or by a level of comfort based on the site's privacy policy. Internet Explorer's privacy settings are located on the Privacy dialog, which can be accessed by selecting the Options item under the Tools menu and selecting the Privacy tab on the dialog. Figure 9.4 shows Internet Explorer's Privacy dialog. The slide bar on the left of the dialog enables users to select their level of comfort with regard to privacy. By default, this level is set to Medium, which blocks third-party cookies and restricts first-part cookies that have a bad or missing privacy policy. A restricted cookie can be used only as a session cookie, and it is not permanently stored on your computer.

The Advanced button on the dialog enables the user to specify how first-party, third-party, and session cookies are handled. The Edit button enables users to select Web sites that should always have their cookies accepted or blocked. The Import button enables users to load an XML-formatted file that can be used to predefine a user's privacy preferences. You can find more information on implementing a customized import file at http://msdn.microsoft.com/workshop/security/privacy/overview/privacyimportxml.asp.

When using Internet Explorer to visit a Web site that uses cookies and either does not have a compact policy or the compact policy conflicts with your privacy preferences, IE displays the eye icon shown in Figure 9.5. By double-clicking this icon, you can see which cookies have been blocked or

---

8. http://www.microsoft.com/windows/ie/default.asp

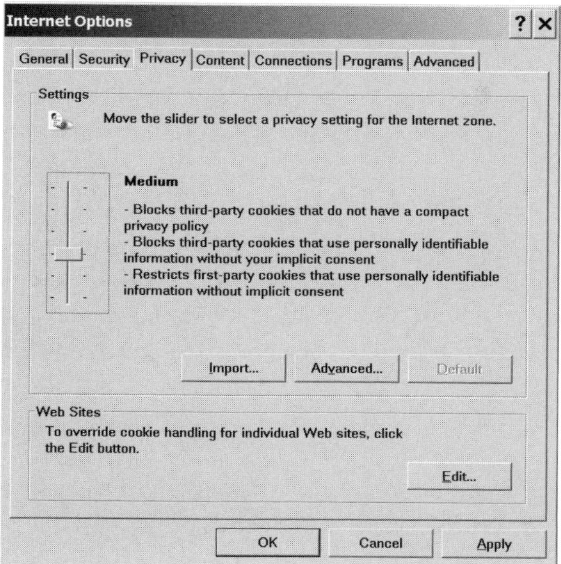

Figure 9.4 The Internet Explorer Privacy dialog

restricted. The first time a privacy problem is detected, the dialog in Figure 9.6 displays. By clicking the Settings button on this dialog, you have the option of adjusting your privacy settings. When creating a Web site, integrate P3P and make sure that your policy does not cause the eye to show up on the Internet Explorer status bar.

Figure 9.5 The Internet Explorer privacy warning icon

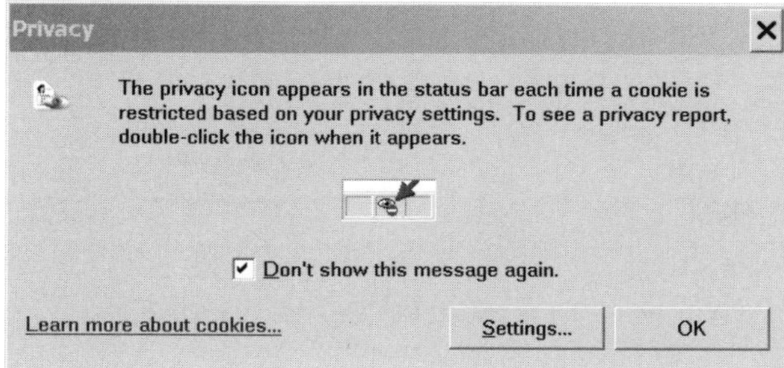

Figure 9.6 The Internet Explorer Privacy warning dialog

Opera

Although the Opera[9] browser provides cookie management, it has no P3P integration. This means the browser cannot control cookies based on a Web site's privacy policy as expressed using a P3P policy file or compact policy. According to the browser's help text, Opera doesn't have P3P integration because of open issues with how well P3P protects a user's privacy.

Figure 9.7 shows Opera's Privacy dialog. It permits cookie management, referrer logging, and automatic redirection. Opera's Privacy dialog also helps protect your passwords by keeping login pages and password protected pages out of the history, and they are removed from its cache when you exit.

Mozilla

This is the original browser created by the Mozilla Organization[10]. Netscape based their browser on the same source code. The Mozilla browser has a set of Privacy dialogs that contain several settings, including some for cookie management. The browser also has P3P integration. Figure 9.8 shows the Mozilla Preferences property sheet. In the tree view on the left, several items provide access to security and privacy settings. Clicking each item displays a dialog that provides you access to settings for the item that you selected.

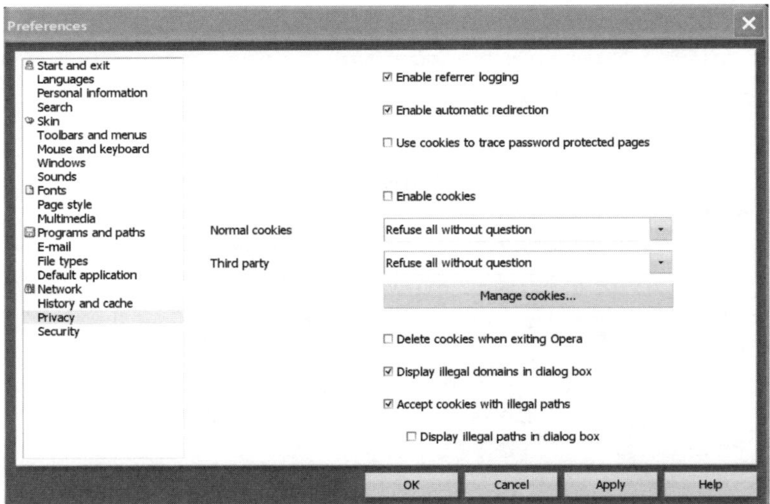

Figure 9.7 The Opera Privacy dialog

9. http://portal.opera.com/

10. http://www.mozilla.org/

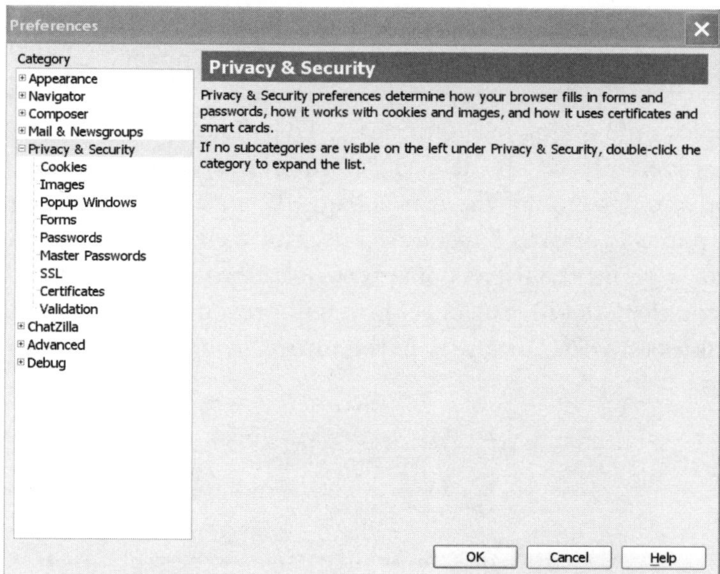

Figure 9.8 The Mozilla privacy/security settings

Clicking the Cookies item and selecting the View button on the Cookies dialog will bring up the dialog shown in Figure 9.9. This dialog enables you to control the use of cookies based on a site's P3P policy. This dialog provides you with more granular control over what is acceptable with regard to a site's P3P policy than Internet Explorer's Privacy Settings dialog.

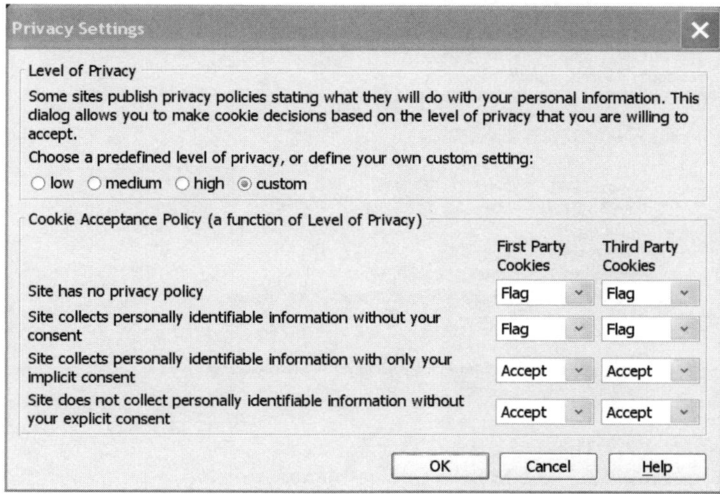

Figure 9.9 The Mozilla Privacy Settings dialog for cookie management

When a page is accessed from a Web site that disagrees with your privacy settings, the eye icon shown in Figure 9.10 appears. Clicking the icon displays the dialog in Figure 9.11. Clicking the View Cookie Manager button displays the dialog in Figure 9.12. This dialog provides a list of cookies that were placed on the user's computer. By selecting a flagged cookie, you can determine why it was flagged. For example, in Figure 9.12, the cookie named xon was flagged because the Web site stores identifiable information without the user's consent. Clicking the Remove button will get rid of the cookie. Clicking the checkbox will prevent the Web site from setting cookies on your computer in the future.

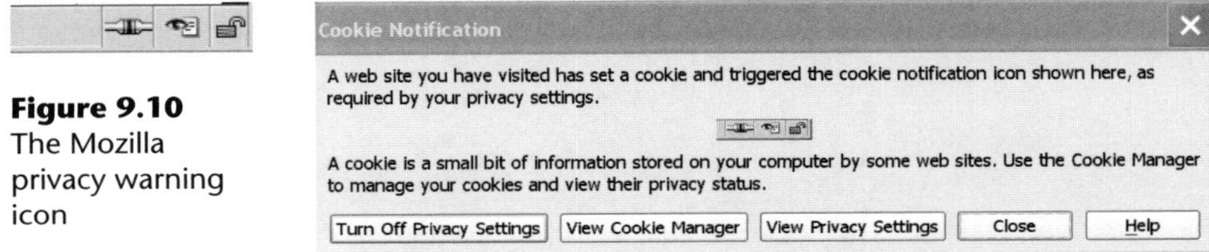

Figure 9.10 The Mozilla privacy warning icon

Figure 9.11 The Mozilla Cookie Notification dialog

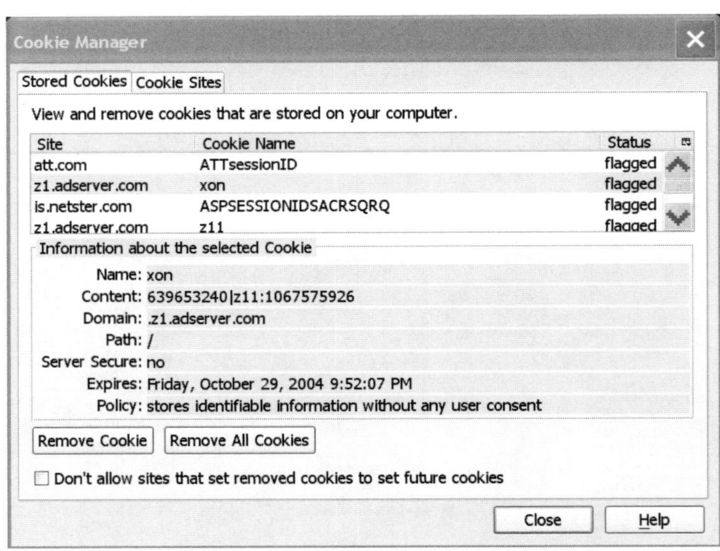

Figure 9.12 The Mozilla Cookie Manager dialog

Mozilla Firebird

The Mozilla Firebird[11] browser is a variation of the original Mozilla browser. It provides a Privacy dialog that offers cookie management as well as the ability to manage passwords and clear history information. Figure 9.13 shows the Privacy dialog. This browser also comes with a built-in popup blocker and what is called an annoyance eliminator, which some advocates view as important privacy tools. Although P3P support has been removed from this version of the browser, it still provides the Cookie Manager dialog to enable the viewing of a Web site's P3P policy for a specific cookie. Future plans include support for P3P compact policies and a P3P policy viewer.

Netscape

The Netscape[12] browser is a licensed version of the Mozilla browser that was put together by AOL. It has the same basic features of the Mozilla browser, including P3P support. For a brief description of the privacy

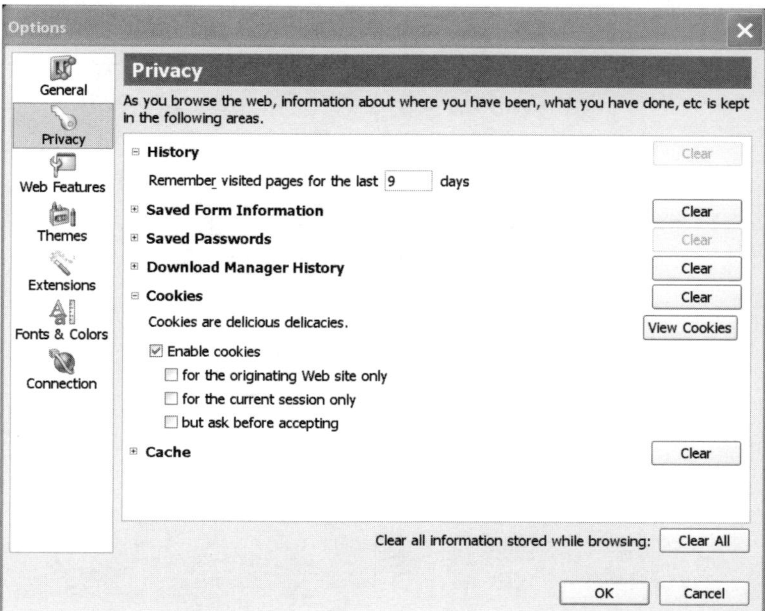

Figure 9.13 The Mozilla Firebird Privacy dialog

---

11. http://www.mozilla.org/

12. http://www.netscape.com

features for this browser, read the section earlier in this chapter on the Mozilla browser.

Avant

The Avant [13] browser is one of the coolest browsers that I have used to date. It has features that you will really enjoy. Anderson Che created this browser. For the most part, this is an extension of Internet Explorer 6.0, described earlier. It has no additional privacy features outside of the one to block popups, which some people think are privacy invasive. However, you will enjoy the way the browser handles Web pages and the way in which it has incorporated the mouse buttons into the browsing experience.

AT&T Privacy Bird

The AT&T Privacy Bird[14] is a user agent designed to work in conjunction with Internet Explorer. By default, it places itself on the right side of the title bar of Internet Explorer after it is installed. Figure 9.14 provides an example of this.

This user agent is the only one discussed in this chapter that reads a Web site's full P3P policy file to determine its privacy policy. This enables users to get a more accurate view of what a Web site is doing. The browsers mentioned earlier look only at a Web site's compact policy, which at best can provide only a superficial view of a Web site's privacy policy. Because of

Figure 9.14 The AT&T Privacy Bird

13. http://www.avantbrowser.com/

14. http://privacybird.com/

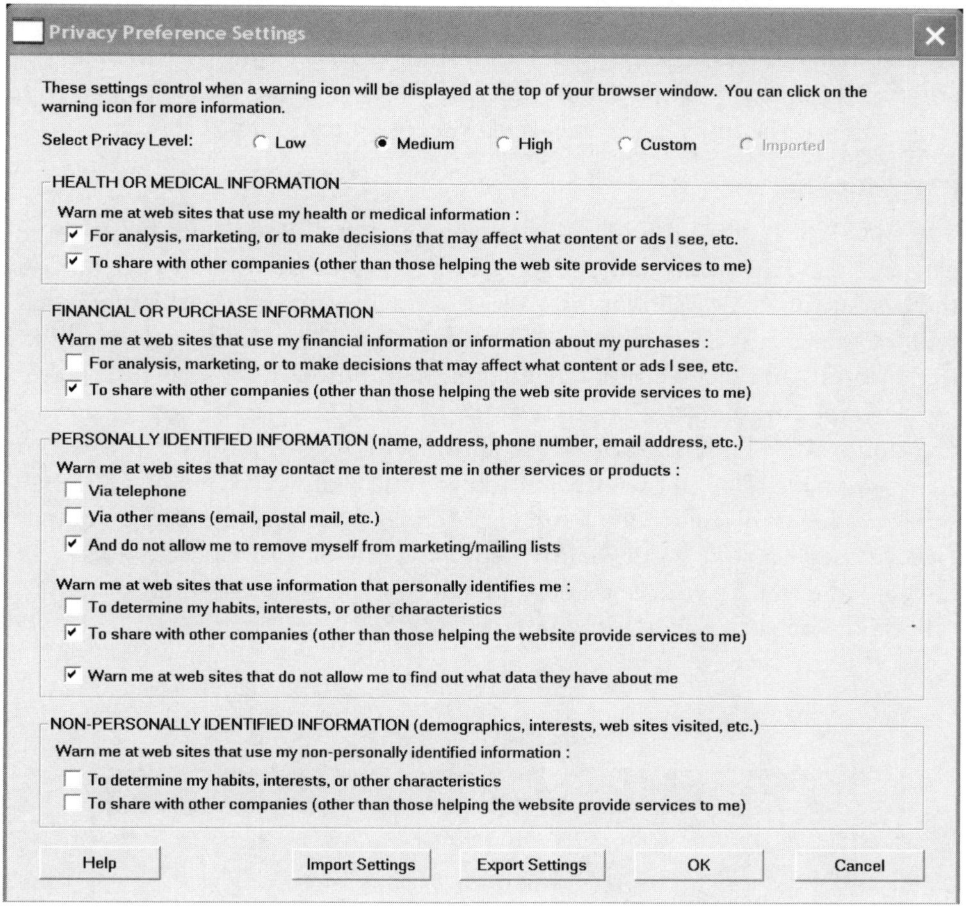

Figure 9.15 The AT&T Privacy Bird Privacy Preference Settings dialog

this, the user agent is able to offer a richer set of privacy settings that map more closely to the elements found in a P3P policy file. This is demonstrated in the Privacy Preference Settings dialog in Figure 9.15.

P3P Creation Tools

If you are not technically savvy or not familiar with XML, creating P3P content can be difficult. Understanding how to create the P3P compact policy can be exceptionally challenging. Several companies have created tools to make the task of creating and testing P3P content easier than creating it manually. This section describes some of those tools. You can find more tools at the links in the *References* section at the end of this chapter.

P3P Policy Editor

The IBM P3P Policy Editor[15] is IBM's version of a P3P tool that helps you generate the content needed to deploy P3P for your Web site. If you look at the header for AT&T's P3P policy file, provided earlier in this chapter, you will see that it was created using this tool. This tool can be downloaded for free by going to the Web site indicated in the footnote.

This tool presents a series of wizards to guide the user through the creation of P3P content. Figure 9.16 shows a dialog from the startup screen. After you have filled in the information for this tool, it can create a P3P reference file, P3P policy file, a full HTML privacy policy file, and a compact policy based on your input. Before deploying any of this content, always have it validated by your legal department to make sure that it accurately reflects the privacy policy for your company.

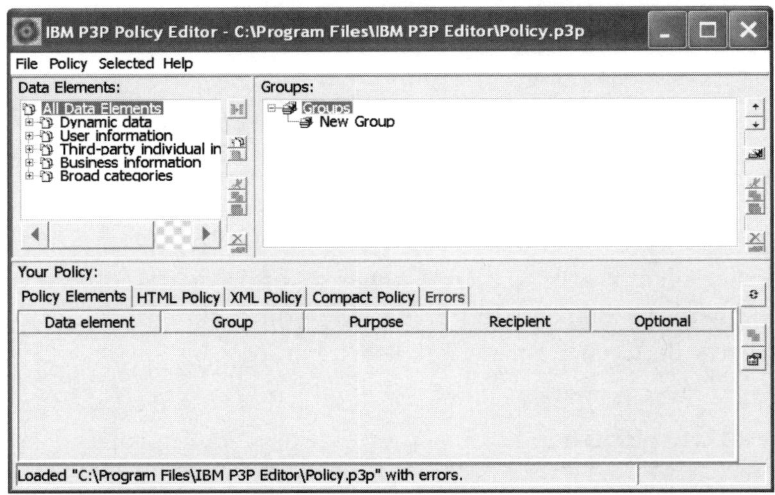

Figure 9.16 The startup page for IBM's P3P Policy Editor

15. http://www.alphaworks.ibm.com/aw.nsf/download/p3peditor

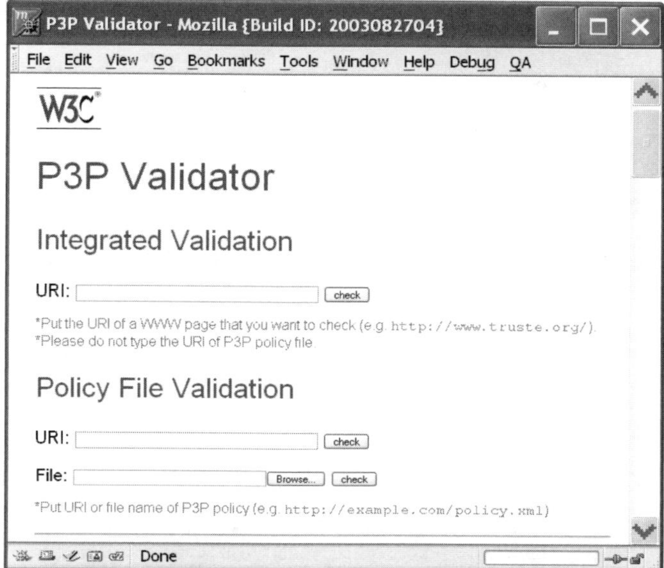

Figure 9.17 The Web page for the W3C's P3P Validator

P3P Validator

The Web site for the W3C has a tool[16] that enables you to validate your P3P implementation at not cost. You can see the Web page for this tool in Figure 9.17. After entering the Web address that you want tested, click the Check button. Upon completion, a Web page displays containing a P3P analysis of your Web site. You can also use this tool just to validate a policy file and view the headers for a Web site.

P3PEdit

The P3PEdit[17] tool was created by Code Infusion to permit the creation of P3P content for a Web site. You can purchase this tool from their Web site listed in the footnote. The creators state that the policy file generated by this tool will satisfy the requirements of IE6 and will validate correctly using the W3C's P3P Validator tool. This is important because improperly generated P3P content can force IE6 or other user agents to falsely indicate that your

16. http://www.w3.org/p3p/validator
17. http://p3pedit.com/

Figure 9.18 The page from the P3PEdit Wizard[18]

Web site has bad privacy practices. After you have completed the wizard, the tool will create a P3P policy file, HTML privacy statement, and compact policy based on your input. The purchase price also includes technical support and a staff review. See Figure 9.18 for a view of one of the P3PEdit pages.

Joint Research Centre

The Joint Research Centre (JRC)[19] is an organization of the European Commission whose mission is to provide scientific and technical support for the conception, development, implementation, and monitoring of European Union policies. The JRC developed a P3P resource center[20] to educate the public, increase consumer confidence, and provide a means to study the impact of P3P. They have the only user agent that has a full implementation of the P3P standard. They provide a proxy that integrates with Internet Explorer, Netscape, and Linux browsers. They have created a proxy and a

18. P3P Edit authored by Carter St. Clair, Spanish-text version translated by Christiane St. Clair
19. http://www.jrc.it
20. http://p3p.jrc.it/index.php

test Web site to permit testing of P3P user agents. They also provide a set of toolkits to help you create your own P3P user agent, P3P proxy server, and an evaluator to permit the testing of an APPEL definition.

A P3P Preference Exchange Language (APPEL)

This chapter has devoted a lot of time to P3P, which enables Web sites to express their privacy policy. APPEL[21] is an XML-based language that provides a means for individuals to indicate their privacy preferences, which can be compared against a Web site's policy. The user can use APPEL rules to instruct a Web browser to complete, limit, or block the request for a Web resource. Limiting a request results in cookies and referrer headers being blocked.

When defining a rule, the behavior must first be defined. The choices are continue, limited, or block. The user can choose to be prompted when a rule fires, to be given a chance to override the specified behavior. The remainder of the APPEL rule specifies P3P elements that should be compared to the P3P statements of visited Web sites. When there are multiple values for an element, the appel:connective attribute indicates whether all or any of the values must match for the rule to fire.

The following example indicates that all Web requests should be limited if the site to be visited collects physical or online contact information and shares the information with unrelated third parties or in public forums:

```
<appel:RULE behavior="limited" prompt="no"
 description="Block cookies and referrer headers from sites
 that collect contact information and share it in public
 forums or to unrelated third parties.">
 <p3p:POLICY>
   <p3p:STATEMENT appel:connective="and">
     <p3p:RECIPIENT appel:connective="or">
       <p3p:public/>
       <P3P:unrelated/>
     </p3p:RECIPIENT>
     <p3p:DATA-GROUP>
       <p3p:DATA>
         <p3p:CATEGORIES appel:connective="or">>
           <p3p:physical/>
           <p3p:online/>
         </p3p:CATEGORIES>
```

21. http://www.w3.org/TR/P3P-preferences/

```
      </p3p:DATA>
    </p3p:DATA-GROUP>
  </p3p:STATEMENT>
 </p3p:POLICY>
</appel:RULE>
```

Rules can be much more complex than this sample and can be applied to specific domains or parts of a domain. Users are not expected to create their preferences by creating a series of XML elements. User agents should provide a user interface to simplify the procedure. When using the Privacy Preference Settings dialog for the AT&T Privacy Bird, shown in Figure 9.15, the settings can be exported in APPEL format and imported on another machine.

Conclusion

The W3C created the P3P protocol to enable Web sites to express their privacy policy in a machine-readable format. By deploying P3P for your Web site, you will permit P3P-enabled user agents such as Internet Explorer and Netscape browsers to manage cookies based on your Web site's policy and the user privacy preferences. Implementing P3P can also help you avoid negative warnings that user agents may display to users when visiting your Web site.

Web site developers who have passed on implementing P3P should take an additional look at doing this. Based on my conversations with members of the W3C, there are certain to be more advanced Web services that will make decisions, such as the Web sites with which to connect, to solicit services based on the site's P3P implementation.

The implementation of P3P requires a short reference file, a policy file (which is the XML version of your privacy statement), and a compact policy (which is an abbreviated version of your XML policy). Several tools and books are available to help you with creating these three pieces of content. Always have your legal department review this content.

APPEL is an XML-based language that enables you to define your privacy preferences. A file containing an APPEL definition can be loaded by a user agent to define its privacy settings.

Several tools are available on the Internet to help you develop and test your P3P implementation and even create APPEL scripts. See the *References* section for links to more information on implementing P3P and APPEL.

References

Web Privacy with P3P, by Dr. Lorrie Cranor
http://www.p3pbook.com

Web Site Privacy with P3P, by Helena Lindskog, Stefan Lindskog
http://www.wiley.com/WileyCDA/WileyTitle/productCd-0471216771.html

P3P Tools
http://www.w3.org/P3P/implementations
http://www.p3ptools.com/
http://www.p3ptoolbox.org/

10 Integrating Privacy into the Development Process

Developing solutions can be very demanding. It's difficult to create the right combinations of features that will persuade the marketplace to become excited about your product enough to purchase it. You are constantly getting input from consumers, enterprises, partners, analysts, marketing, and even your own product groups. There are also concerns about reliability, usability, availability, supportability, compatibility, security, accessibility, legality, and ship schedule. There has been a growing focus on the security of applications because of the interconnectivity of systems and increasing threats from hackers. Now you get yet another task called privacy awareness added to your already full plate. Few development teams are staffed to handle the intricacies of privacy awareness. Trying to fit it into the schedule with everything else without having to delay shipping is almost impossible.

One of the biggest questions you have to ask yourself is, "Will building privacy awareness into my application be enough of a differentiator to offset the time investment?" Measuring the financial benefit from adding privacy awareness is not always easy. Measuring the barriers to sales should be easier. For example, would product sales to companies that are concerned about Health Information Portability and Accountability Act (HIPAA) compliance be affected? Would privacy-sensitive countries such as Germany and Denmark resist deployment of your product? One sure way to avoid sales barriers caused by privacy issues is to add privacy awareness to the development process.

Getting Started

So when should the privacy process start? As soon as possible. When does it end? When all of the privacy issues have been identified and mitigated. Mitigation may simply mean providing a privacy statement that addresses any privacy concerns users may have. Each time your team starts a new version of your component or a patch, you start the process again. Building privacy-aware applications is an iterative process that should continue as long as development is taking place. During the development process, developers should always look to perform a privacy analysis on each feature and mitigate all known privacy risks. You then send out your results for review, and then take the feedback and incorporate it back into the development process, refining your work until you have a set of deliverables with which you and your customers are comfortable.

A privacy analysis, like a security-threat modeling analysis, can be performed at any phase during the development cycle, including on software that has been deployed. Although companies may not always be in a position to update software that has already deployed, they will be better positioned to support the software if all of their support personnel understand what data is being collected by the company's solutions and how it is being handled.

The *Privacy as Part of Development* section discusses how privacy fits into each phase of a development project. The following sections provide guidance in learning what you need to do to be successful at privacy development.

Start with a Solid Infrastructure

All great initiatives start with the assignment of the right resources. Developing a privacy process is not any different. To be successful at building privacy-aware applications, the following things should be in place:

- A relationship made with the corporate privacy group (CPG)
- A privacy council
- A privacy lead assigned for each component
- A privacy standard

Understand that in small organizations there may not be a CPG, privacy council, or even a privacy lead. For small organizations, developers or project managers need to add the role of privacy lead to their list of duties.

These topics are covered in Chapter 7. Be sure to read through each topic for a better understanding of how they impact the product-development process.

Get Privacy Training

Before making any progress on privacy, everyone on your team should have a thorough understanding of what privacy means and how it can impact your customers. Chapter 7 discussed developing a training program for your company. Your training program should include guidelines on building solutions and protecting customer data that reflect the company's privacy policies. During the development process, there are often programs that include collecting customer feedback, which is often stored in unprotected databases and computer systems. These types of practices should be covered during privacy training. A training program should be mandatory for each member of a development department.

There are organizations such as Deloitte and Touche, Ernst and Young, The Privacy Council, and MediaPro[1] that offer privacy training. These companies can assist with producing a training curriculum and providing formal training classes for your company. Developing an online training program is one of the most effective ways to reach employees.

A training program should be patterned after an organization's written privacy policies. Several books make excellent reading material for individuals desiring to improve their knowledge of privacy:

- *Writing Secure Code*, Second Edition, by Michael Howard and David LeBlanc (Microsoft Press, 2002)
- *Windows Security Resource Kit*, by Ben Smith and Brian Komar (Microsoft Press, 2002)
- *Privacy Handbook: Guidelines, Exposures, Policy Implementation, and International Issues*, by Albert J. Marcella and Carol Stucki (John Wiley and Sons, 2003)
- *The Privacy Payoff*, by Ann Cavoukian Ph.D. and Tyler J. Hamilton (McGraw-Hill Ryerson, 2002)
- *Protect Yourself Online*, by Matthew Danda (Microsoft Press, 2001)

---

1. MediaPro offers a pretty cool online training suite that is media driven and interactive. Information on their offerings can be found at http://www.mediapro.com/privacy.

Create a Plan

Now that your team has acquired some background in privacy, assigned a privacy lead, and you have a privacy standard to follow, the privacy lead needs to devise a plan for complying with your privacy standard in the development of your component. In devising a plan, the privacy lead should work with the other privacy leads (PLs) in your organization to get their ideas and ensure that your plan integrates well with theirs. Consult the privacy council whenever you need clarification or just need to have your plan validated.

The first step in developing a plan is to take an inventory of all of the products for which your team is responsible and where they are in the development cycle. Follow the flowchart in the next section and the material in this chapter as a guide to the development and execution of your plan. At a minimum, create a privacy statement for each of your team's products and Web sites. Remember, privacy is not a part-time job, but a full-time commitment. Plan your privacy work, then work your privacy plan. When you have completed everything for the current product cycle, review your successes and areas that need improvement and then prepare for the next development cycle.

Privacy-Process Flowchart

The set of flowcharts in Figures 10.1 through 10.5 guide you through the creation and execution of a privacy plan for your organization. The letters *A* through *D* in Figure 10.1 refer to the flowcharts in Figures 10.2 to 10.5, respectively. Details on each of the tasks in the flowchart can be found later in this chapter. Some sections of the flowchart may not apply to your component(s). For example, if your component does not collect, store, or transmit data, there is no need to create a privacy-deployment guide.

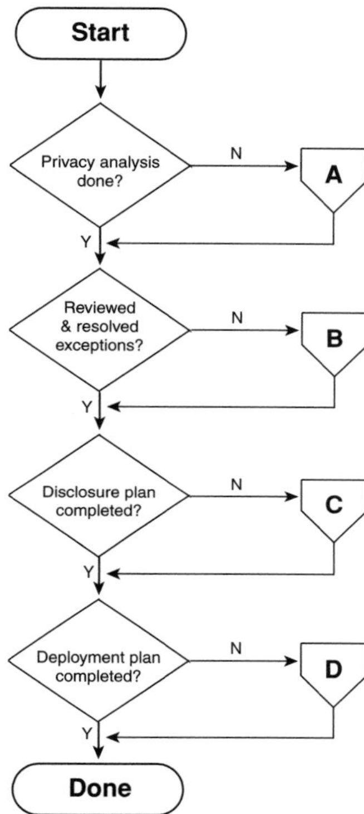

Figure 10.1 Top-level flowchart for building a privacy-aware component

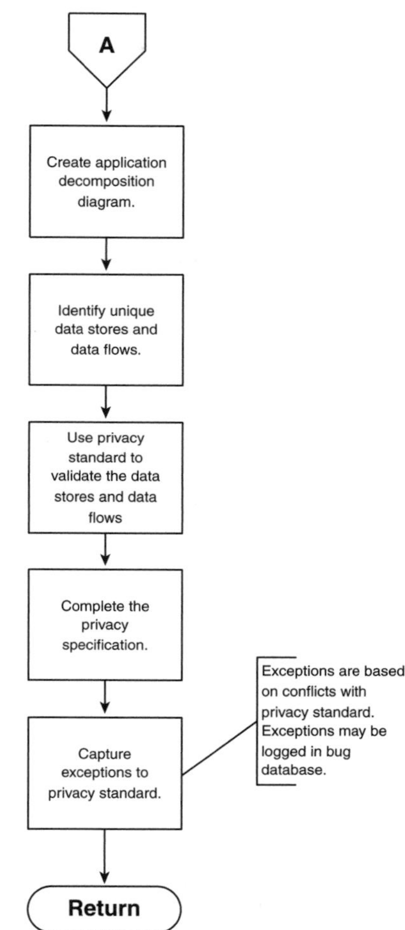

Figure 10.2 Flowchart for performing a privacy analysis

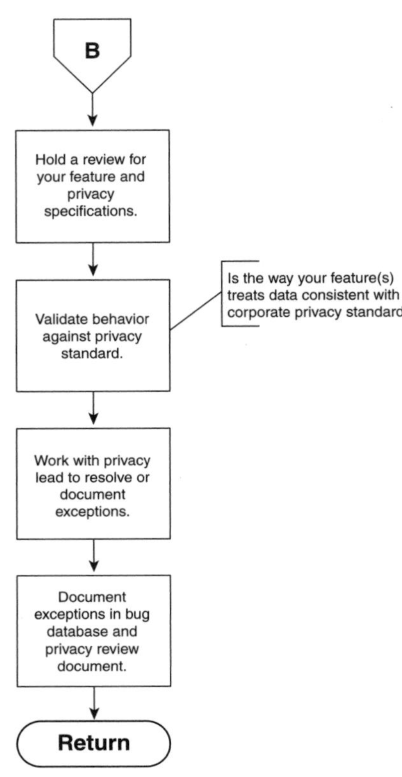

Figure 10.3 Flowchart for analysis exceptions

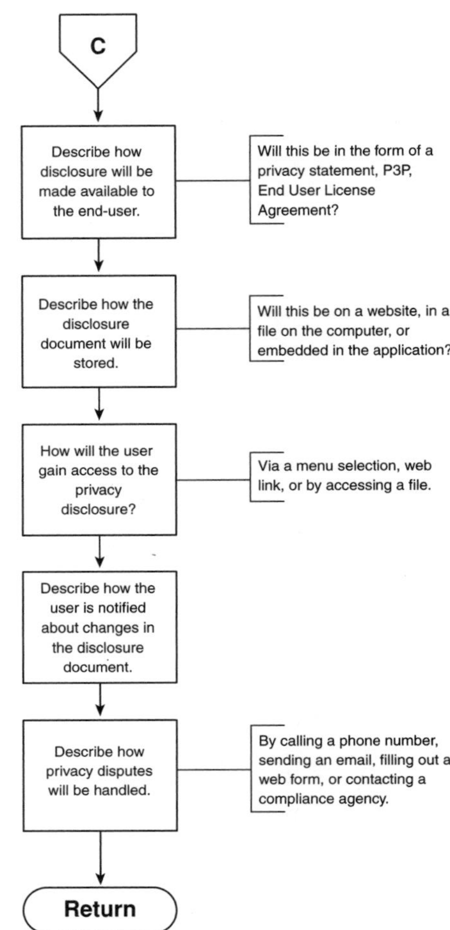

Figure 10.4 Flowchart for creating a disclosure plan

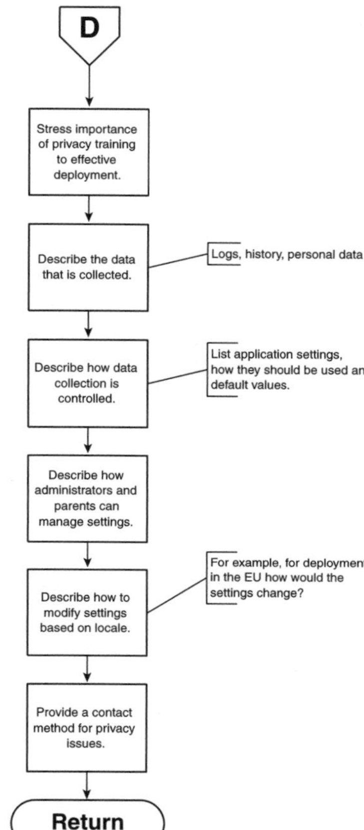

Figure 10.5 Flowchart for creating the privacy-deployment guide

Integrating Privacy into Development

Whether you are building products, Web sites, or services, each has a set of steps that you go through that denote the beginning, intermediate, and end phases of development. During each phase, a set of privacy tasks must be performed to ensure privacy compliance.

This section provides an example of how privacy can be integrated into various phases in the development of a product. The example may not map 100 percent to the way that you are building a product, but it should be useful as a guide for determining privacy integration points. Figure 10.6

depicts how a development process can effectively integrate privacy during product development. For companies with a simpler development process, focus on producing a privacy specification and privacy review to resolve open issues.

The Documents

The privacy documents identified in Figure 10.6 represent the deliverables of the phase(s) to which they are connected. For example, the feature specification document is a deliverable of the design phase and feeds some of the content in the privacy specification document. Each document should be created during the indicated phase, but not necessarily completed. A more detailed description of each document is provided later in this chapter.

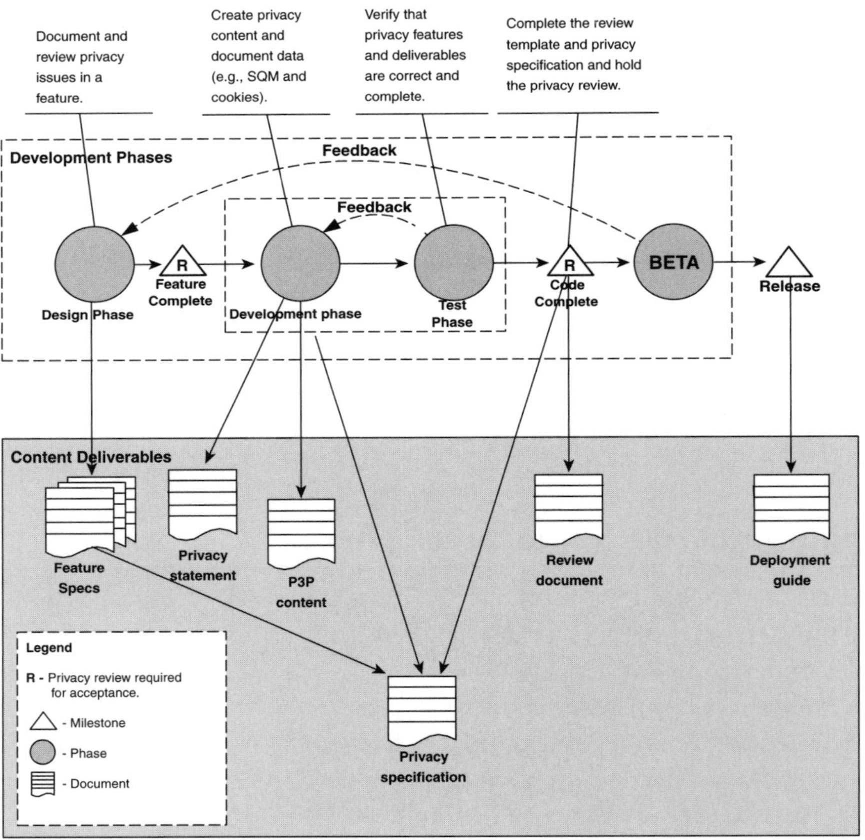

Figure 10.6 Integrating privacy in each phase of development

Each document shares a relationship with the others; the contents of a later one are driven by the contents of a previous one. Although you could create each document in isolation, it is recommended you create the documents in succession to avoid excluding information needed for later documents. Whenever a document changes, make sure to update any documents that may derive from it. Figure 10.7 shows the relationship between privacy documents in more detail. The arrows show the flow of dependency from one document type to the next. The following sections describe the purpose of each document and how it feeds into successive documents.

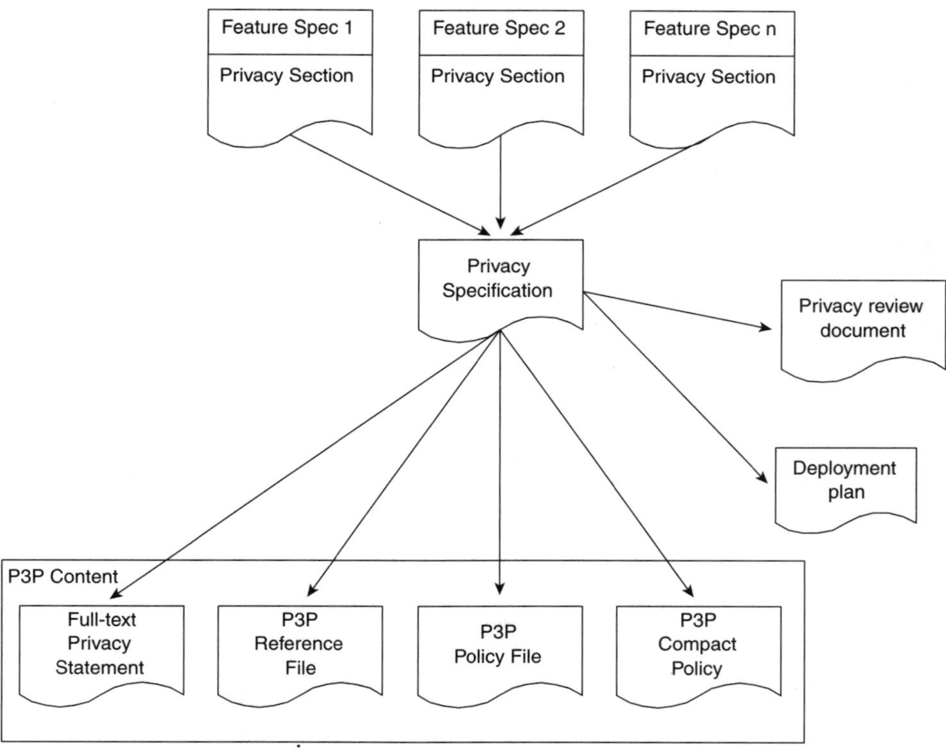

Figure 10.7 Relationship of privacy content

Localization/Globalization

Most user readable privacy material (for example, privacy statements) will need to be localized when being deployed to other countries. Once the privacy content has been translated it should be turned over to privacy experts in each foreign subsidiary to validate the language. Localization is not simply a matter of translating the documents. Consider the privacy practices of the local market and/or regime when performing localization. Default values for components may even need to be modified to satisfy local requirements. For example, the collection or transmission of data by default may be permissible in the United States, but not in other countries.

Feature Specification Document

The feature specification document provides a detailed description of a feature that is to be incorporated into a component. Each feature specification should include a privacy section. This section should describe the privacy aspects of the feature. For example, it should include the following information where appropriate:

- A list of the data that is collected, stored, shared, and transmitted
- The method used to protect the data
- Methods of accessing the data
- The user interface (UI) that can be used to control the data capture, storage, and transmission

To avoid duplication and inconsistent documentation, it is acceptable to reference other sections in the privacy specification or other specifications. Follow the instructions provided later in this section or ask your privacy lead for assistance. Features that do not have any privacy consequences should simply state, "not applicable" in this section. The information from the privacy section should be used to fill out the privacy specification. Read the section *Design Phase* for information on uses of the privacy section during a feature review.

Privacy Specification

The privacy specification is a compilation of the privacy information captured in the privacy section of each feature specification, as well as a rollup of the privacy analysis performed on a component. It includes a description of the privacy disclosure, settings, features, and data. The information contained in the privacy specification is used to drive the contents of the privacy statement, privacy review document, and deployment guide. It should be created by the privacy lead or a program manager (PM) on the feature team who is familiar with the component. It is described in detail in the section *The Privacy Specification.*

Full-Text Privacy Statement

This is a public document for consumption by end users. Its purpose is to notify users of what data is collected and how it is used. Information from the privacy specification can make creation of this document simpler and thorough. The contents of this document can be used as a basis for the P3P content for a Web site. More information on privacy statements can be found in the section *Creating a Privacy Statement.*

A good example of a privacy statement can be found at Hewlett Packard's Web site at http://welcome.hp.com/country/us/en/privacy.html. Here is a list of the features that make this privacy statement particularly appealing:

- It informs you of the data HP collects, why it's collected, and with whom it is shared.
- HP is transparent about the cookies, Web site beacons, and advertising they use.
- It indicates how your data is protected during transfer, storage, and usage.
- It provides a method for accessing your data.
- It documents a means for opting out of communications from HP.
- It lists a privacy certification with which HP is affiliated.
- It provides a set of links for easily navigating the privacy statement.
- It lists a method for contacting HP.

P3P Reference File

This file contains an eXtensible Markup Language (XML) document that points to the XML version of a company's privacy statement. This file can be created manually or by using a tool such as IBM's P3P Policy Editor. The P3P reference file should be placed in the W3C subdirectory of your Web site's root directory. See Chapter 9 for more information on P3P and how this file is used.

P3P Policy File

This document is the XML version of a company's privacy statement that is created using the P3P privacy vocabulary. This document can be created manually or by using various tools. See Chapter 9 for more information on P3P and how this file is used.

P3P Compact Policy

This content is used to express a Web site's privacy policy in an abbreviated form that can be read by P3P-aware browsers. It consists of codes that reflect a condensed version of the P3P XML document. The compact policy is placed into the HTTP header of a Web site. This content can be created manually or by using one of many P3P tools. See Chapter 9 for more information on P3P and how this file is used.

Deployment Guide

Each product that you ship should have a privacy-deployment guide, which ensures that all privacy collateral is accounted for and that the customer using the component is able to make the best use of the product's privacy settings. Deployment data for each component and feature should be included in this document. The deployment guide is driven by the content in the privacy specification. For more information on building a deployment guide, go to the section *Creating a Deployment Guide*.

Privacy Review Document

This document is used as a basis for formal privacy reviews. It contains a summary of each privacy issue for a product along with a proposal on how to mitigate the issue where appropriate. Issues are ordered from highest severity (S1) to lowest severity (S3). The thorough completion of the privacy specification makes it easy to create this document. More information on this document can be found in the section *The Privacy Review*.

Design Phase

During the design phase of development, the privacy section of each feature specification should be filled out by the PM who is responsible for the feature, describing all privacy-related information that may exist in the feature. Use the privacy checklist in Appendix E as a guide to filling out this section. If there is an associated privacy statement or privacy feature description, it should be indicated in the feature specification under the "User Assistance Issues" or similar section. A sample privacy section can be found in Appendix A.

Review your privacy documentation with the appropriate privacy experts (for example, other privacy leads, your privacy council, or legal) to ensure it's complete and accurately reflects all privacy risks. Identify possible ways to mitigate the risks (include development and test estimates).

A single privacy specification for your component should be created during this phase by your privacy lead, if one has been identified; otherwise, the PM for the product is accountable for creating it. Information from each feature specification should be fed into the privacy specification for your component. It will contain the results of a privacy analysis that was performed on your component. A thorough description of the privacy specification is provided in the section *The Privacy Specification*.

During the review of your feature specification, present your privacy evaluation to those in your organization who are accountable for the delivery of your component, such as your development manager, director, or general manager for your product. Make sure they understand and accept any privacy risks that may exist prior to approving the feature.

Feature Complete

Feature complete represents the end of acceptance of new features. Before feature complete has been designated, each feature should have gone through a review that included an evaluation of the privacy risks. This means that every feature must include a privacy section that has been filled out.

Development Phase

During the development phase, each developer is responsible for creating the privacy features for a component. This can include encryption, privacy settings, and Group Policy scripts. During this phase, the documentation department should create the privacy content for a feature, such as the privacy statement and any P3P content for Web sites. These documents should go through legal review before they are released. The privacy lead should ensure that the review is carried out. The contents of all cookies, logs, and any data sent to the Internet from the application should be documented, along with a description of how they are used. Technical writers should include a description of privacy features in the documents that they create. Appendix D contains a list of possible privacy content.

Moreover, each developer is responsible for ensuring that relevant sections of the privacy specification accurately reflect the implementation of their features. Make sure that the code you develop is in line with the Safe Harbor Privacy Principles.[2] Review the data that you are storing and make sure it is documented. Filling out the specification will help you identify any weaknesses in your privacy strategy.

When privacy issues arise, add them to the privacy review document along with a suggested mitigation plan, if one exists.

Test Phase

During the test phase, testers should validate the privacy implementation and deliverables for their components. All privacy documents should be correct and complete. This should include ensuring that legal has reviewed the wording of any privacy documents that have been created. Understand that legal may take several weeks to complete a review. All discrepancies found with the privacy implementation should be entered in a bug-tracking database for resolution by developers. Be sure to indicate a privacy code when creating the bug report to permit the tracking of privacy-related bugs.

When testing each component, ask the following questions:

- Is data being collected by the component?
- Does the component track usage, most recently used file lists, histories, cache, or logs?
- Does the component transmit any information to the Internet?
- Is there an unintended privacy exposure when the component is used improperly?
- Does the component comply with the corporate privacy standard?

If the answer to any of these questions is yes, verify that these things have been documented in the privacy specification. It may be prudent to run a "packet sniffer" on the network connection of the computer under test to be 100 percent sure that all information being transmitted by your application is documented. A packet sniffer is a tool that is cable of monitoring the data that travels over a network. The Network Monitor tool, which comes with Windows Server operating systems, is an example of a packet sniffer.

2.The Safe Harbor Privacy Principles can be found at http://www.export.gov/safeharbor/sh_overview.html. Safe Harbor is also covered in Chapter 3.

Be sure to verify that the contents of all data files have been documented. Use the checklist in Appendix E to guide you in the verification of the completeness of the information in the privacy specification. The ultimate goal of privacy testing is to ensure that each component complies with the Safe Harbor Principles.

If you find any privacy issues that need to be reviewed by your management team, add them to the privacy review document. Be sure to follow up on any open issues to ensure that they are resolved.

Code Complete

Code complete is the milestone that typically marks the end of code changes based on feature submissions. Before this milestone is completed, a formal privacy review should occur. During the review, verify that the following tasks have been completed:

- The first draft of all privacy documents is available.
- A feature exists for displaying the privacy disclosure to the user.
- Privacy settings exist to enable users to control their privacy.
- Each privacy setting has an equivalent Group Policy setting.
- All sensitive data that is transmitted or stored is protected with security and encryption.

The PL must play a prominent role in ensuring that these tasks are accomplished. Each privacy lead should perform a review for his or her area and present the results at the privacy review meeting. Use the review template in Appendix B as a guideline. See the section *The Privacy Review* for more information on conducting a privacy review.

The PL for your team should work with the PMs to ensure that the privacy specification and privacy review document are completed. When these documents are complete, the PL should hold the privacy review. A completed review where all privacy issues have been mitigated should be a requirement for the signoff of code complete. This does not necessarily mean that the issues have all been fixed, but that a resolution has been determined.

Beta Release

Before a public release such as a beta or other intermediate release, a privacy review should have been completed. Make sure that the product's feature list description contains a category for privacy features so they are clearly visible to reviewers. During these releases, you may get feedback from customers, analysts, or the media on your privacy implementation. This feedback should be fed back into the design phase and the appropriate changes should be made to your products.

Product Release

The RTM or RTW (release to Web) of a product marks the end of development and the release of the product for distribution to the market for which it was designed. Part of the release requirements for a product should be the privacy-deployment guide, which acts as a road map for deploying the product within an enterprise or the home of a consumer. A support plan that includes a means to respond to possible privacy issues should also be developed for products. Lessons learned from the deployment and use of your product by customers should be analyzed to improve the product's next version.

Privacy Response Team

Every product group should have a privacy response process in place for handling privacy issues with its products. This process should be tied to the description provided to users of the product as part of the privacy-deployment document. New issues may come into the company's privacy response center and then be assigned to a product team. A new privacy issue could also be generated by the product team itself. All issues should be reported to the company's privacy response center for tracking.

The person in each product group appointed to be in charge of the privacy response process should understand the process and know who the responsible people are in your organization for each major component, associated Web sites, databases, and third parties. This person should work closely with the company's privacy response center for vetting the issue. This will avoid delivering messages to customers that may be inconsistent with corporate guidelines. Including the privacy response center in issue closures will also permit quicker resolution of similar issues that may come in later. Chapter 8 contains more information on developing a privacy response process.

For smaller companies, there should still be a process in place for handling privacy issues. The manner in which you handle normal customer-support issues can be expanded to handle privacy issues. Support personnel should be trained on privacy. Privacy issues should be reviewed by senior management to ensure that they are resolved in a manner that will not cause harm to the company's image.

Creating a Deployment Guide

When a product is released, it may contain dozens of features. Customers will want to know how each of those features works and how each feature may affect their privacy. Product documentation should include sections on privacy-related features and how to manage privacy settings in the home and in an enterprise. The following types of content should be part of the privacy documentation for a product when it is released:

- **Privacy statement**—Each product should have its own privacy statement. It should describe what personal or sensitive data is being collected, what connections are being made to the Internet to transmit or receive data, which privacy settings exist for the application, and what are the defaults. There should be a clear and conspicuous mechanism for accessing the privacy statement from the application. Web sites associated with the product should include P3P integration.
- **Privacy deployment**—This paper should indicate the privacy-related features that should be taken into account when the product is deployed. This paper should discuss the best practices for deploying the application with regard to privacy. What are the different privacy settings? What are the default and recommended values based on locale? For example, in some countries, certain types of behavior, such as sending data over the Internet without explicit consent from the user, may not be permitted. What settings control history and log collection? What clear-tracks features exist? How can Group Policy be used to control privacy settings in an enterprise?
- **Privacy enforcement**—This document should provide information to the end user about how they can contact your company in case a privacy violation occurs. It should also indicate any subscriptions that exist to third-party compliance organizations such at TRUSTe.[3] The privacy-enforcement process should tie into the privacy response team for issue resolution. Even though this information may be covered in the privacy statement, additional information on this process should exist in other product documentation, possibly under the support section.

The resources required to produce the deployment guide should be minimal as long as the privacy features have been tracked in the privacy specification. This will also depend on the complexity of your product and the amount of data that is collected by it. It will probably go through several iterations that

3. http://www.truste.org/

map to each public release that is part of your development schedule. It can be started soon after *feature complete*. Starting it sooner could cause unnecessary churn because of features being cut or modified before they are reviewed and approved. The deployment guide should be created by the product's PL in conjunction with PLs from other groups.

The Privacy Specification

Each component should have a privacy specification that describes all privacy data, transmissions, features, and dependencies. The privacy specification should be started by the component team's PL during the initial design phase for the component and be completed before the first public release of the component. This specification acts as the master working document on privacy for a component. All privacy-related information should be detailed by this document. Even if a piece of privacy content is not contained in this document, it should be referenced by it. For example, a link to the privacy statement should be included in this document. Here are the major sections that should exist in the privacy specification:

- Data analysis
- Usage analysis
- Security analysis
- User control analysis
- User access analysis
- Disclosure plan
- Dependency analysis

Figure 10.8 shows the sequence for completing the various sections of a privacy specification.

Determining all of the information that needs to go into a privacy specification can be difficult at times. Diagramming your component can assist you in pinpointing the data that is used by your application and how it is used. Chapter 11 describes how to perform an analysis with diagrams created using application decomposition. The results that you get from analyzing your data usage will directly tie into the information that is needed by the privacy specification. Figure 10.9 shows an example of a diagram used to document the dataflow for an imaginary application. The examples used later in this section refer back to this diagram. Although the diagram is useful, it should not be considered a requirement for completion of the privacy specification.

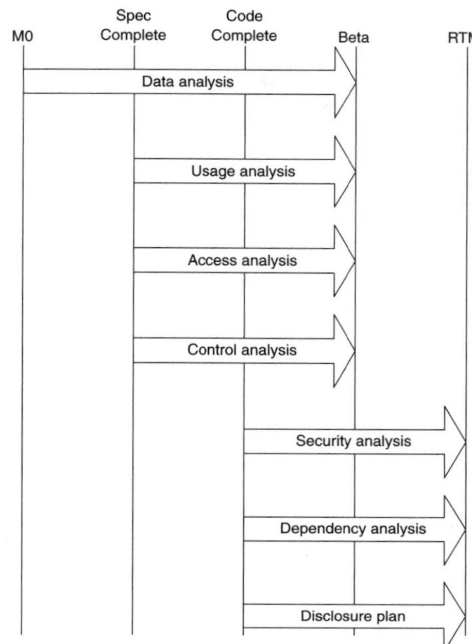

Figure 10.8 Sequence chart for completing a privacy specification

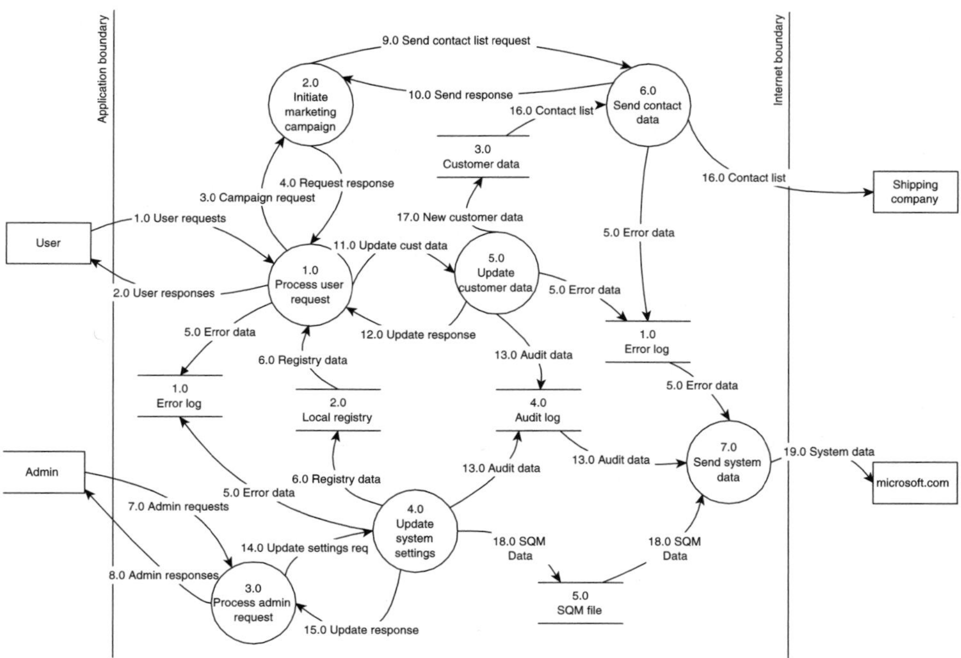

Figure 10.9 Sample dataflow diagram

Data Analysis

The data analysis task is used to determine what data is collected and transmitted by your component. For companies that perform threat-modeling analyses for security, the data analysis section of the privacy specification can be filled out during the security-threat modeling process. Use the application decomposition diagrams to aid you in determining how data is used by your component.[4]

During the data analysis phase, scrutinize the application decomposition or other diagrams looking for occurrences of application data. Look for values used as keys in multiple data stores to clue you in if data can be correlated or commingled. For example, in Table 7.1, the GUID is used in the customer data and audit log storage locations. If a person has access to both of these, a more complete picture of the user could be built. Try to avoid propagating keys where possible.

Examine what data is stored and transmitted by the application. Use the data analysis template to track the name and privacy properties of your data. A sample template is in Appendix C. Following is an example of a partially filled template based on the previous application decomposition diagram. Here is a description of the columns in the template example:

- **Item name**—The number and name of the process from the application decomposition (AD) diagram that owns the section of data being described. This column may also contain the name of the value or data item.
- **Notice given**—Was notice given in the privacy statement about the collection and use of this value?
- **Sent to Internet**—Is this value sent to an Internet site (i.e., your Web site)? If it is sent to a third-party Web site, indicate that in the next column. All transmissions to the Internet should be indicated in the product's privacy statement.
- **Sent to third party**—Is this value sent to a third-party Web site? If so, this fact should be indicated in the privacy statement. If the third party is acting as an agent of your company, this does not have to be mentioned separately, because it should be covered by the description-of-use section of the privacy statement.
- **In use**—Is the value used at all? Even though the value is collected and passed around, it may never be used.

4.Threat modeling is defined in detail in the book *Writing Secure Code*, Second Edition. Application decomposition is described in Chapter 11.

- **User control**—Does the user have control over the collection or use of this value? If so, the user's means of control should be described in the privacy statement. If not, a solution should be investigated.
- **Central control**—Can control over the collection and use of this value be managed by Group Policy or some other mechanism accessible to a network administrator? If so, the means should be described in the component documentation.
- **Access provided**—Is access to the value provided to users? If so, the means to access the data should be described in the privacy statement. Access can be local for applications and online for Web site services.
- **Security exist**—Are there security settings, encryption, or other means to protect the data? If so, it should be mentioned in the privacy statement and described in the help documentation.

Following is a sample entry:

TABLE 10.1 EXAMPLE DATA ANALYSIS TABLE

	Notice Given	Sent to Internet	Sent to Third Party	In Use	User Control	Central Control	Access Provided	Security Exist
Item name								
D_3.0 Customer data								
GUID	Y	Y	Y	Y	N	N	N	Y
User name	Y	Y	Y	Y	Y	N	N	Y
Address	Y	Y	Y	N	Y	N	Y	Y
Credit card number	Y	N	Y	Y	Y	N	Y	Y
F_19.0 System data								
Audit file	Y	Y	N	Y	N	Y	N	Y
Error data	N	Y	N	Y	Y	Y	N	N
SQM file	Y	Y	N	Y	Y	Y	N	N

Item name	Notice Given	Sent to Internet	Sent to Third Party	In Use	User Control	Central Control	Access Provided	Security Exist
D_3.0 Customer data	Y	Y	Y	Y	N	N	N	Y

Sent to Internet

Our contact management team manages the database, which is accessed by various marketing groups.

Sent to Third Party

We partner with Accenture to provide a small-business solution, and they have access to this data based on our partnership. This is described in the disclosure section.

Security Exist

This data is stored in a SQL Server database. Security restrictions have been placed on the table to restrict access and the credit card information is encrypted using 64-bit RC5 encryption.

The fields that contain an N are priority 2 work items that we will attempt to get into the M5 release.

Usage Analysis

The usage analysis section should describe the use for the collected data and who uses it. If there are multiple purposes, indicate who is involved in the use for each purpose. Make sure that every data store defined on the diagram is listed here.

A user's data should be collected only if there is a bona-fide business purpose or regulatory requirement for collecting it. For regulatory requirements, you should be able to cite the relevant regulation for presentation to a customer. In addition, you should be able to articulate a clear customer benefit for such collection (for example, access to a cool feature or better service). If you cannot find one, you should not collect the data.

Following is an example entry based on the diagram in Figure 10.9:

D_3.0 Customer data

This represents a database table used to store information about a customer who has registered this information because he or she purchased our product or is interested in doing so. Each piece of the data that is collected is used. The information is used for the following purposes:

> **Problem reporting**
>
> The engineering team uses the information to send updates and report problems to the customer.
>
> **Marketing e-mails**
>
> The marketing department uses the information to send brochures on new product releases and associated products. The information is also used to send targeted e-mails to warn users when their subscription is about to end.

Security Analysis

This section is used to indicate the type of security associated with each set of data collected. Here you should indicate whether encryption is used during transfer and storage, if physical protection is provided for the data, and if access to the data is protected via an authentication and authorization mechanism. If the data is sent to third parties, indicate their data protection plan. Following is an example of what this section would look like:

D_3.0 Customer data

This is the security analysis for the customer data table.

> **Transmission security**
>
> Collection of this data is protected by SSL over the Internet and internally. When the data is sent to third-party agencies via the Internet, it is protected using SSL.

Storage security

Each item of data is encrypted when it is stored using the Triple-DES algorithm. It can only be decrypted using our client application. Access to the data is protected by roles. Users are only able to access the data that is necessary to fulfill their role.

Physical security

The servers used to hold this data are kept in a secure data center with limited access. The building is continually monitored by guards and cameras.

Third-party handling

Each agent who uses this data is required to store it in an encrypted fashion. They are not permitted to transfer this data to other parties or use it for any purposes other than for the fulfillment of this service.

User Control Analysis

This section is used to describe the settings that are available to users to enable them to control the application's ability to collect their data or its uses. Indicate the default value for each of the settings. Also indicate whether there is any Group Policy integration or other means of centralized control that would assist an IT administrator in managing these settings for the enterprise. When describing the controls, indicate whether they are opt-in or opt-out. For sensitive information, the default should be opt-in. Following is an example of what the definition would look like:

D_3.0 Customer data

Customers are compelled to provide this information to complete their purchase transactions. In addition, when a product is purchased, the transmission of product problem report e-mails is turned on, because they could warn the user of problems that could affect their business or data loss.

Available settings

Product update e-mails—Controls sending product update e-mails to users.

Marketing e-mails—Controls sending marketing e-mails to users.

Partner sharing—Controls sharing contact information with our partners.

Access to settings

Each of the privacy settings listed here is presented to the user during the first-run experience for each user; the settings are not visible during setup. The user can also access these settings on the privacy property page, which is accessible either by selecting Privacy on the Help menu or the Privacy tab when displaying the Options dialog after selection Options on the Tools menu.

Group Policy

Each of the privacy settings is accessible via Group Policy by selecting the CRM application node under Windows applications.

Defaults

Product update e-mails—This is on by default; opt-out.

Marketing e-mails—This is off by default; opt-in.

Partner sharing—This is off by default; opt-in.

User Access Analysis

This section describes how a user can view and change the information that has been collected about him or her. Indicate whether this access can be delegated to another user. Describe how this access is protected to ensure that only the user or delegate can make changes. For example:

D_3.0 Customer data

The user can view all of his or her information by accessing our Web site and entering an ID and password. Each field, except the name and ID, can be modified by the user. Access to this information can be delegated by providing the ID and password. The user can also change this information by calling our customer-support line and providing his or her name and account ID. Verification of identity is done through e-mail.

Disclosure Plan

This section of the specification should describe your plan for disclosing to users of your solution what data about them you collect and how it is used. Where possible, add links to the disclosure content. See Appendix D for a list of possible privacy content that you can create. Following is a set of things to resolve when creating your disclosure plan.

Displaying the Privacy Statement

This part of the plan describes how you will display the privacy statement or privacy-related content. For this part, answer the following questions:

- Which component will be responsible for displaying the privacy statement?
  - Your component
  - An external component in your application
  - A third-party component
- When will the privacy statement display?
  - During the installation process
  - During the first use by each user on a computer
  - On demand through your application or a Web site
- How will the statement display?
  - Using an application such as Notepad or Word
  - Inside of a custom UI that you deliver
  - From a Web page

Storing the Privacy Statement

This part should describe how you will store the privacy statement. Indicate whether it will be stored in a file on the user's computer, a Web site, or by some other means. If you are storing the statement on a Web site, consider what happens when the user requests the privacy statement while offline.

Accessing the Privacy Statement

This part should explain how the user will access the privacy statement. The mechanism should be easy for the user to discover. If it is displayed as the result of a menu selection, ensure that the menu item is easy to find. If it is part of a Web site, ensure that the page is easy to navigate to.

Changing the Privacy Statement

This part explains how the privacy statement will be changed and how the user is notified about the change. Consider the following things when filling out this part:

- How will changes be deployed?
  - In a service pack
  - In version updates
  - By updating a Web site
- How will users be notified of changes?
  - New date at the top of Web site page
  - E-mail message
  - Updated tag
  - Popup after an update
- How will the user determine what changes occurred?
  - Visual inspection
  - Via a summary of the changes in an e-mail
  - Via a summary as part of the privacy statement
  - Change bars or other markings in the text

Documenting Details in the Privacy Statement

This part explains the detailed information that you will disclose as part of your privacy statement. This can include a technical description of data stores or transmitted data. Use the following questions as guidelines for this part:

- What detailed information will you include in the statement?
  - All network traffic
  - Cookie contents
  - Contents of files or the registry
  - Contents of databases or other data stores
- How is detailed information accessed by the user?
  - System tools or applications such as RegEdit or SQL Server
  - Custom UI
  - Hyperlinks

Handling Disputes in the Privacy Statement

This part describes what measures a customer can take to resolve disputes. You should provide an e-mail address, Web site form, phone number, or mailing address. Also consider participating in the TRUSTe program, http://www.truste.org. Contact your corporate privacy group to determine if your company subscribes to this service.

Dependency Analysis

This section should describe privacy dependencies between your component and other components. There may be components that your component is inherited from and components that inherit from your component. In each case, privacy dependencies should be addressed. Create a diagram to help indicate the dependencies that exist between your component and others. Figure 10.10 provides an example of a dependency diagram that shows the relationship between the CRM application and other components.

Components That You Inherit From

Ensure that the privacy requirements of each component that you inherit from are understood and accepted by your team. There may be disclosure, control, and access requirements that you need to fulfill and document. If you do not interact with or expose any privacy features of another component, you are not obligated to do anything.

Components That Inherit From You

For these components, ensure that other internal product groups and external parties that are integrating with your component understand your privacy requirements and are willing to adhere to them. Where appropriate, include your privacy requirements in the license agreement, terms of use, memorandum of understanding, or other document that governs the use of your component.

Phone Home Disclosure

Phone home refers to the practice of an application connecting to the Internet to receive information from or transmit information to the manufacturer of the software. Regardless of how innocuous the data you are transferring may be, it may concern a user if your application connects to the Internet without a clear description of why it is being done and what

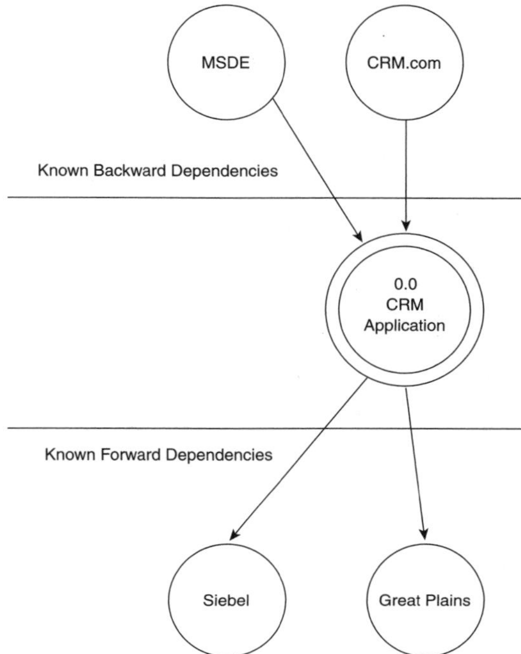

Figure 10.10 A dependency diagram

data is being transferred. Internet connections should be indicated on your dataflow diagram (DFD) by a dataflow. This dataflow should be documented in the previous sections of the privacy specification. In this section, just list the dataflows that connect to the Internet so that they can be easily referenced in the privacy specification. Following is an example entry:

Dataflow name	Destination
F_19.0 System_data	Corporate error reporting team

Entity Description

Each entity included in a diagram should be described to indicate the part that it plays in the component's data handling. In general, an entity will be an application, Web site, or company that sends data to or receives data from your component. This description should include what data is shared with the entity and how the data is handled. Include a description of any contracts or agreements with third parties. For example:

Direct Marketer

This entity is the company West Corp Data Services that provides mailing services for our company. They are managed by the marketing team. There is a contract in place that covers this transfer of data.

The Privacy Review

The privacy review should be viewed as the mitigation process for unresolved problems found during the privacy analysis of each component.[5] If no problems were found during the privacy analysis of each component, the review document will have no issues associated with it. However, the formal review should still be held to make sure everyone is in agreement with the findings.

Starting the Privacy Review

So where does one get started with a privacy review? For legacy products, you will want to perform a privacy review of each released component to see where you are before starting the next development cycle. List each of the privacy risks along with proposed solutions to mitigate the risks. This requires a privacy analysis of each component. Although this will take a bit of time, it will be time well spent. For products that are well into the development cycle, examine the areas that may have the maximum risk. These will be areas that collect personal data or transmit data to the Internet.

For brand new products, follow the development process described in the section *Integrating Privacy into Development*, and hold the privacy review before the first public beta for your product. Use the privacy review template as a placeholder for documenting your unresolved privacy issues. The privacy specification that you create during the product development cycle can be of great assistance with the content for the privacy review. A description of the privacy review template and how to use it is provided in the section *Privacy Review Template*.

Management by Exception

To streamline the process of the privacy review, base it on management by exception. This means that as long as your component follows the guidelines outlined in the privacy standard created by your privacy council, a

5. The privacy-analysis process is described in Chapter 11.

formal review meeting is not necessary. Whenever there are cases where the standard was not followed (exceptions), a review must be held to manage the exception. Your component's compliance with the privacy standard should be validated by your privacy lead. When there are exceptions to the guidelines of the privacy standard, they should be indicated in the privacy review template and discussed during your formal privacy review meeting.

To get an understanding of the types of things that should be in the standard, I have listed each type of privacy analysis and provided an example of what kinds of privacy items should be expected for each analysis. Your privacy council should decide what is acceptable based on your corporate privacy policy. Anything that does not agree with the standard should be placed in the review document for discussion during the review.[6] The types of analysis and the items that correspond to them are as follows:

- **Data analysis**—During the data analysis, make sure that each of the analysis points in the spreadsheet is appropriately marked. If any of the values differ from the ones suggested here, it should be indicated in the review document. The suggested values are as follows:
  - Notice given—This value should always be yes.
  - Sent to Internet—If this analysis point is yes, verify that it is mentioned in the privacy statement.
  - Sent to third party—If this analysis point is equal to yes, verify that the third party is an agent or the user can provide consent for the data transfer.
  - In use—If this analysis point is no, the value should not be collected.
  - User control—If this analysis point is no, indicate when a setting is planned to be implemented.
  - Central control—If this analysis point is no, indicate when control is planned to be implemented.
  - Access—If this analysis point is no, ensure that senior management is aware of it and have a good justification for it.
  - Security exist—If this analysis point is no, indicate why security is not important for this value.

6. Understand that these are merely suggestions from the author and that your company should decide what is acceptable during a review.

- **Usage analysis**—If there is a value that is not being used, it should be placed in the privacy review document for later discussion. Usage should include requirements from any group in the company. Any usage of collected data by any department in your company should be documented. Any requests made after the product ships should be reviewed and added to the privacy statement.
- **Security analysis**—All sensitive data that is collected should have some form of security. Exceptions should be added to the review document.
- **User control analysis**—If there are no privacy settings to manage the collected data for either the consumer or enterprise, it should be mentioned in the review document.
- **User access analysis**—The user should have a simple means to modify or delete data that is collected locally. Exceptions should be added to the review document.
- **Disclosure plan**—If there is no disclosure plan in place for the product, this should be mentioned in the review document.
- **Dependency analysis**—If there are forward or backward dependencies for this product that have not been resolved, this should be mentioned in the review document. Resolution means that the product teams on which your product is dependent or that depend on your product have been contacted to ensure that privacy obligations have been met for collected data. For example, if you have a component that collects data and passes it on to another component that sends it to the Internet, the team working on the other component has an obligation to mention this in the privacy statement.

Who Should be Involved?

Everyone who is working on the product should understand that privacy compliance is part of the job. When it comes to the privacy reviews, the key stakeholders for your organization should be involved in it. Members of the team may work separately preparing for the review, but they should all be present at review meetings. The following is a list of essential attendees:

- Key program managers, developers, and testers
- A representative from the documentation team
- The project leader for the product
- The privacy lead for each component team

Depending on how the meetings are organized, you will want only individuals who are involved in the component(s) being reviewed for the product. Senior management should be involved only when the review team is unable to come to a consensus about how to mitigate a privacy issue or when a decision may negatively affect the business. For example, the team may have decided to continue to send information from your client application to your Web site because it never was an issue in the past. Considering the recent privacy regulations, you will want to ensure that senior management wants to continue to assume this risk.

In small companies, one developer may be the entire development team. In this case, review any concerns you have regarding your privacy plan with senior management. Enlist the assistance of a consulting company such as Pricewaterhouse Coopers or Deloitte and Touche to assist in reviewing your privacy statements and assisting with other areas of concern.

Running the Meeting

The meeting should be run by the product's PL. Try to cover one component at a time, unless they are simple components that don't collect data. Work on the severity-one[7] issues first, and then move to the severity-two issues. The job is to agree on a mitigation plan for each issue and then remove the issue from the review document after it is mitigated. Severity-three issues should just be verified to make sure they were appropriately leveled.

Plan on the review meeting taking at least two hours, with subsequent meetings being held to go over decisions that were postponed.

Note

I've been in many review meetings for large and small components. The only ones that lasted less than two hours were the ones that didn't collect any data.

---

7. Severity levels are described later in this section.

Keep track of time, and if it looks like the time allotted for the meeting will run out, enough time should be provided before the end of the meeting to determine what should be covered in the next meeting. If the meeting members find themselves flailing and not making much progress, the meeting attendee list for the next meeting should be narrowed to only those essential for a component or even an area within a component.

Privacy Review Scope

Privacy reviews can take a great deal of time and resources. The PL should focus each component team on reviewing only those components that directly affect them. Large applications should be broken down into isolatable components. Here, *component* means a standalone deliverable for a product group. You may even want to split out areas of these components, especially if they are common components such as an encryption component.

After you have identified the granularity of the components that you are going to review, make sure you include all the pieces that make up the component. This will be similar to a threat analysis where you determine all the interfaces and connections between your component and the outside world. For example:

- Web sites
- Data stores
- Shared memory
- Configuration files
- Registry settings
- Communication links

Privacy Review Template

The privacy review template acts as a guide for describing an application's privacy exceptions and can include several components, which can themselves be divided into multiple areas. The privacy template should be used to ensure that every possible privacy risk has been reviewed and mitigated. All privacy content and settings should be accounted for. The PL should drive the completion of this document. Any action items that come out of the review of this document should be resolved before release of the product. You can find a sample privacy review template in Appendix B.

The privacy review template has several PowerPoint slides defined in it. These should be looked upon as an example that can be used to pattern a review template that PLs can create for their own company and products. Following is a description of each slide to help understand their purpose:

- **Title slide**—This slide should hold the name of the product and the owner for the file. For complex products, you may want to use a separate file for each component.
- **Definitions**—Here describe any acronyms or words that will help a reviewer understand your product or privacy issues better.
- **Overview**—On this slide, indicate any general positions or issues that the reviewer should be aware of. For example, there are no prominent controls available to manage data going to the Internet, so your product cannot be shipped to Germany until that issue is resolved.
- **Assumptions**—List any assumptions about data handling practices, products, market, or intended customers that will help the reviewer. For example, all data sent to the Internet is aggregate and cannot be traced back to the user, so no encryption is used.
- **Open issues**—List the issues that have not been resolved and the reasons for the lack of resolution.
- **Privacy-issue severities**—This slide should be used as a guide to reviewers to help them understand how severities were determined.
- **Instructions for component slides**—This slide provides instructions for creators of the file to understand how they should order and complete each slide.
- **Severity one**—This represents a severity-one level slide.
- **Severity two**—This represents a severity-two level slide.
- **Severity three**—This represents a severity-three level slide.
- **Follow-up**—This slide is used to indicate the decisions that were made during the meeting and the decisions that were postponed until further investigation is completed.

Severity One

Component: Area

- **Issue Description**
  - Describe the issue
- **User Value**
  - Indicate any benefit for each user class
- **Privacy Data Description**
  - Describe in general terms the content of the privacy data
- **When data is captured**
  - Describe when the data is acquired from the user
- **How data is used**
  - Describe why the data is being captured
- **Disclosure plan**
  - Describe how users are informed that their data is being captured
- **Default State**
  - Indicate if the data is captured or not captured by default. List any variations
- **User Control**
  - List any control the user has over the capture and access of the data
  - Indicate if there is control through group policy

Figure 10.11 Sample review template slide

Within the privacy review file, a slide should be created for each privacy issue, as shown in Figure 10.11. The component for the application and area within the application should be listed. To assist you with flushing out privacy issues, use the checklist in Appendix E. When listing each privacy issue, mark its severity as one, two, or three. Use the following categorization to help you in assigning the correct severity level to a privacy issue:

- **Severity one**—These issues must be resolved before shipping the product.
  - Inadequate disclosure (for example, no privacy statement is ever presented)
  - Inadequate control over how data is handled
  - Inadequate security on sensitive data
- **Severity two**—These issues should be resolved before shipping the product.
  - Data not encrypted when stored
  - Inadequate user control over privacy settings
  - Inadequate user access to data
  - No P3P implementation

- **Severity three**—These issues can be postponed until the next release.
  - No warning given to users before data is transmitted
  - No clear tracks feature
  - No retention plan in place for removing stale PII

Conclusion

If you or your company is building software solutions, take a serious look at building privacy awareness into them. This means focusing on privacy during development, when establishing defaults, and when planning deployments This means the following three things:

1. All members of your development team are focused on protecting a user's privacy as they are developing products.
2. Product features that may share a user's information are off by default.
3. In deploying a solution, users are provided with prominent disclosure of privacy features and risks.

Reviewing how your solutions collect, store, and share data is an important part of the development process. Also look at how data that is sent to your company by your solution is protected and accessed. This process should be documented as part of the privacy disclosure that you provide to users of your solution.

There are companies that are committed to complying with privacy regulation such as HIPAA. Using applications that send information to the Internet could violate a regulatory requirement and cause litigation against the company. There are also regional considerations. Applications that are acceptable to sell in the United States may be prohibited from sale in other countries because of the way that they handle data.

The most important things to do with regard to privacy when building applications are to provide prominent disclosure about the application's data usage practices and an easy mechanism for users to manage these practices.

Document your privacy-development process in a predictable manner for trend analysis and process improvement. You'll want to pass on your privacy process as well as what you have learned to other development teams in your company or even write a book about it.

11 Performing a Privacy Analysis

In the book *Writing Secure Code, Second Edition*, Michael Howard and David LeBlanc use dataflow diagrams to demonstrate the technique of completing a threat-modeling analysis. They even go on to say, "The overriding driver of threat modeling is that you cannot build secure systems until you evaluate the threats to the application with the goal of reducing the overall risk." A similar statement can be made about building safe systems from the viewpoint of protecting the user's privacy.

Dataflow diagrams (DFDs) are not a new concept. Tom Yourdon first introduced them in 1976, in his book *Piecewise Decomposition and Application Specification*.[1] The use of DFDs for threat modeling is described in Chapter 4 of the book *Writing Secure Code, Second Edition*. In the book, this process is called application decomposition (AD). DFDs are used to help simplify the security-analysis process.

Although another diagramming technique would work just fine, DFDs seem to lend themselves to analyzing areas of weakness in the handling of data. Feel free to choose or continue to use another diagramming method to track the flow of data in your software. The important point to make is that these diagrams can be used to perform a privacy analysis. This chapter describes how to perform a privacy analysis using DFDs.

This chapter describes some of the elements of a DFD and their usage. This will provide you with the basics you need for understanding DFDs and how they can be used in performing a privacy analysis. There are also some guidelines for documenting these diagrams.

1. http://www.yourdon.com/books/msa2e/CH09/CH09.html

These diagrams permit an easy means for graphically validating that all data being collected, stored, and shared is captured. Although they don't take the place of written documentation, they do offer a simpler means for depicting and validating all the data for a software component during a review. Bruce Schneier also discusses an approach for finding security vulnerabilities in his book, which uses an attack tree that could be applied to privacy analysis.[2]

Helpful Hints for Diagramming

A DFD consists of the following main elements:

- **Process**—A software module that transforms or manipulates data.
- **Data store**—A location for storage of data. This can be a registry, file, log, usage history, or most recently used list.
- **Entity**—This is a consumer or creator of data. This can be a person, Web site, company, or external process.
- **Dataflow**—An arrow that depicts the flow of data to or from a data store, entity, or process.

This section provides tips and techniques to make the basic DFD more readable.

Number Processes, Data Stores, and Dataflows

Using numbers on the various elements helps remove any ambiguities that may exist when there are multiple elements with the same or a similar name. These numbers can also be used in the place of titles for brevity and clarity when writing documentation. Elements should have unique numbers assigned to them. The exception occurs when multiple dataflows or data stores consist of the same data.

Use Underscores to Connect Words in a Title When Creating Documentation

To make the names of elements clear, use an underscore to connect each word in the title of a construct. For example, when describing process 1.0 in Figure 11.2, format the title as Process_user_request.

---

2. *Secrets and Lies*, by Bruce Schneier. (John Wiley & Sons, 2000). http://www.schneier.com/book-sandl.html

Use a Prefix on Names or Identifiers to Avoid Confusion

When using the names of different dataflow elements in your documentation, use prefixes for clarity. For processes, use the prefix P_. For data stores, use D_. For dataflows, use F_. For entities, use E_. For example, based on Figure 11.4, when P_Send_contact_data receives an update request via F_Send_contact_list_request, it retrieves data from D_Customer_data and sends it to E_Direct_marketer. Another method of documenting a DFD is to use the element number—for example, D_3.0 is used to store the contact information for customers.

This rule is not necessary to follow in the DFD itself because it is easy to distinguish between types of elements. It should also not apply to documentation, where the type of element being described is called out.

Adornments

Many of you will use some type of diagram to convey what data your components store, collect, or transfer. You may also want to depict specific attributes graphically. To make it easier to do this, the icons shown in Figure 11.1 can be used. You can find a file with these icons on the accompanying CD-ROM for your use. Here is a description of the icons:

- **Policy**—This icon represents a privacy statement or other type of disclosure. Placing it on a dataflow indicates that the transmission or collection of data over the dataflow is documented in the privacy statement. Placing the icon on a data store indicates that the storage of the data is documented in the privacy statement. When other icons are used in conjunction with this icon, it should mean that their use is also documented in the privacy statement.
- **Trash can**—This icon is used to indicate that there is a retention policy for the data that is stored in the data store to which this icon is attached. The retention policy indicates how long data will be stored in the data store before it is deleted. This policy should be described in the privacy statement.
- **Lock**—This icon indicates that the data stored in the data store to which it is attached has security associated with it to protect access to the data. This can be physical and or programmatic security. The type of security being used should be documented in the privacy statement.

- **Checkbox**—This icon is used to indicate that there is a privacy setting available to the user. If the checkbox is attached to a dataflow, it means that the collection or transfer of data over the dataflow can be controlled through a privacy setting. If the checkbox is attached to a data store, it means that the storage of data can be controlled through a privacy setting.
- **Letter G**—This icon indicates that group policy can be used to manage the collection, storage, or transmission of data. If the letter is attached to a dataflow, it means that the collection or transfer of data over the dataflow can be controlled using Group Policy. If the checkbox is attached to a data store, it means that the storage of data can be controlled using Group Policy.
- **Slashed eye**—This icon indicates that encryption is used to protect the data. If the icon is attached to a dataflow, it means that the transmitted data is encrypted. If the icon is attached to a data store, it means that the stored data is encrypted. All of the data may not be encrypted, so it is important to document exactly what is encrypted in the privacy statement.

Figure 11.2 provides an example of how these icons can be used to adorn a DFD.

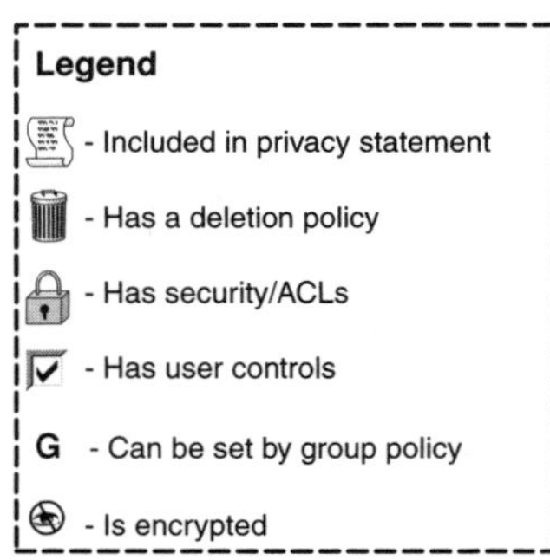

Figure 11.1 Adornments for use in a DFD

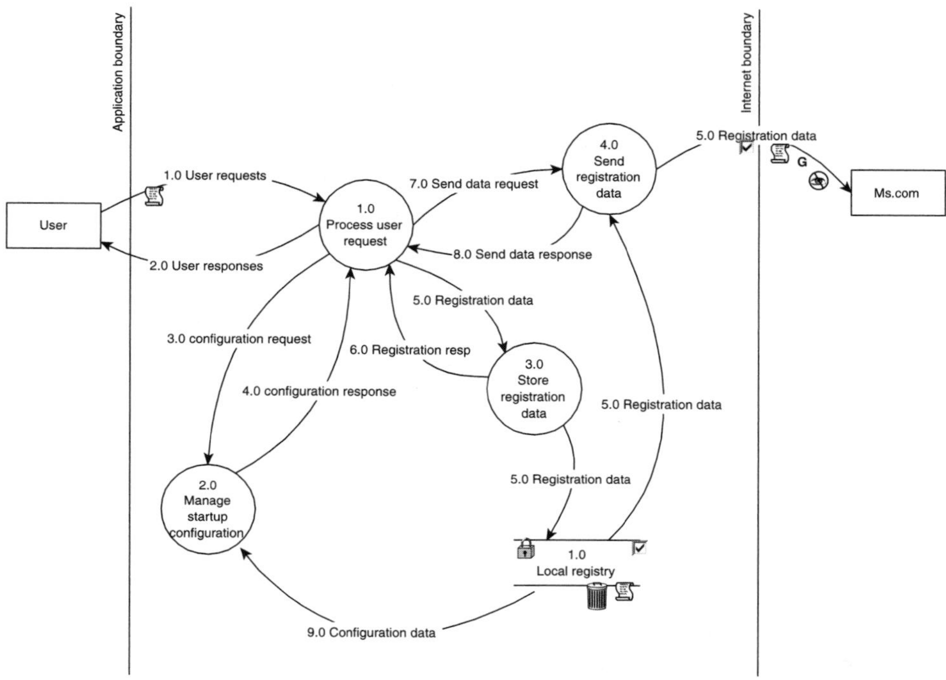

Figure 11.2 Example of using adornments in a DFD

Context-Level Application Decomposition

The context level of a DFD that is used in application decomposition shows the high-level architecture for a component. Figure 11.3 shows an example of a context-level AD diagram.

This diagram shows the interface between the component and external components or entities. The vertical lines represent boundaries between the user, the machine, and the outside world. These lines will help you determine which approach to use for protecting the data. For example, if the boundary represents data leaving the machine for the Internet, you will probably want encryption on any dataflows that cross it. Unfortunately, this level of decomposition is not granular enough to expose internal data structures and is thus not very useful for data analysis. One or two more levels of decomposition are usually required.

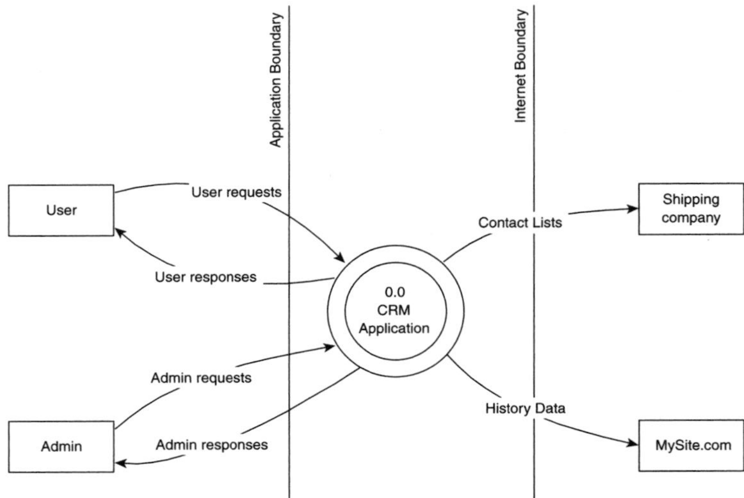

Figure 11.3 Context-level DFD

Level 0 Application Decomposition

In a level 0 AD diagram, you should be able see the underlying data structures for a component. As you can see in Figure 11.4, the CRM application interacts with the registry, system log file, audit log file, History file, and customer database. The numeric identifiers for these data stores can be used in the privacy specification as a tracking mechanism to ensure that each data store is accounted for and as a reference for those who want to see where a data store fits into the AD.

Other members of your team should review this diagram to ensure that each data store and dataflow is accounted for. Because this diagram will play a major role in the privacy analysis you will be performing, it should be as accurate as possible. If this level is not detailed enough, feel free to advance an additional level. However, be careful not to overcomplicate the diagram by having too many levels. The purpose of the diagram is to simplify the view of your data; so, stick with simplicity.

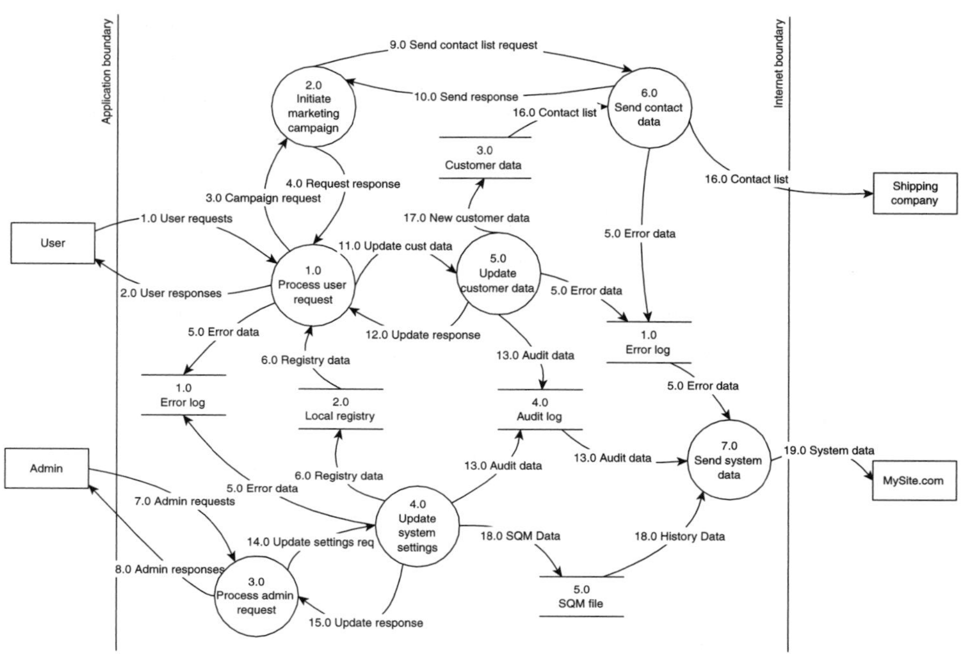

Figure 11.4 Level 0 DFD

Privacy Boundaries

To make it easier to perform and document a privacy analysis, privacy boundaries can be used to group parts of a DFD that exhibit the same types of privacy behavior and to indicate the area of control. A privacy boundary is characterized by a region drawn on a DFD that encapsulates selected processes and data stores. All data stores within the region must be accessed only by processes developed by the group performing the analysis. This removes concerns that they may be susceptible to privacy issues from another group. Dataflows that enter selected processes are included in the privacy boundary and do not have to be documented separately, because they are covered by the description of the data stores. This is to say that these dataflows do not carry any data that is not already covered in a data store description that is part of the privacy analysis.

In Figure 11.5, you can see that a region has been drawn that includes several processes and data stores. This depicts the sphere of control for the CRM application. The data stores Local_registry and Customer_data are not included in this region because they are accessed by processes outside of the control of the group that owns the CRM application. Dataflows 2.0, 3.0, 8.0, 9.0, 10.0, 16.0, and 19.0 should be described separately and indicated in the dependency section of the privacy specification. The description of a dataflow is similar to the description of a data store.

A dataflow that terminates at a data store does not require a unique description, because its data will be included in the description of the data store.

Entities, although they may be entirely controlled by a group, should always have a separate description. Entities differ from processes and data stores in that there may be agreements made between the component group and the entity that need to be described.

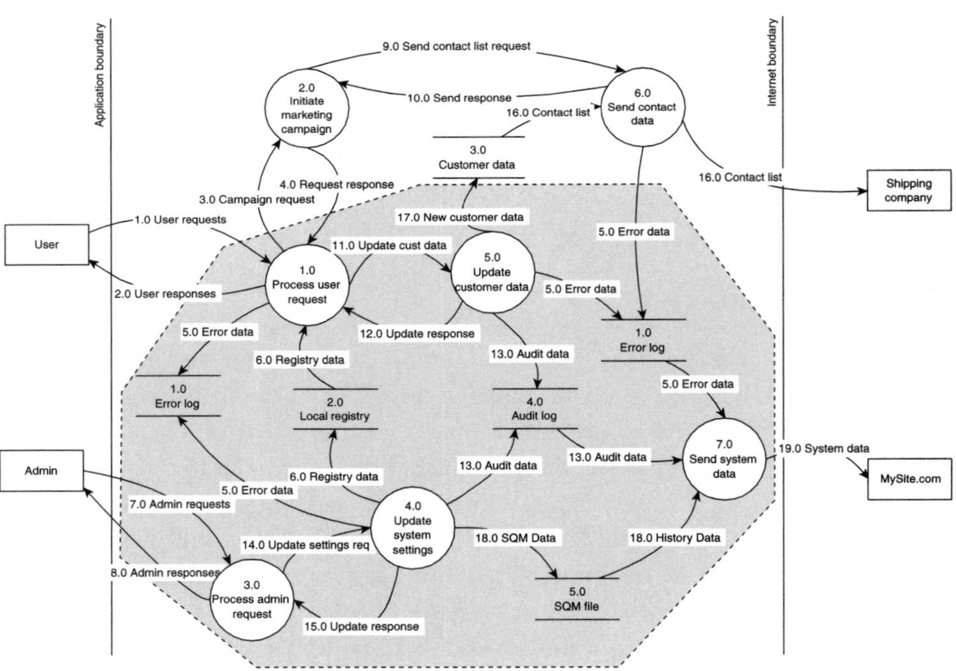

Figure 11.5 Privacy boundary example

Rolling Up an Application Decomposition

Many teams perform their threat-modeling analysis at different levels, some at the feature level and some at the subcomponent level. Eventually these analyses need to be rolled up into a single analysis diagram to better capture the privacy risks that present themselves across the entire component. The question is how to do this effectively. It is not a simple matter of combining the diagrams; often they will overlap or have inconsistencies because features or subcomponents may be designed without awareness of what the entire component looks like. It is the job of the privacy lead with assistance from the feature team to reconcile the individual subcomponent diagrams into a single component diagram.

When performing a privacy analysis at a lower level, use a separate privacy specification to capture the results of your privacy investigation. When combining diagrams, the privacy specifications will have to be combined. Reconciling multiple privacy specifications can be difficult work. However, it can also be difficult trying to create one privacy specification for multiple subcomponents and keep all of the descriptions and designations straight. The exception, of course, is if your subcomponent is already a part of the full-component diagram. At this point, you can perform your analysis using the full diagram and capture your findings in the privacy specification for the component.

If you use a separate privacy specification, migrate your privacy data, after your subcomponent is rolled up into the component diagram, from the subcomponent's privacy specification to the privacy specification for the component. Reference the component's privacy specification in your document and make future updates to the component's privacy specification.

An Application Decomposition Rollup Example

This section provides an example of a component that consists of four subcomponents. The purpose of the component is to collect registration and configuration information about a product from a user. The registration information is sent to the company Web server after the user installs the product.

Notice that in the subcomponent diagrams, in Figures 11.6 to 11.9, each element starts off with the label 1.0. If the number of subcomponents is known from the start or there is a system in place to assign numbers to subcomponents, you can use the assigned number rather than 1.0. However, it is difficult to know how many data stores or dataflows may be created for a subcomponent as the design evolves, and the administration of numbers can be tricky and time-consuming. You may find it easier to have subcomponents use a separate numbering system for simplicity.

Each subcomponent will have its own privacy specification that is filled in by the program manager (PM) who owns the subcomponent. After the rollup is done, this data should be moved to the component's privacy specification and future updates should be made there. This example, depicted by Figures 11.6 to 11.9, shows a separate diagram for each subcomponent. However, in the case where a PM owns multiple components, he or she is free to combine them into one diagram to simplify the analysis and documentation process.

The first subcomponent, shown in Figure 11.6, takes in requests from the user and passes them on to other subcomponents for processing. The user requests should be examined to ensure that all data being collected is described in the subcomponent's privacy specification and that the user is informed of its use and handling in a privacy statement. The teams that own the components consuming the data should be contacted to ensure that they are abiding by the company's privacy policy for the handling of data.

The second subcomponent, shown in Figure 11.7, obtains configuration data from the user and stores it in a local data store. The configuration information should be documented along with its attributes in the privacy specification. The security for the data store must be documented as well as who normally has access to its contents.

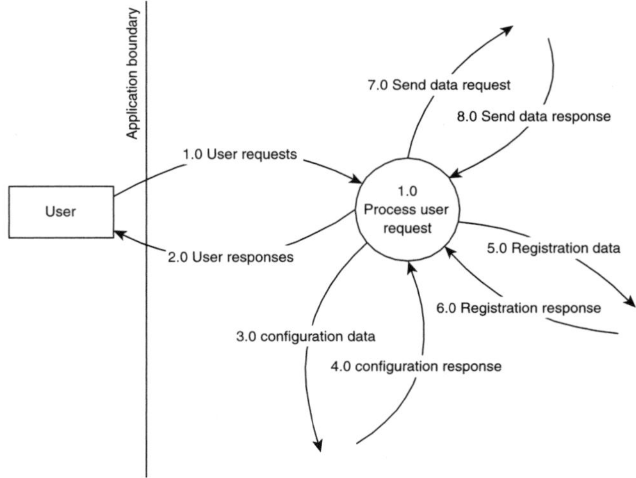

Figure 11.6 DFD for subcomponent one

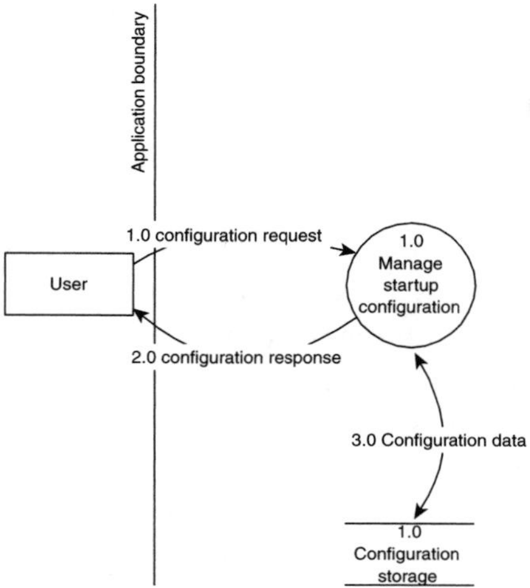

Figure 11.7 DFD for subcomponent two

The third subcomponent, shown in Figure 11.8, is responsible for collecting the component's registration information from the user. The registration information should be documented along with its attributes in the privacy specification. The security for the data store must be documented as well as who normally has access to its contents.

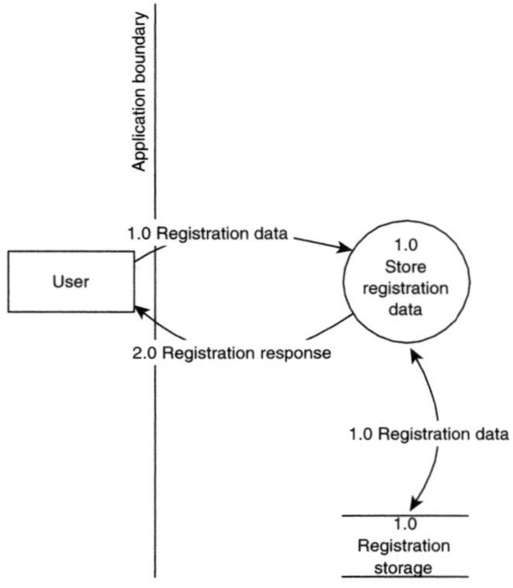

Figure 11.8 DFD for subcomponent three

The fourth subcomponent, shown in Figure 11.9, sends registration information from the registration data store to a company Web server. The link used to transfer the data should be examined to ensure that the appropriate security precautions are maintained to protect the data and validate that the data is being transferred to the correct site. If third parties access the registration data after it is stored at the company, there should be a separate agreement made with them to ensure that they will abide by the company's privacy policy with regard to the storage and handling of the data. All of this information must be placed in the privacy statement for the component so the user is aware of how his or her data is being used.

The diagram in Figure 11.10 combines the diagrams from the four subcomponents. This diagram should be created by the privacy lead (PL) in conjunction with a member of the feature team that is familiar with the overall component design. Notice that at this level it is possible to see how data flows across the entire system. The type of data store is known, and it can be seen that the registration and configuration data are stored in the same location. The numbering of the entities is completely different from that of the subcomponents. These numbers could be applied back to the diagrams of the subcomponents, but it is not necessary to do so because future updates to the subcomponents should be documented on the component diagram.

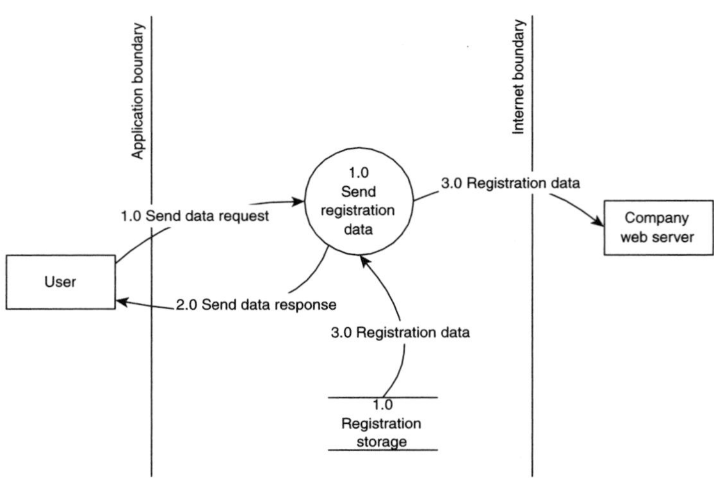

Figure 11.9 DFD for subcomponent four

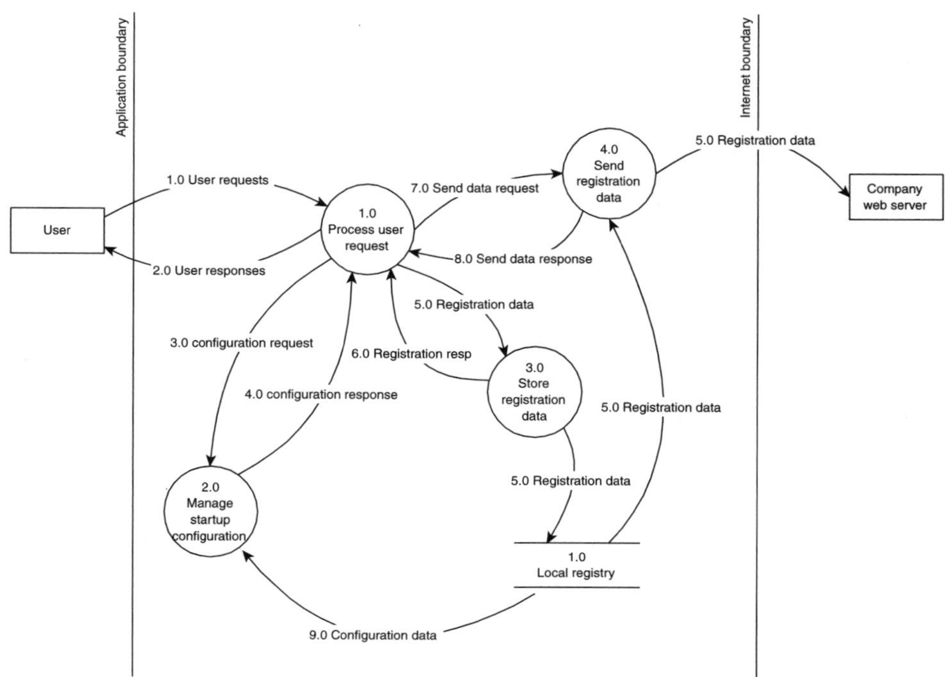

Figure 11.10 DFD for the combined subcomponents

The detail that may have been missing from the description in the subcomponents' privacy specifications can be filled in at this level. Be careful to move data from the subcomponents' privacy specifications to the component's privacy specification and update the subcomponent privacy specification to reference the one for the component. After the subcomponent has been rolled into the component's diagram, reflect future updates to the subcomponent using the component's diagram and privacy specification.

Complex Rollups

In cases where rolling up the subcomponents causes the creation of a diagram with so many entities that they are just too difficult to manage, feel free to cut the diagram into sections and examine one section at a time. You can also stick to the subcomponent diagrams if that is where you started. You should still be able to label each entity on the diagrams so that they have a unique number and name. Continue to place the description of each entity along with the diagrams in a single privacy specification document. Figure 11.11 shows a complex AD diagram that has been divided into four pieces for easier evaluation.

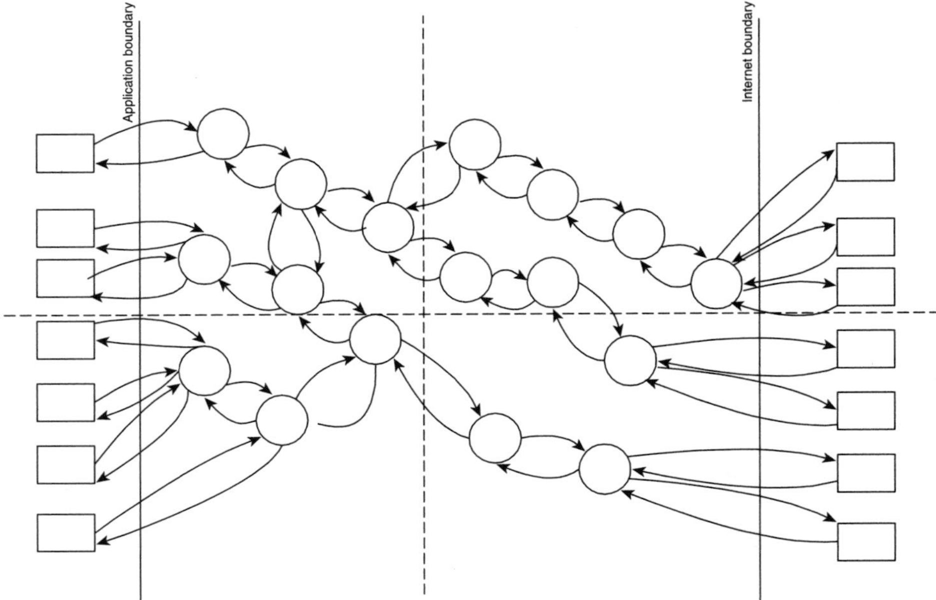

Figure 11.11 AD for complex rollups

Conclusion

Diagramming the data that your application collects, stores, and transmits is a good way to visually validate the data during a review. It can also form the basis for the input to a privacy specification by providing a visual reference for the documentation. Dataflow diagrams are a good method to use to diagram your data. This same methodology is used to perform threat-modeling analyses to mitigate security issues. This helps to streamline privacy and security analyses by using a method that works for both.

Each feature team should diagram the data used by its application and document its findings in a feature specification. This process should eventually be rolled up into a single diagram that represents the data used by a component, which should be viewed as a standalone deliverable.

Standard DFDs can be augmented using icons as visual queues to make it easier to understand how data is being treated by an application. The goal should be to make diagrams as informative as possible without *un*necessarily cluttering them.

12 A Sample Privacy-Aware Application

Previous chapters considered the importance of creating privacy-aware applications and building special features in to an application to improve its privacy awareness. This chapter looks at a sample application, called PSample, that has many of the privacy features that should be included in applications. Although the sample application may give the impression that it connects to the Internet, in reality it doesn't. Its features are provided merely for demonstration purposes. The source code was written using Visual C++ 7.0. Although it was written for the Windows platform, these concepts can be applied to programs written for any platform. This program could have just as easily been written in Java for the UNIX platform. The entire set of source code for this sample application can be found on the CD-ROM that accompanies this book.

This application provides minimum functionality. It was written mostly to demonstrate the following privacy-awareness features that should be part of an application:

- Privacy disclosure
- P3P integration
- Local privacy settings for use by end users
- Centralized privacy settings for use by administrators (using Group Policy)
- Encryption of stored data

Program Design

The PSample program uses a set of menus to interact with the user. When creating a Microsoft Visual Studio Microsoft Foundation Class (MFC) application, a default set of menus is provided. Some extra menus were added to provide access to the program's features. These menus provide access to dialogs that enable the user to interact with the program. In one instance, a browser window is opened to permit the display of the online privacy statement. The menus and dialogs are described later in this chapter.

Figure 12.1 shows the dataflow for the program. Annotations illustrate the attributes that apply to the data being transferred and stored by the program. The following sections describe the dataflow diagram.

F_1.0 User requests

This dataflow represents the requests that can be made by the user. These requests are passed on to a local process to handle or on to the PSample Web site for processing. The user can request the following:

- Display the privacy statement
- Create a privacy issue
- Perform an online search*

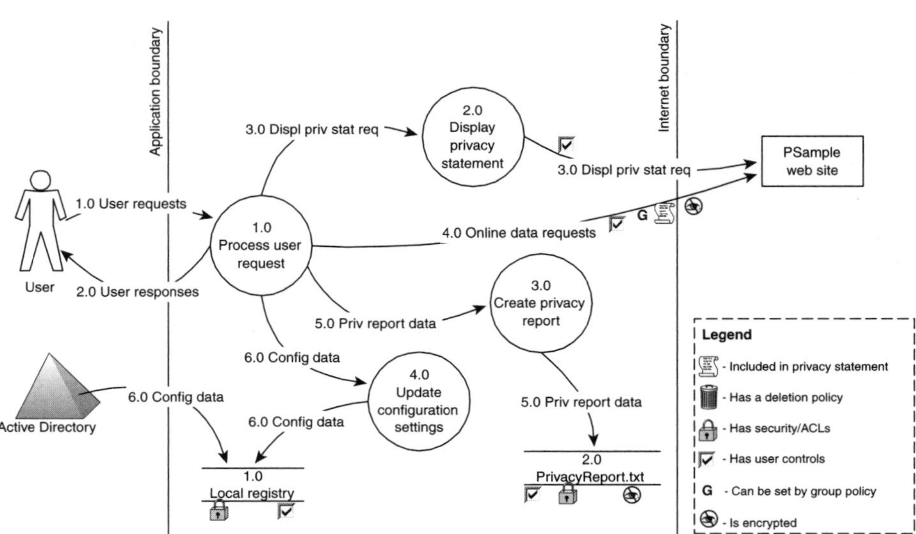

Figure 12.1 PSample program design

- Request online help*
- Perform an application update*
- Modify the configuration settings

* This functionality has not been implemented, but is mentioned for illustration purposes.

F_2.0 User responses

This dataflow represents a response to the user on the success or failure of each request.

F_3.0 Displ priv stat req

This dataflow represents a request to display the online privacy statement. No data is passed on this dataflow. If the computer is online, the request is passed to the local Web server for processing. Otherwise, a dialog displays requesting that the user go online to obtain access to the privacy statement.

F_ 4.0 Online data requests

This dataflow represents the three requests that could go to the PSample's Web site: online search, online help, and automatic update. The checkbox icon on the dataflow indicates that the user can control these requests. This control is provided by the Privacy dialog. The letter *G* on the dataflow indicates that these requests can be controlled by an administrator by Group Policy. The document icon on the dataflow indicates that these requests, along with the data that accompanies them, are described in the program's privacy statement. The eye icon on the dataflow indicates that the data sent during these requests is encrypted during transfer.

Note

There is no code in the PSample program to implement or even simulate this functionality.

F_ 5.0 Priv report data

This dataflow carries the information captured from the user and used to fill out the privacy report. The information that is captured in the dialog is copied to a local file named PrivacyReport.TXT.

F_6.0 Config data

This dataflow carries the configuration data from the user and from Group Policy that is used to manage the features that send data to the Internet. This information is copied to a hive for the program in the local registry.

D_ 1.0 Local registry

This data store represents a hive in the local registry. The checkbox icon on the data store indicates that the user can control this storage. This control is provided via the Privacy dialog. The lock icon on the data store indicates that an access control list (ACL)[1] is placed on the data store to prevent other users on the computer from accessing the registry settings. The data is stored in the registry based on the currently logged-on user. The ACL is not created by the program.

D_ 2.0 PrivacyReport.txt

This data store is a local text file named PrivacyReport.TXT and is used to hold the information that comes from the Privacy Report dialog. The checkbox icon on the data store indicates that the user can control this storage. This control is provided via the Privacy Report dialog. The eye icon on the data store indicates that the data stored in the file is encrypted during storage. The lock icon on the data store indicates that an ACL is placed on the data store to prevent other users on the computer from accessing the file. The ACL is not created by the program. The file is placed in the same directory as the application.

1. ACL stands for access control list. An ACL is used to indicate the users and groups who have access to a resource and the type of access that they have. For example, an ACL may indicate that the product development group has read access to marketing report files.

Installing the Application

The application can be installed on any Windows 2000 and above operating system with Internet Information Server running on it. The Group Policy file must be installed on a Windows 2000 or Windows 2003 operating system with Active Directory installed. The installation of the application consists of copying the file sample.exe to a directory on the computer.

Place the W3C and Privacy folders into a folder beneath the root of your Web server. If you are running the IIS Web Server, place the W3C and Privacy folders in the directory wwwroot.

Use the Group Policy Object Editor (GPOE) to load the file PSample.adm so that Group Policy can use it. If you have installed the Group Policy Management Console (GPMC), bring it up by running gpmc.msc on the Run menu or at the command line. Right-click a Group Policy object in the Group Policy Objects folder and select Edit to bring up the GPOE. If you have not installed the GPMC, bring up the MMC for Active Directory Users and Computer, right-click the Domain Controllers folder, and select Properties. Select the Group Policy tab and select Edit to access the GPOE.

After the GPOE is up, right-click the Administrative Templates folder beneath the User Configuration folder and select Add/Remove Templates. On the dialog that appears, click the Add button and go to the location where you copied the file PSample.adm and select it. Close the dialogs and the file should be loaded and ready to use. Open the Privacy Sample settings in the GPOE and modify the values to manage the privacy settings in the sample application. For your changes to take effect right away, you need to run **gpudate** from the command line. If this is too confusing, obtain an administrator's guide for Windows 2000 or Windows 2003 Server or ask an administrator for assistance.

Sample Files

The following files are part of the sample program. I am listing only the files created or modified by me. The remaining files are created by default by Visual Studio when creating a new MFC project. The files are listed by the folders where they are stored.

Privacy Folder

- **PrivacyStatement.html**—This file contains the privacy statement for the sample program.
- **PSample.adm**—This is the administrative template file for the sample program.

W3C Folder

- **P3P.XML**—This file contains the P3P reference file for the sample program.
- **Policy.XML**—This file contains the P3P policy file for the sample program.

PSample Folder

- **PrivacyDialog.cpp**—This file contains the code that manages the Privacy Settings dialog.
- **PrivacyDisclosure.cpp**—This file contains the code that manages the dialog for displaying the application's privacy statement.
- **PSampleView.cpp**—This file contains the code for managing the menu selections made by the user.
- **ReportDialog.cpp**—This file contains the code for managing the dialog that creates the sample privacy report and stores it in an encrypted file.

PSample/Release Folder

- **PrivacyReport.TXT**—This file contains the encrypted output from the Report dialog. A sample is provided with the code.
- **Psample.Exe**—The executable file for the sample program.

PSample/Res Folder

This folder contains the resource files for the sample application. These files hold the descriptions for the dialogs and other objects used by the application.

Privacy Disclosure

As mentioned in a previous chapter, the privacy disclosure is the most important piece of an application with regard to privacy. It informs users about the data being collected, stored, or transmitted by the application. Although the sample application does not collect any data from the user, it provides a disclosure about the simulated features. A description of the disclosure is provided below.

The Privacy Statement

The Help menu of the application contains a menu item beneath it labeled Online Privacy Statement. The word *online* is added to let the user know that this command will connect with the Internet. Selecting this command executes the OnHelpPrivacystatement() function, whose source code is in the file PSampleView.cpp. This function first determines whether there is an Internet connection. This is done to ensure that the user always has the most current privacy statement. The following code segment is used to determine whether an Internet connection exists:

```
bConnected = InternetCheckConnection("http://www.ietf.org/",
➥FLAG_ICC_FORCE_CONNECTION, 0);
```

If there is a connection to the Internet, the privacy statement displays in a browser. In actuality, the privacy statement is retrieved from the Web server on the local computer. The application's privacy statement displays from the URL http://localhost/privacy/PrivacyStatement.html. This is a simple privacy statement that describes the data collection practices and the privacy settings of the application. The following code is used to display the online privacy statement:

```
CreateProcess(NULL,
  "Explorer http://localhost/Privacy/PrivacyStatement.html",
   NULL, NULL, FALSE, 0, NULL, NULL, &si, &pi)
```

If there is no connection to the Internet, the application displays a simple dialog telling the user where to find the privacy statement for the application on the Internet.

P3P Integration

Like all good Web sites, this one includes P3P integration. The P3P integration is deployed by placing the two eXtensible Markup Language (XML) files in the W3C directory modifying the header on the Web server. The first file is the P3P reference file named p3p.xml, which is placed in the directory c:\inetpub\wwwroot\w3c. This file points to the P3P policy file. See Chapter 9 for a description of these elements. Here is a listing of the file:

```
<META xmlns="http://www.w3.org/2000/12/p3pv1">
 <POLICY-REFERENCES>
    <POLICY-REF about="Policy.xml">
       <INCLUDE>\*</INCLUDE>
       <COOKIE-INCLUDE name="*" value="*" domain="*" path="*"/>
    </POLICY-REF>
 </POLICY-REFERENCES>
</META>
```

The next file is the P3P policy file named Policy.xml, which is placed in the same directory as the P3P reference file. See Chapter 9 for a description of these elements. As the following listing of the file shows, the file contains two statement definitions to simulate the collection of two sets of data. The first statement represents the clickstream and HTTP protocol data that is collected. The second statement represents the demographic data that is collected. The discuri attribute points to the full privacy statement. The opturi attribute is supposed to point to the page that describes the opt-in or opt-out settings for the Web site. Because this program doesn't collect any data, the attribute just points to the same privacy statement page. The Netscape and Mozilla browsers are the only ones I have found that take advantage of the opturi attribute. To see how this works open a Netscape browser and select the Page Info option from the View menu. On the Page Info property page, select the Privacy tab and click the Options button at the bottom of the dialog.

```
<POLICY xmlns="http://www.w3.org/2000/12/p3pv1"
    discuri="../privacy/PrivacyStatement.html"
    opturi="../privacy/PrivacyStatement.html ">
 <ENTITY>
  <DATA-GROUP>
   <DATA ref="#business.name">Peeps and PJs Business Center</DATA>
   <DATA ref="#business.contact-info.postal.street">1201 Main
➥Street</DATA>
   <DATA ref="#business.contact-info.postal.city">Detroit</DATA>
```

```
    <DATA ref="#business.contact-info.postal.stateprov">MI</DATA>
    <DATA ref="#business.contact-
➥info.postal.postalcode">48213</DATA>
    <DATA ref="#business.contact-info.postal.country">U.S.A.</DATA>
    <DATA ref="#business.contact-
➥info.telecom.telephone.intcode">1</DATA>
    <DATA ref="#business.contact-
➥info.telecom.telephone.loccode">313</DATA>
    <DATA ref="#business.contact-
➥info.telecom.telephone.number">5551212</DATA>
   </DATA-GROUP>
 </ENTITY>
 <ACCESS><all/></ACCESS>
<STATEMENT>
  <PURPOSE><admin/><develop/></PURPOSE>
  <RECIPIENT><ours/></RECIPIENT>
  <RETENTION><stated-purpose/></RETENTION>
  <DATA-GROUP>
    <DATA ref="#dynamic.clickstream.server"/>
    <DATA ref="#dynamic.http.useragent"/>
  </DATA-GROUP>
</STATEMENT>
<STATEMENT>
  <PURPOSE><pseudo-analysis required="opt-in"/></PURPOSE>
  <RECIPIENT><other-recipient/></RECIPIENT>
  <RETENTION><indefinitely/></RETENTION>
  <DATA-GROUP>
      <DATA ref="#user.home-info.postal.postalcode">
        <CATEGORIES><demographic/></CATEGORIES>
      </DATA>
  </DATA-GROUP>
</STATEMENT>
</POLICY>
```

The compact policy that represents the abbreviated version of the P3P policy file is stored as a custom IIS header using the IIS Manager. Figure 12.2 shows how this is done. The first five tokens of the compact policy represent the first STATEMENT element in the P3P policy file. The remaining four tokens of the compact policy represent the second STATEMENT element in the P3P policy file.

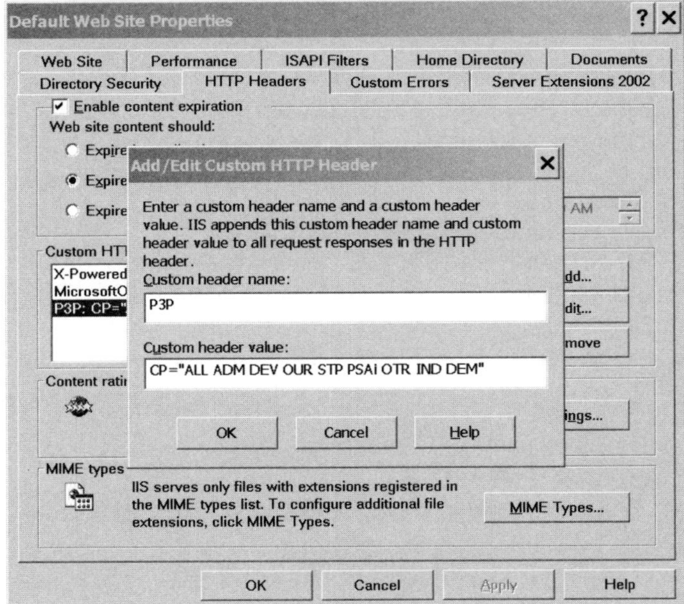

Figure 12.2 Adding the compact policy for the sample program

Privacy Settings

The application settings that could affect a user's privacy should be placed together in an easy-to-find dialog. If you have a Properties or Tools property page for your application, add a Privacy tab to it and place your settings there. The sample application has only one set of settings that are for privacy, so it is implemented as a single dialog, which can be displayed by selecting the Options item under the Tools menu. The Privacy dialog is shown in Figure 12.3. The values for the three fields on the dialog are stored in the Registry under the key HKCU/Software/Privacy/Sample with names that correspond to their captions in the Privacy dialog.

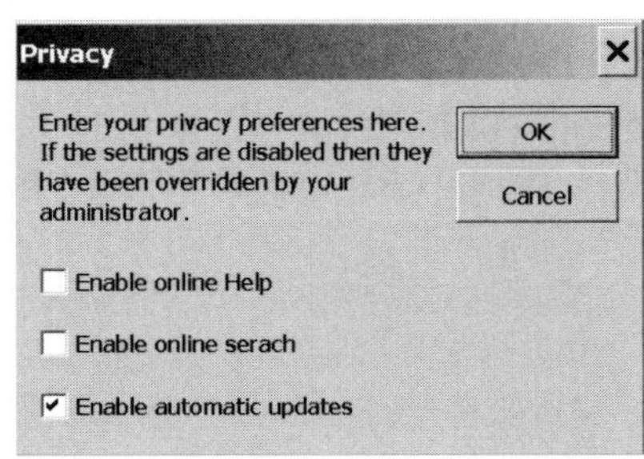

Figure 12.3 The Privacy dialog for the sample application

Tying Privacy Settings to Group Policy

Privacy settings for an application should be tied to Group Policy to enable administrators in a company to manage the settings. These settings should override any settings entered by the user. In that respect, user settings are considered preferences and Group Policy settings are considered policies. To implement this functionality, the Group Policy settings are stored in the Registry under the key HKCU/Software/Policies/Privacy/Sample. Storing the Group Policy settings in a separate location preserves the user's settings. When your application detects the existence of the Group Policy settings, they should be read in and the dialog should be disabled to prevent the user from modifying the values. In the sample program, this code can be found in the OnInitDialog() function, whose source code is in the file PrivacyDialog.cpp.

To create the Group Policy settings, the administrative template file PSample.adm is used. The file consists of some simple script and descriptive text to inform administrators how to use the settings. The text of the file is as follows:

```
CLASS USER

CATEGORY “Privacy Sample”
KEYNAME “Software\Policies\Privacy\Sample”

POLICY “Manage the privacy settings for the sample application.”

EXPLAIN “This setting is used to manage the privacy settings for
the sample application.

If the setting is enabled then the user’s preferences will be
overwritten by the values selected here. To use this setting
select the enable button and select the checkboxes based on
whether you would like the particular feature enabled or disabled.

If this setting is disabled, then each privacy setting will be
cleared and the user’s preferences will be overwritten.

Your selections will be reflected on the settings of the sample
application’s privacy dialog once the Group Policy settings have
been read or the user logs in.
```

```
If this setting is not configured then the user's preferences will
be used for the sample application.
 "
 PART "Enable online help." CHECKBOX
    VALUENAME "Enable Online Help"
    VALUEON NUMERIC 1
    VALUEOFF NUMERIC 0
    END PART

  PART "Enable search help." CHECKBOX
    VALUENAME "Enable Online Search"
    VALUEON NUMERIC 1
    VALUEOFF NUMERIC 0
    END PART

  PART "Enable automatic updates." CHECKBOX
    VALUENAME "Enable Automatic Update"
    VALUEON NUMERIC 1
    VALUEOFF NUMERIC 0
    END PART
END POLICY
END CATEGORY
```

The CLASS statement indicates that the settings are to be applied to the user. The CATEGORY statement is the folder name where the settings will be stored beneath the Administrative Template folder in the Group Policy Object Editor (GPOE). The KEYNAME statement indicates the Registry location to store the settings. The POLICY statement is the label for the setting object in the right pane of the GPOE. The EXPLAIN statement describes how the settings should be used. This is displayed on the Explain tab when editing the setting or on the left side of the setting object when the object is selected in the right pane of the GPOE. Figure 12.4 shows what the setting object will look like when it is stored in the GPOE.

The PART sections define the fields that will be placed on the GPOE dialog and the values that will be placed under the Registry key. Figure 12.5 shows the dialog that is created when the administrate template file is loaded using the GPOE.

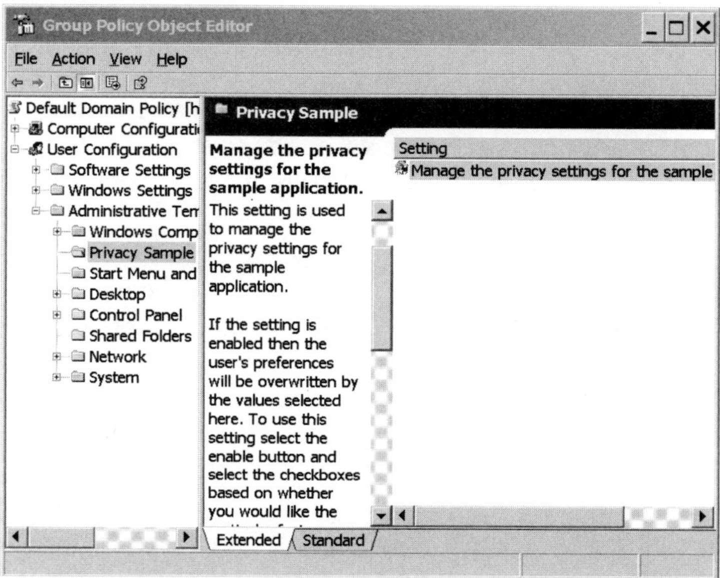

Figure 12.4 The sample application settings defined in the Group Policy Object Editor

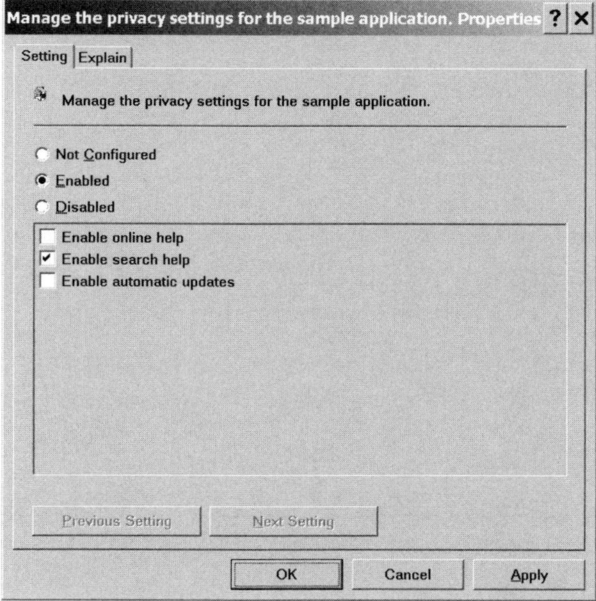

Figure 12.5 The GPOE Settings dialog for the sample application

Encrypting Local Data

When storing application data on the user's computer, consider the possibility that the user may be sharing the computer with others at home or at work. ACLs can be used to protect access to the data file, but an additional way to protect the file is to encrypt it. One easy way to do this is to use the Encrypted File System feature that comes with the Windows operating system. (Of course, other mechanisms can be used to encrypt files.) The sample application has a command under the Help menu labeled Privacy Report. Selecting this command brings up a dialog that a support person might use to log a privacy issue. The data in the dialog is used to capture the different aspects of the issue. The data that is entered is stored in a text file that can be read using Notepad. Figure 12.6 shows the dialog.

To protect its contents, the file is created using the CreateFile() function with the encryption flag set. This code is implemented in the OnInitDialog() function of the file ReportDialog.cpp. The call to the CreateFile() function appears as follows:

```
m_hFile = CreateFile("PrivacyReport.TXT",
                     GENERIC_READ | GENERIC_WRITE,
                     0, NULL, OPEN_ALWAYS,
                     FILE_ATTRIBUTE_ENCRYPTED, NULL);
```

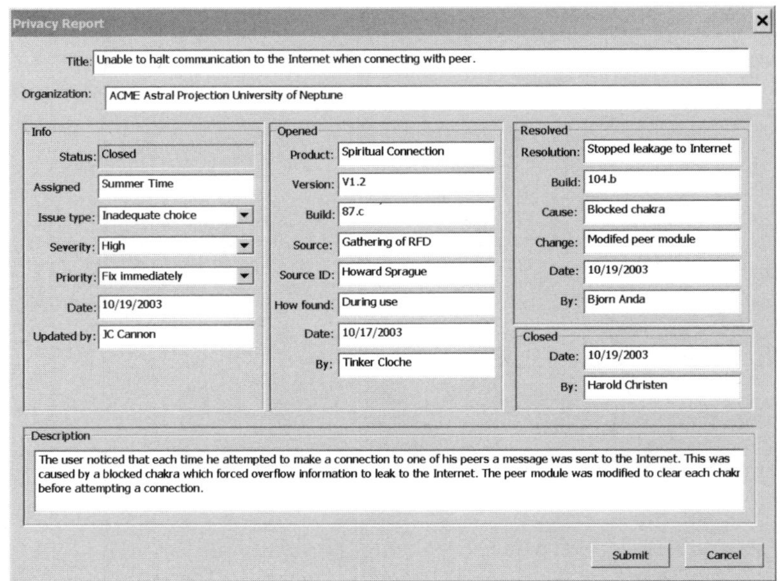

Figure 12.6 The Privacy Report dialog for the sample application

This encryption will prevent other people who log in under a different account from seeing the contents of the file. This encryption stays intact only while the file remains in the same file system. Copying the file to another computer or a file system that does not support NTFS will remove the encryption.

Conclusion

Use this program as an example of how to add privacy awareness to your code. Don't just copy and paste the code into your production code without getting it reviewed. I took several shortcuts for brevity, and you should be sure to add validation code and to check all code for security vulnerabilities.

The key messages to remember from this chapter are as follows:

- Provide a privacy disclosure for users.
- Create privacy settings to enable users to control their privacy.
- Integrate the privacy settings with Group Policy to enable administrators to manage their enterprise.
- Protect data that is stored locally on the user's computer.

13 Protecting Database Data

Databases are used extensively in our daily lives. Just about every time we make a purchase, withdraw money, log in to a computer, or use a badge to activate an electronic door, data about us is being captured in or retrieved from a database. Everyone who gets one of your checks or reads your credit card to fulfill a transaction has an opportunity to add your information to a database. Think about when you buy an item at a yard sale with a check. That person has the opportunity to capture all the personal information on your check in a database. Some nightclubs are even making electronic copies of their patrons' driver's license information when they enter the club. Although sophistication in the ways data collection happens has been advancing at a rapid pace, the mechanisms to protect this data haven't kept up. Not that the technology doesn't exist, but companies have been disinclined to take the steps to implement the technology because of costs. It is still far too easy for people to gain access to sensitive data. Often the people responsible for identity theft work for the companies that were given the responsibility of protecting the data.[1]

According to a September 2003 Federal Trade Commission survey on identity theft, thieves acquired on average about $4,800 in goods and services from each victim of identity theft. On average, victims incurred $500 in out-of-pocket expenses and 30 hours of time dealing with identity theft.[2] The total cost to companies was near $50 billion. Six percent of the nearly 10 million victims of identity theft indicated the theft was caused by

1. Bob Sullivan, "Help-Desk Worker Alleged Point Man in Theft of 30,000 Ids," MSNBC, November 25, 2003.

2. FTC, "FTC Releases Survey of Identity Theft in U.S. 27.3 Million Victims in Past 5 Years, Billions in Losses for Businesses and Consumers," September 2003.

an employee of the company that had access to their personal information. According to the FTC's yearly report for 2003, identity theft complaints are in first place, with more than 500,000 complaints (an increase of 50 percent over 2002).[3]

Identity theft prevention is not the only motivation for data protection. There are many companies with corporate secrets or intellectual property, such as the formula for Coke, that they want to protect. The government has an endless number of secret documents and pieces of data that it would like to protect. Think about the generals who have to manage troop movements during a war or encryption keys for secure communications. There is a great need to distribute sensitive information to those who need it while preventing others from accessing it.

For the most part, the various options available to protect data can be reduced to simply implementing straightforward data protection features and processes. Many identity-fraud incidents occur because of simple things, such as computers being accessible by too many people, computer accounts for employees not being disabled after they leave the company, and computer and database accounts that are allowed to have a blank or simple password.[4]

This chapter covers some basic and some more complicated approaches you can take to protect data in your company and some features that you might want to add to your database-based solution. To protect access to its data, an organization's system administrators should use all of the following approaches:

- Physical security
- Programmatic security
- Transaction auditing
- Data minimization

These approaches should be taken for any data being stored in a database. Don't make the assumption that the data you are collecting is not worth protecting or that your employees would never take the data. Most of these features are easy to implement and well worth the investment.

3. FTC Releases Top 10 Consumer Complaint Categories in 2003, http://www.ftc.gov/opa/2004/01/top10.htm.

4. Will Knight, "You Are the Weakest Link in Network Security," CNET News.com, May 2, 2001.

Some additional approaches are more technical than the previous ones and may require the assistance of an experienced database administrator (DBA) or programmer to implement. These are also features that you can find in applications on the market today. They are as follows:

- Data obfuscation
- Data quantization
- Query limitation
- Data suppression
- Data encryption
- Data perturbation

This chapter elaborates on each of the approaches listed here and takes a look at a couple of enterprise-level applications that provide a more sophisticated means for protecting data. This chapter provides only a high-level view of methods for restricting access to database data. Throughout this chapter you will find a list of books, documents, and Internet links that will provide access to more detailed information on the concepts being described here.

Physical Security

One of the most rudimentary ways to protect sensitive data is to provide physical security for the computers that hold the data. Physical security includes keeping computers in a locked, monitored area with limited, tracked access. Only people on the access list should be allowed access to the data center. Review access lists at least once a month to ensure that each person on the list still requires access. Monthly should be a good enough interval, because assignment changes typically do not occur more often than that. Anytime an employee leaves the company, all of the employee's computer accounts and building-access permissions should be revoked right away. In some cases, you may want to revoke access before the employee is made aware of the termination to avoid retribution from a disgruntled employee.

Everyone entering into the data center should either use a badge to access it or sign in on an access sheet. Review access logs daily to ensure that nothing looks out of the ordinary, such as accesses outside of normal business hours or excessive accesses by someone. You may even want to prohibit access to your data center altogether during hours when access isn't needed for business purposes. Be cautious about giving data center users free rein to access any computer either physically or through shared monitors. Also track the removal of equipment from the data center. Where possible, remove floppy drives, disable USB ports, and limit the use of writable CD and DVD drives to limit the means to walk off with data. Be sure to remove backup media from the premises and store it in a secure location.

Although the practices mentioned here may be pretty obvious, many companies overlook the departments that use data for development, testing, or customer service purposes. After spending an enormous amount of time and money perfecting the security practices of their data center, a company will enable a developer to copy sensitive data to his or her office computer for testing. Often these computers are sitting open in an unlocked office with access available to anyone during the course of the day. These computers often are shared locally or remotely with other colleagues. Where possible, use dummy or anonymized data for development and testing. Computers holding sensitive data should always have limited access and not allow transfer of data to local computers. Have customer service personnel use diskless workstations that access data from a remote server in a protected area.

Programmatic Security

Programmatic security simply requires that credentials be entered before permitting access to data. Most database applications permit the assignment of a user ID and password to users who need to access data. You are even permitted to indicate the role that a particular user may have, and which tables and even which rows in a table a user can access. These database features are only useful if there is a set of procedures in place to take advantage of them. Consider these points for controlling access to a database:

- The complexity of passwords
- The lifetime of passwords
- The roles that will be defined for your database
- The level of access permitted for each role
  - Indicate whether the role can read, update, or delete data
  - Indicate which tables or even rows a role can access
- The disposition of backup tapes

- The procedure for employees that transfer to different departments
- The procedure for employees that leave the company

Using Row-Level Security to Protect Data

Row-level security applies to restricting access to a row of data in a table. This restriction limits the range of data that a person can view. Rows of data can be grouped into categories based on the customer's name, demographic information, or other criteria. For example, you can categorize your customers by last name or region and assign employees a range of names based on category. This will limit the exposure of customers from one malicious employee. This method, although it limits the exposure of a range of customers, does not address the problem of limiting the exposure of sensitive information within a record when an employee only needs to access nonsensitive data. Column-level security can resolve this issue.

Using Column-Level Security to Protect Data

Column-level security applies to restricting access to specific fields within a database record. This type of restriction should be applied based on an employee's role. For example, shipping clerks should have access only to a customer's name and address information, whereas billing personnel should have access only to a customer's credit card information. Column security alone does not prevent employees from browsing through all the records, but it will when combined with row-level security.

This approach is, of course, limited to databases that support column-level security. See other techniques discussed later in this chapter, such as encryption or isolation, which can provide a more robust means for protecting column data.

Transaction Auditing

One of the ways to keep honest people honest is to track what they are doing. If people know there is a camera watching them, they are less likely to engage in any inappropriate behavior. When you are evaluating databases and applications, make sure that they have rich auditing and reporting capabilities. Set the granularity of audits at a level that is practical for detecting data access abuses. For example, only look at certain access types to important tables such as the salary table. Otherwise, you could get too many logs to process effectively.

When evaluating logs, look for bulk reads, multiple backups, or access during off-hours. Though it is very difficult, try to have audit logs stored in a manner that is inaccessible by the database or network administrator. There are tools, such as Align 3.0 from Synomos, that can monitor database access remotely. A discussion of this tool is provided later in this chapter.

Attempt to avoid collusion between employees by having your investigative and administrative personnel on different teams. Bring in a consultant to assist with internal investigations instead of using a staff member who could be involved in an incident. Use tools that can search logs for abnormalities rather than trying to do it by hand.[5]

Data Minimization

Chapter 2 discussed the importance of the constant pursuit of anonymity for privacy professionals. A corollary to that principle is the minimization principle. This principle refers to the minimization of identity and data collection. Companies should seek to collect the minimum amount of information that is needed to provide their services to their customers. Solution developers should collect the minimal amount of information with their products and services. If the user's identity is not needed, don't collect it. Use a pseudonym or an account ID instead.

Collecting too much data can cost a business in many ways. The extra resources, software, and personnel needed to manage excess data are only a portion of the problem. There is also the risk of exposure of the extra data you are collecting. Suppose that a famous celebrity comes to visit your facility regularly and you log the visits. This could be information that an employee might want to sell to a stalker or a newspaper.

Your mantra should be "Less is More." That is, the less data you have, the more you are protected against data handling issues. The remainder of this section will provide further information about how to minimize data collection.

The process of data minimization should continue throughout the entire lifecycle of data until all the data is eventually purged from the system. After the data has been collected, an administrator can use a number of techniques to ensure data minimization. This section examines some of those techniques.

5. Lumigent Technologies makes a product that can do this, http://www.lumigent.com.

Data Reduction

At the point where data is collected, determine whether all the data collected needs to be kept. For example, look at the log settings for your Web server to determine whether all the data being stored in the log needs to be collected. In IIS, the data logged can be controlled via the Advanced tab of the Logging Properties dialog of each Web site's Properties dialog.

When departments in your organization need to gain access to the data in a database, don't give them access to the entire database or to a Web site that may provide access to the data. Only give them access to the minimal amount of data that they need to fulfill their business needs. They should not need to see every entry in the database nor every item in a record. Disable access to the data when it is no longer needed.

Data Retention Policy

One of the biggest problems for data, whether it be electronic or on paper, is how long to keep it. Most of us have problems clearing our garages where the clutter is visible. Think about how much less clutter there would be if we could assign an expiration date to junk and it would automatically disappear if it wasn't used before the expiration data. Data should be treated this way. Many free e-mail services work that way; after a fixed number of days of inactivity, the e-mail account is disabled.

All data that you collect should have an expiration date associated with it. Never plan to keep data forever. Each department in your organization that collects data should understand their business and regulatory needs for persisting the data and define a retention policy based on that understanding. When the expiration date has passed, all the data should be deleted. Include your retention policy in your privacy statement when it affects customers and in your employee manual when it affects employees.

When backing up data to tape or another medium, try to store permanent data separately from data you want to eventually erase or destroy when it has passed its expiration date. When you can't separate out the data, make it difficult to retrieve the data. For example, don't permit the retrieval of records that are older than their expiration date. Although it is impractical to go back to archives and attempt to remove unneeded data, likewise it should not be easy for an employee to pull up old data that the owner may expect to have been deleted.

Note

All data that is placed on backup tapes or other medium should be encrypted to mitigate any exposure of the data due to theft or loss.

Data Classification and Isolation

The sensitivity of data can warrant different storage techniques. Place the data you collect in categories and apply your privacy policies to the data based on its category. Personally identifiable information (PII) is a category that applies to information that can be used to identify or contact an individual. Strict requirements are placed on the treatment of this type of data. For example, most countries prohibit the sharing of PII with third parties without the express consent of the owner. PII includes data such as a person's name, address, and phone number.

The association of PII with other data also makes the latter PII, requiring that it be protected in the same manner. For example, having a database table with records that reflect a person's medical condition and no identifying data is not PII and can be stored in a less-secure manner than if you associated the owner's name with the data. Read the section later in this chapter on data isolation and other means to separate attribute data from PII.

Exposing certain forms of sensitive information can leave a person susceptible to financial ruin or cause undue legal complications. Information such as credit card numbers, national identity numbers, or other data that can enable identity theft falls into this category. Even when this information is separated from its identifiable information, it can still be used in a malicious fashion. This type of information should always be encrypted when stored in a database.

When working on your data protection strategy, first categorize the data, separate the data by category, and then protect it based on its sensitivity level. Of course, the safest thing would be to encrypt everything. Unfortunately, this can cause additional overhead when retrieving data and make all but the simplest of queries difficult to perform. So the most practical approach is to be selective about the encryption that you use. This is covered further in the section on encryption.

Table 13.1 provides an example of how data could be categorized, along with how to treat the data based on its category and the condition that should be placed on the data use.

TABLE 13.1 DATA CATEGORIZATION TABLE

Category	Protection	Condition of Use
PII	Restricted access	Consent from owner
Sensitive	Encryption	Consent from owner
Medical	Access based on role	Isolated from PII
Financial	Access based on role	Isolated from PII

When storing data, try to separate identifiable information (PII) from the attribute and transaction information that often is part of a record. That is, don't include the medical or financial information for an employee or customer in the same database record that identifies the person. When there is an ID that is used to connect the data in two tables, use a one-way hash of the ID as an index into the table holding the additional information. In this manner, you are able to permit people access to the table with the identity information for contact purposes, other people access to the medical information for reporting, and a third set of people access to both tables to perform operations that require both tables. Separating the tables in this way provides two levels of protection: the security protection that restricts access to the table, and the hashed key that prevents direct correlation of the data in the two tables.

If you have multiple types of data that need to be isolated, use a different hash key to create the index for each additional table. This prevents a person who has the hash key for one table from accessing data in another table. Using this isolation fits into the minimization rule because you are minimizing the data to which users have access.

Translucent Databases

The American Heritage Dictionary 1983 defines translucent as, "Transmitting light but diffusing it sufficiently to cause images to become blurred." For example, walking through a thick fog provides a limited view of surrounding objects. A translucent database[6] provides controlled access to its data. Sensitive data is protected while innocuous information is made available to those who want to access it.

In Peter Wayner's book *Translucent Databases*, he states, "The most secure database is one that immediately forgets everything stored into it … Translucent Databases are a compromise between complete transparency and complete opacity."

Many of the techniques described later in this chapter show how to reveal parts of the data in a database while leaving the remainder of the data hidden. The goal here is to not leave all the data in your database exposed to a rogue who hacks his way into your database or even to the administrator who has legitimate access to the database.

Data translucency will take you a step closer toward fully protected data. When building translucency into your database, look for ways to increase the level of security while maintaining the database's utility. For example, using extremely long passwords or slow-performing encryption can decrease productivity to the point that the safeguards are impractical.

Data Obfuscation

Obfuscation is a means for concealing data by hiding it. The difference between obfuscation and encryption is that obfuscation typically employs a simple and insecure mechanism that does not produce a performance burden on the database. Although this may not be a hindrance for a sophisticated hacker with plenty of time to browse through a small database, it can be enough of a barrier for a database with dozens of tables to convince a malicious person to find an easier target. Obfuscation should not be used in the place of a more secure mechanism where possible.[7]

6. The term translucent databases comes from Peter Wayner's book with the same name. Peter Wayner, *Translucent Databases*, Flyzone Press, 2002.

7. Sybase offers a database obfuscation feature for their UltraLite database. http://manuals.sybase.com/onlinebooks/group-sas/awg0800e/dbwnen8/@Generic__BookTextView/3561

For databases, simple obfuscation can be performed by mangling the table and column names to make it difficult to discern their purpose. For example, Table 13.2 shows a standard table used to store credit card information. As you can see, based on the name of the table and of the columns in the table, it is easy for anyone who has brief access to the database to find where the credit card information is stored.

TABLE 13.2 STANDARD CREDIT CARD TABLE

Credit Card Table

Name	**Card Number**	**Exp Date**
John Doe	1234-5678-1122	12/2003
Jane Doe	1234-5678-2233	12/2003
John Q. Public	1234-6789-3344	11/2004

In Table 13.3, less-obvious names were chosen for the table and column titles. You can see how this makes it more difficult to find the useful data in a database. One of the downsides to this method is that it makes it difficult to perform ad-hoc queries. However, it is better to control what users can have access to programmatically rather than letting them run their own queries against the database. As long as all access to the data is controlled by an application, there will be less of a threat from users browsing through the database.

TABLE 13.3 OBFUSCATED CREDIT CARD TABLE

Table *XX*

Col XX1	**Col XX2**	**Col XX3**
John Doe	1234-5678-1122	12/2003
Jane Doe	1234-5678-2233	12/2003
John Q. Public	1234-6789-3344	11/2004

In Table 13.4, an additional step was taken to also obfuscate the credit card number by removing all but the last four digits. In this manner a customer service person could still verify a credit card transaction with a customer without exposing the entire credit card number.

For sensitive data where the entire value needs to be stored in a table, obfuscation by itself is not a practical approach. A stronger method such as encryption or data perturbation, which are discussed later, should be used.

TABLE 13.4 FURTHER OBFUSCATED CREDIT CARD TABLE

Table *XX*

Col XX1	Col XX2	Col XX3
John Doe	1122	12/2003
Jane Doe	2233	12/2003
John Q. Public	3344	11/2004

Data Quantization

Quantization of data is the practice of categorizing data or making it less precise so that the original value is not known. This method is typically used in statistical databases where the exact values of data are not needed. For example, take a billing service that charges customers based on the city from which they are requesting the service. Because the specification of the city is all that is needed, it should not be necessary to provide the street address.

Suppose that you want to be able to permit the benefits department at your company to assign insurance benefits based on an employee's age and salary. Most of these benefits are based on where an employee's age and salary fall within a certain range. For that reason, there is no need to give the benefits department the exact values of an employee's age or salary. Table 13.5 is an example of a standard employee table with the exact age and salary specified.

Before giving the data to the benefits department, it is copied to another table and modified. Table 13.6 shows the same entries with the age and salary mapped to an age and salary category such that the actual values are not known. Of course, a table with quantized data is only useful for performing certain functions. Although using ranges in this manner hides the real data, it may be more practical to use numeric values.

TABLE 13.5 STANDARD EMPLOYEE TABLE

Employee Table

Name	Age	Salary
John Doe	34	$58,000
Jane Doe	28	$83,460
John Q. Public	56	$66,500

TABLE 13.6 QUANTIZED EMPLOYEE TABLE USING CATEGORIES

Employee Table

Name	Age	Salary
John Doe	Level2	Bracket2
Jane Doe	Level1	Bracket3
John Q. Public	Level4	Bracket2

Table 13.7 has the same entries as the original table with the age and salary mapped to a fixed value in an age or salary range. By using this type of quantization, the employee can still assign the appropriate benefits to the employee, but the range is large enough to make it difficult to discern the original value. The amount of precision required for the queries will determine the amount of exposure for the data. Once again, a table with quantized data is only useful for functions such as statistical analysis.

TABLE 13.7 QUANTIZED EMPLOYEE TABLE USING FIXED VALUES

Employee Table

Name	Age	Salary
John Doe	39	$60,000
Jane Doe	29	$80,000
John Q. Public	59	$60,000

Other types of quantization include rounding, where you might round a value to the nearest hundred or a distance to the nearest mile. Precision reduction is the act of making a series of values less precise. For example, you might indicate the county that a person is from instead of the city, or only store four digits from the user's social security number or credit card number.

Query Limitation

Query limitation places restrictions on the types of queries that can be run by a user. When choosing restrictions, you will want to maximize security while minimizing loss in utility.[8] What this means is that a set of restrictions should be used that will minimize the risk of exposure of sensitive data while still permitting the queries against a set of data to be useful. Determining the right restrictions to make can be difficult. Your decision should be based on the total number of records you have stored, the uniqueness of the data, and the number of sensitive columns. These techniques make the assumption that the tables under which the queries are being performed do not contain any user identifiable information from the database, such as the name, employee number, or account ID.

Data Re-identification

When designing your query-limitation algorithms, be wary of the possibility of re-identification[9]. It is possible that a query returns enough information to permit a savvy or even a novice user to determine the original identity of the user based on the returned data. For example, say that your class at college wants to perform a study of grade levels based on the demographic information of the class. If the student's age were included, it would probably be easy to determine what grade belonged to the only person over 60 in the class.

---

8. Rathindra Sarathy and Krishnamurty Muralidhar, "The Security of Confidential Numerical Data in Databases," Information Systems Research Vol. 13, No. 4, December 2002.

9. The United States General Accounting Office created the report titled "Record Linkage and Privacy," which discussed the problems several local and foreign government agencies have had with the re-identification of individuals based on the data that was returned from databases.

Re-identification becomes unusually tricky when multiple databases are used and the results can be linked together. Consider the previous example, where the age is not included in the original study. However, a second study was performed that included the town in which someone grew up and the year that they graduated from high school in order to determine the average number of years that students waited before entering college. If the original study also included hometown, it would be quite easy to correlate the two sets of results to determine the grade of the oldest or youngest person in the class.

The best way to mitigate this risk is to limit the number of databases that are accessible at a time and the data returned for each query. Remember the minimization rule. Another approach is to use perturbation, which is discussed later in this chapter.

Result-Set Limitation

One mechanism of query restriction is limiting the minimum number of records that can be returned in a query. Suppose you are working with a medical database table with ten columns that catalog terminal diseases based on four categories: a patient's age, gender, ethnicity, and Zip code. Although a query for male Libyans over the age of 40 with a Zip code in Detroit might return a lot of records, running the same query for a small city in Iowa may only return one record and thus permit the identification of the individual. Setting the minimum returned records to 100 would prevent that type of easy identification.

Of course, a minimum limitation must be combined with a maximum limitation. Otherwise all of the values could be returned and sorted, making it easy to browse the data and find whatever you need.

Column-Count Limitation

Limiting the number of columns that can be used in a query is one way to limit exposure to sensitive data. For the same medical database table, suppose you limit the columns that could be used in a query to three out of the four categorical columns. The same limitation would be placed on the result set, so that only the categorical columns used in the query can be included in the result set. This helps to reduce the risk of exposure. If the result set is permitted to include every column, the person performing the query could still sort the data, making it simpler to expose someone's identity.

Query-Type Limitation

Most statistical research is only interested in aggregate information. For example, what is the total number of people with scurvy, or what is the average age of females with rickets? The value of individual records does not offer any significant benefit to a researcher. Therefore, limiting queries of a statistical database to those that include aggregate functions such as COUNT, AVG, and PERCENT maintains the utility of the database while minimizing disclosure.

However, this limitation stills has risks when the result set is sufficiently small. Say, for example, you looked for the count of males who were over 40 and from Bosnia with an artificial heart in a small city in Idaho. It would probably be easy to deduce the identity of the person. Therefore, look at using a result-set limitation along with the query-type limitation.

Suppression

Suppression merely refers to either removing any sensitive data from the database or preventing a user from accessing any sensitive data. When removing sensitive data, be sure to not only remove identifying data such as names and IDs, but to remove data that might permit the deduction of someone's identity due to the uniqueness of a record. One test you might want to perform is to ensure that for every combination of each categorical attribute, a required minimum number of records are returned.

Encryption

In general terms, encryption is a way to transform readable information into an unreadable form. One of the earliest forms of encryption involved adding a constant number to each value in a string, such as 4. This is also known as Caesar's cipher, after Julius Caesar, who used it to send messages to his armies in the field.[10] For example, using a shift value of 4, the string ABC would become EFG. If you are new to cryptography, the book *Applied Cryptography* would be a great book to add to your collection.[11]

---

10. The Caesar's cipher, http://www.trincoll.edu/depts/cpsc/cryptography/caesar.html. A tool to create or decrypt Caesar's ciphers can be found at http://codebreaker.dids.com/caesar.htm.

11. *Applied Cryptography: Protocols, Algorithms, and Source Code in C, Second Edition*, by Bruce Schneier, John Wiley & Sons, 1996. Information about the author can be found at http://www.schneier.com/.

Encryption is a good way to protect data in a database from people who have access to the database for administrative purposes, but should not necessarily be viewing customer data. Encryption is also a good way to make it more difficult for hackers to benefit from accessing tables with sensitive data. Encryption can also be used to protect data that has been backed up to tape or exported to local files. However, there are issues with using encryption that you should investigate before deploying encryption, including the following:

- What data should be encrypted?
- Which encryption algorithm should be used?
- Which length of encryption key should be used?

These are not easy questions to answer. It really depends on what is important to your business or the application you are developing.

Determining What to Encrypt

There is an inordinate amount of data stored in some databases. Much of the data could be considered sensitive. Encrypting everything in a database is often not practical. At best, it would be arduous. Executing queries, creating reports, and maintaining transaction performance on encrypted data is difficult to the point that it is cost-prohibitive. But there are times when encrypting all of the data is appropriate and practical, as when backing up data or transmitting sensitive data across a communications link.

Encrypt data that you think is sensitive, such as credit card numbers. If you need to use a column for sorting or searching, create a separate column that stores a subset of the numbers, such as the last four of the credit card number. When there is a great deal of data that is considered sensitive, such as a patient's medical history, use the data isolation technique mentioned earlier to protect the data.

Selecting the Right Encryption Algorithm

There are basically three types of encryption algorithms: symmetric, asymmetric, and hashing. The algorithm you use will usually be based on your performance needs, desired level of security, and whether you need to decrypt the data. Following is a brief description of the three types of encryption:

- **Symmetric encryption**—This type of encryption involves using the same key for encryption and decryption of data. Use this type of encryption when you are concerned about performance. The downside to using this method is that you have to be concerned about the safe transportation of the key to the parties that need access to it. DES, IDEA, and Blowfish are three types of symmetric encryption algorithms.
- **Asymmetric encryption**—This type of encryption uses two keys: one public key that is shared with individuals who need to decrypt your messages, and a secret key that is never shared and is used to encrypt messages. To keep every holder of a public key from decrypting your messages to a specific individual, each message is encrypted using the recipient's public key so that the recipient is the only one who can decrypt the message. Although asymmetric encryption is very secure, its downside is that the encryption process takes longer than symmetric encryption. Examples of asymmetric algorithms include RSA, PGP, and DSS.
- **Hashing**—This encryption method is used to perform encryption on values that you never want to decrypt. (Hashing makes it computationally infeasible to determine the original value from the hashed value.) Hashing is a great way to store sensitive data as a key when it does not need to be returned in a query. For example, you may want to store the index to a patient's medical information in a separate table from the patient table using a hashing algorithm. The unencrypted index is stored in the patient's record. To find a patient's medical data, you would hash his or her index and do a lookup in the table that stores medical information. This prevents users with access to the medical condition database from browsing the patient database to find out who has specific medical conditions. The only downside to hashing is that you can never decrypt a value, which may be okay. Examples of hashing algorithms include MAC, MD5, and SHA. The section of code that follows shows how to use the CryptoAPI, which can be accessed using Microsoft Visual Studio, to hash a social security number:

```
int _tmain(int argc, _TCHAR* argv[])
{
 HCRYPTHASH hHash;
```

```
HCRYPTPROV hCryptProv;

// Get the handle to the Digital Signature Standard
// provider. Use the CRYPT_NEWKEYSET value as the last
// parameter to create the key container
if (CryptAcquireContext(&hCryptProv, "PSample",
                        MS_DEF_DSS_PROV, PROV_DSS, 0))
{
   if (CryptCreateHash(hCryptProv, CALG_SHA, 0, 0, &hHash))
   {
     // Use a dummy social security number as the data
     const BYTE *pHashData = (const BYTE *)"123-45-5678";

     BOOL   bResult;
     DWORD  dwBufferSize, dwValue;
     BYTE*  pBuffer;

     CryptHashData(hHash, pHashData, 11, 0);
     dwBufferSize = sizeof(DWORD);

     // Get the size of the hashed data
     CryptGetHashParam(hHash, HP_HASHSIZE,
                       (BYTE*)&dwValue,
                       &dwBufferSize, 0);
     dwBufferSize = dwValue;

     // Create a buffer to hold the hash value.
     pBuffer = (BYTE *)new char [dwBufferSize];

     // Get hash value.
     CryptGetHashParam(hHash, HP_HASHVAL,
                       pBuffer, &dwBufferSize,0);

     // Store the value in a database or other data store
     // or use it to retrieve a record.

     CryptDestroyHash(hHash); // Release hash object.
   }
   else
   {
     DisplayLastError("Error during CryptCreateHash()");
   }
   CryptReleaseContext(hCryptProv, 0);
}
else
```

```
    {
        DisplayLastError("Error during CryptAcquireContext()");
    }
    return 0;
}
```

Note

A user with access to the hashed values and the hashing algorithm could generate a lookup table to determine the social security number that matches the hashed value. For the SHA-1 algorithm used in this code, it would take ~19GB of storage to create the lookup table. Adding a salt, or extra value, to the input value can avoid this type of attack as long as the salt can be hidden from the attacker.

Determining the Encryption Key Length to Use

In general, use the longest key possible based on the type of encryption you are using. The problem with doing this in some cases is performance problems, depending on how the encryption is used in the application. You can always use shorter keys to improve performance, but that could increase the risk of someone decrypting the data. You should use the recommendations of the algorithm provider on the minimum key length to use. For example, the RSA company suggests that you use at least a 1024-bit key when using their RSA algorithm.

Data Perturbation

Data perturbation, as the expression implies, is the act of perturbing or disturbing data. This technique is typically used in statistical databases, where it is important to obtain accurate analysis while protecting sensitive data. A census or medical database is an example of a database with lots of statistical information that could be used for good or evil. There are many ways to perform perturbation on data. However, you will want to be careful that the perturbation does not affect the results of any data mining that you would like to perform. The effect that perturbation has on a set of data is typically called bias. The four main types of bias that can occur with perturbation are classified as types A, B, C, and D.[12] Each is discussed here. When designing your database, determine what level of bias will be acceptable to you.

Type A Bias

Type A bias occurs when the data perturbation increases the variance of the data. This can cause the standard deviation to change. This may permit queries that return the average or median value to remain unchanged, whereas a query that looks for the average salary for the top 10 percent of citizens, for example, returns a different value.

Type B Bias

Type B bias occurs when the data perturbation causes the relationship between confidential values within a table to change. This type of bias can be caused when swapping confidential values in rows independently of each other.

Type C Bias

Type C bias occurs when the data perturbation causes the relationship between confidential and nonconfidential values within a table to change. This type of bias can be caused when confidential values are moved around independent of the nonconfidential values.

Type D Bias

Type D bias occurs when the data perturbation causes the distribution of the data in the database table to change. This type of perturbation will cause aggregate functions to return biased results.

Perturbation Techniques

This section looks at some samples of perturbation. Table 13.8 is an original table with some demographic information from Armenian respondents. From the table, you can see that the average age of each individual is 40.25, and the average salary is $65,000. Looking at the data in the original table,

---

12. *Protecting Data Through "Perturbation" Techniques: The Impact on Knowledge Discovery in Databases*, by Rick L. Wilson and Peter A. Rosen, Idea Group Publishing, 2003.

an intruder may be able to identify an individual based on the information or use it for his or her own marketing purposes. The sample table only has four entries, whereas in reality a census table, for instance, would have thousands of entries. So keep that in mind when looking at these examples.

TABLE 13.8 ORIGINAL CENSUS TABLE

Census Table

Ethnicity	Zip Code	Age	Salary
Armenian	49444	34	$50,000
Armenian	49444	28	$80,000
Armenian	98009	56	$60,000
Armenian	98009	43	$70,000

In Table 13.9, the ages have been swapped within the same Zip code. By doing this, we still maintain the same average age and average salary based on ethnicity and location. However, the salary per age has changed, which may or may not be important to the statistics you are analyzing. The important thing to look at is that the data can be used for some kinds of statistics, whereas the information may not be useful to an intruder looking to steal data

TABLE 13.9 CENSUS TABLE AFTER SWAPPING

Census Table

Ethnicity	Zip Code	Age	Salary
Armenian	49444	28	$50,000
Armenian	49444	34	$80,000
Armenian	98009	43	$60,000
Armenian	98009	56	$70,000

In Table 13.10, noise has been added to the data to make the data unusable for an intruder. Adding noise to a database can consist merely of changing the values of each record in a predictable manner or adding dummy records to make the database less of a target for an intruder. This example shows both kinds of noise addition. First, an additional entry has been added for each entry in the table. In addition, the age and salary of the original entry has been modified to mask the original values. The age and salary of the new entries were adjusted so that the average age for all of the records is still 40.25 and the average salary is still $65,000. However, the average age for a subset of the data has changed. You will find that for large databases, the margin of error may be acceptable.

TABLE 13.10 CENSUS TABLE AFTER ADDING NOISE

Census Table

Ethnicity	**Zip Code**	**Age**	**Salary**
Armenian	49444	36	$60,000
Armenian	49444	32	$40,000
Armenian	49444	30	$90,000
Armenian	49444	26	$70,000
Armenian	98009	58	$70,000
Armenian	98009	54	$50,000
Armenian	98009	43	$80,000
Armenian	98009	43	$60,000

Advanced Perturbation Techniques

There are essentially three advanced perturbation techniques that use additive data perturbation: SADP, CADP, and GADP.[13]

Simple additive data perturbation (SADP) adds noise to multiple confidential values independent of each other. This method causes type A, B, and C bias, because the variance and relationships change. There is no type D bias because the distribution of the data does not change.

Correlated-noise additive data perturbation (CADP) adds noise to each of the confidential values in a correlated fashion. Although this avoids type B and D bias, types A and C bias still persist, because the variance is still affected, and the relationship between confidential and nonconfidential values changes.

---

13. Rathindra Sarathy, Rahul Parsa, and Krishnamurty Muralidhar, "A General Additive Data Perturbation Method for Database Security," Management Science Vol. 45, No. 10, October 1999.

The general method for additive data perturbation (GADP) bases perturbation on confidential and nonconfidential values. This permits the relationship between confidential and nonconfidential values to be maintained, thus avoiding type C bias. When GADP is used with databases that can be described by a multivariate normal distribution, the results will not suffer from any type of bias as long as the appropriate covariance matrices are used. I know that is a mouthful.

If you decide to implement any of the ADP methods, you will want to get a statistician or someone knowledgeable in the field of perturbation to assist you.

The major drawback to each of these advanced perturbation methods is that they require the data to be changed. This makes people feel uncomfortable, even though you may be able to prove that the results are the same. The answer to this problem is data shuffling.[14] Data shuffling starts by performing GADP calculation on all the original data X to form a set of perturbed data Y. Replace the rank ordered values of Y_i with X_i and you are done. This provides the benefits of GADP perturbation while preserving the original values.

Hippocratic Databases

Hippocratic databases[15] go beyond securing data and protecting privacy and attempt to attain the elusive goal of policy compliance. New legislation such as the Health Information Portability and Accountability Act (HIPAA), Gramm-Leach Bliley Act (GLBA), Patriot Act, and the Sarbanes Oxley Act have placed increased pressure on companies to not only limit access to data, but to ensure that all accesses follow the practices prescribed by the various pieces of privacy legislation. Implementing a Hippocratic database can effectuate compliance with privacy legislation as well as privacy guidelines such as Safe Harbor.

A Hippocratic database has the following characteristics:

- **Purpose specification**—The purpose for the collection of all personal data must be defined and associated with the collected data.

---

14. Rathindra Sarathy, Rahul Parsa, and Krishnamurty Muralidhar, "Data Access, Data Utility, and Disclosure are *Not* Always Mutually Exclusive," NSF Workshop on Confidentiality, May 12–13, 2003.

15. Rakesh Agrawal, Jerry Kiernan, Ramakrishnan Srikant, and Yirong Xu, "Hippocratic Databases," Proceedings of the 28th VLDB Conference, Hong Kong, China, 2002.

- **Consent**—All personal data collected must be accompanied by the consent of the data subject.
- **Limited collection**—All personal data that is collected must have a policy defined that permits the collection of the data element for a specified purpose.
- **Limited use**—Queries will only be permitted to retrieve personal data when they are accompanied by a purpose that is consistent with the defined purposes for the data.
- **Limited disclosure**—Personal data can only be retrieved from the database with the consent of the data subject.
- **Limited retention**—Personal data can only be retained for the length of time specified in the retention policy for the data.
- **Accuracy**—Personal data stored in the database shall be accurate, complete, and current.
- **Safety**—Personal data must be protected from internal and external threats by an appropriate amount of security consistent with the sensitivity of the data.
- **Openness**—Each data subject should have the ability to access all information about him or herself that is stored in the database.
- **Compliance**—Each data subject and auditing entity should be able to verify compliance with the aforementioned principles.

IBM and Synomos offer enterprise privacy systems that provide the capability of a Hippocratic database. They are briefly discussed in the following sections.

Synomos Align

Synomos, Inc. makes a privacy solution called Align 3.0 Data Governance Manager[16] that enables companies to define, implement, and manage corporate privacy policies and practices within the enterprise IT environment. Align permits the expression of corporate policy in a machine-readable fashion. Align is built on the client/server model, where the client and server components were designed to run on separate machines. The heart of the solution is the Policy Model component, which interacts heavily with the client and server components. Align provides a sophisticated means for ensuring that role-based access to data follows corporate policy.

16. http://www.synomos.com/

IBM Tivoli Privacy Manager[17]

IBM's Tivoli Privacy Manager (TPM) permits companies to ensure compliance of their corporate data access policies in a programmatic fashion. TPM uses P3P as a means to define the policies that are used by a company to protect its data. IBM includes a service in its solution that controls access to a data store based on defined access rules. Each application that wants to access the database must have the appropriate authentication, role, and purpose for accessing the data. Sometimes there are additional requirements such as user consent, which must be met to access the data.

Tivoli Privacy Manager is considered the premier enterprise privacy solution. TPM, along with IBM's other work in the field of privacy, helped IBM obtain the Privacy Company of the Year 2003 award from The Privacy Manager.[18]

Conclusion

The database is where most privacy breaches occur. Several steps can be taken to limit the risk of exposure of sensitive data, including removing the sensitive data before it is stored in a database or limiting access to it after it is stored in the database. This is part of the minimization principle that should be applied to data throughout its lifecycle. That is, minimize the data that you collect, minimize access to the data, and minimize the amount of time that you keep the data.

The types of protection you can use to protect data in a database include the following:

- Physical security
- Programmatic security
- Transaction auditing
- Data minimization
- Data obfuscation
- Data quantization
- Query limitation

17. http://www-3.ibm.com/software/tivoli/products/privacy-mgr-e-bus/

18. http://theprivacymanager.com/pressreleases/company031210.htm

- Data suppression
- Data encryption
- Data perturbation

Recent privacy legislation makes it imperative that you take action to minimize the risk of exposing sensitive data. There are simple techniques for implementing data privacy as well as advanced ones such as translucent or Hippocratic databases. There are also enterprise privacy solutions such as the ones developed by Synomos and IBM that can simplify the creation and implementation of corporate policies.

14 Managing Access to Data: A Coding Example

Many companies are faced with issues of data governance. Data within an enterprise can be collected from consumers, partners, and other enterprises of all types. Companies are under pressure to not only comply with privacy legislation, but to prove that they are in compliance. Providing physical security is important, but not enough. Adding programmatic security provides additional security, but does not go far enough. Restricting access to data based on a user's role in a way that is inclusive of multiple applications and platforms would be even better. And how about automatic encryption of data based on the category of the data? This is the type of integrated solution that software companies should be building more of.

This chapter presents a simplified version of such an application. This is a Web-based application used to manage patient data and resumés in a doctor's office. This application has two versions. In the first version, the information for the staff of the fictitious doctor's office, along with their role information, is stored in SQL Server database tables. The design of this version is shown in Figure 14.1.

In the second version of this program, the staff of the doctor's office consists of users who have been defined in Active Directory. Their role information is stored in an Authorization Store using Authorization Manager, which comes with Windows Server 2003. All other information is stored in SQL Server. In this manner, authentication and role definition is integrated with the same identity the user is assigned in the operating system. During the provisioning of an employee, the HR admin can assign an employee to a role that can be used in a consistent fashion across applications instead of having to modify each application for a user's role. The fact that the role definition is stored in an eXtensible Markup Language (XML) file means that the definitions are portable. Figure 14.2 shows how the components communicate with each other.

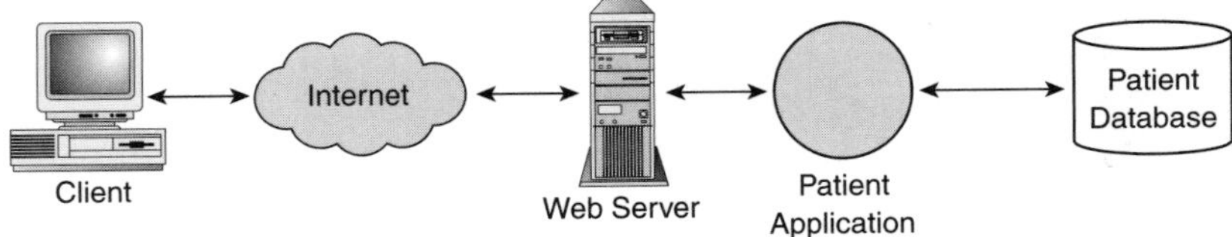

Figure 14.1 Pure database version of patient program

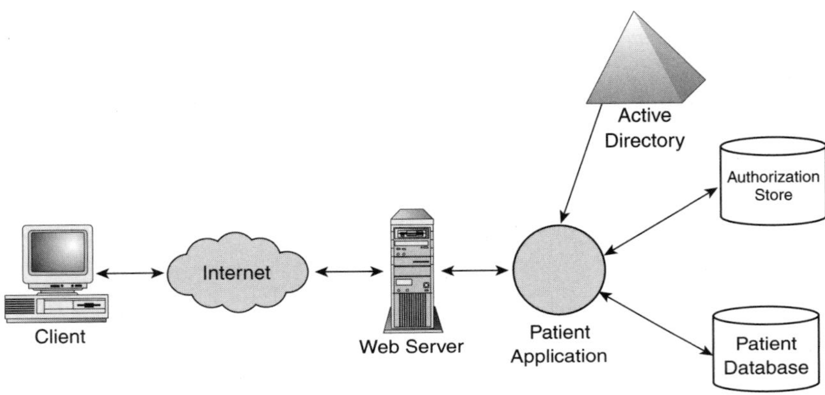

Figure 14.2 Authorization Manager version of patient program

Program Overview

In this fictitious doctor's office, there is a separate network and database administrator. There is also a developer who creates the encryption and decryption code as a COM object. The developer creates the code on a separate machine using dummy data for testing. The users of the application can only access the patient data using the application. They are provided with login IDs to access their client machines, but no SQL Server access. The ASP pages in the program contain the SQL Server ID and password and point to a system DSN. The login ID is limited to performing reads and insertions on only two tables.

Categorizing the Columns of a Table

Each column in the Patient table, shown in Figure 14.13, is assigned a data category. The four categories supported in this sample are Contact, Financial, Medical, and Sensitive. For example, the category Sensitive is used to indicate a column that should be encrypted before being stored in the database or decrypted before being removed from the database. The extended property of each column is used to store the data category.

A mapping table is used to map the roles used in the application to the categories of data that are stored in the Patients table. When an application user retrieves patient records from the database, his or her role is first determined. Data will be retrieved from the database based on the user's role and the category of the data. For example, an accountant will be able to retrieve only financial data. In this program, anyone will be able to enter data for a patient record. Realistically, even patients would be able to enter their own data. Hopefully doctors' offices will evolve to the point where we will never have to fill out a paper form or worry about forms being left out in the open for any passerby to pick one up and examine it.

Categorizing the Rows of a Table

A second approach to data categorization is also implemented in this application. This application enables employment candidates to submit their resumé for a position at the doctor's office. These candidates are able to enter various types of information about themselves in a separate data block. Each data block can be assigned a category to restrict who can view the information. Because each block could have a different category, it would not be practical to store them in the same column with a static category. Each data block is stored as a separate row in the Resumé table and indexed by the candidate's ID. A column is also provided for indicating the data category for each row. When a request is made to view a resumé, each of the candidate's records whose category maps to the role of the current user is retrieved. The administrator is permitted to see all data.

Encrypting Data

If you view the data for the Patients table, you will notice that the social security number column is encrypted. The Crypto Application Programming Interface Component Object Model (CAPICOM) library is used to perform the encryption and decryption of data. You can download the CAPICOM library for free from http://www.microsoft.com/downloads/release.asp?ReleaseID=44155.

Program Files

The following files are part of the sample program. I am only listing the files that were created or modified by me. The remaining files are created by default by Visual Studio when creating a new MFC project. The files are listed by the folders where they are stored.

DrOffice Folder

- **DrOffice.XML**—This file contains the XML file that can be loaded using Authorization Manager. Before running the application, users must be assigned to the roles defined in the file. This file must be placed in the DrOffice folder under the root of the C drive. If the file is placed somewhere else, update the roles.asp file to reflect the new location.

Privacy Folder

This folder contains the Web files that make up all of the code for this application. It can be placed anywhere under the root folder of your Web server. It should contain the following files:

- **AddPatient.asp**—This file takes the data entered on the NewPatient.htm page and places it in the Patients table in the database.
- **Candidates.asp**—This file displays the list of candidate names that have placed a resumé into the Candidate table in the database.
- **default.htm**—This is the home page for the application. It contains the links to the application's other pages.
- **DisplayData.asp**—This file is used to display patient data or resumés that have been added to the database.
- **DisplayPatients.asp**—This file displays the patient information from the Patients table in the database based on the current user's role.
- **DisplayResume.asp**—This file displays the selected resumé from the Resumé table, only returning data blocks whose category matches the current user's role.
- **Header.inc**—This file is included by the pages that display data based on the user's role. It places a header on the top of the page with the user's ID and role.
- **login.asp**—This file looks at the user ID that was selected on the Login.htm page and retrieves the user's role and associated data category from the database.

- **Login.htm**—This file enables the user to select a user ID to be used when retrieving data from the database. This file is called as a result of the user selecting Manual Login on the home page.
- **NewPatient.htm**—This file is used to enter the patient information for a new patient record.
- **Password.inc**—This file contains the VB script to read the database password from the registry. The password is stored in the registry to limit exposure of the password to people that might have access to the ASP files. The file is included by the ASP files that need to access the database.
- **Privacy.reg**—This is a Registry file that is used to initialize the Registry with the database password and the encryption secret. This value must be loaded before the program is run. Double-click the file to load its contents into the Registry.
- **Resume.asp**—This file is used to collect data for a new resumé. It contains multiple data blocks that can be placed into a specific category. This page calls SubmitResume.asp to place the resumé into the Resumé table in the database.
- **roles.asp**—This file retrieves the role for the currently logged-on user from the Authorization Manager store. The data category is retrieved from the DataMap table based on the user's role. This file is called as a result of the user selecting Integrated Login on the home page.
- **SubmitResume.asp**—This file takes the data entered on the Resume.asp page and places it in the Resumé table in the database.
- **Tables.asp**—This file is used to display the data tables in the database for the application.

SQL Folder

This folder contains the database files for this application. They are used to create and initialize the tables in the database.

- **Candidate.txt**—This file contains a sample entry for the Candidate table.
- **DataCategory.txt**—This file contains sample entries for the Data Category table.
- **DataMap.txt**—This file contains sample entries for the DataMap table.
- **Patients.txt**—This file contains sample entries for the Patients table.
- **Resume.txt**—This file contains a sample entry for the Resumé table.

- **Scripts.sql**—This file contains the scripts for creating the database, each of the tables, the login ID, and the column initialization needed for this application. It must be the first one run from this folder.
- **Staff.txt**—This file contains sample entries for the Staff table.

Setting Up the Application

To run this application, you need to be running Windows Server 2003. Active Directory, IIS, and SQL Server 2000 must also be installed. The application can be run from a single machine or using a client machine attached to the server over the network.

Setting Up the Web Files

The Privacy folder contains the Web pages for the application. Place this folder beneath the wwwroot folder. Using IIS manager, select the properties for the Privacy folder. Under the Directory Security tab, click the Edit button to bring up the Authentication Methods dialog and clear the Enable anonymous access checkbox. Click OK and exit IIS manager. See Figure 14.3 for an example of the dialog with the checkbox cleared. This enables the user to be identified when a Web page is accessed. Double-click the file Privacy.reg to place the database password and the encryption secret into the Registry.

Setting Up the Database

The files needed to set up the database are located in the SQL folder. Start by running the SQL Query Analyzer application. Open the file scripts.sql and run it. This will create the DrOffice database, the Candidate, Data Category, DataMap, Patients, Resumé, and Staff tables. The DBTest user account will also be created and assigned the appropriate access. You will still need to set the password for the DBTest account to DB$#4aX in the Logins section of the SQL Server Enterprise Manger. You can verify that the extended properties were set by right-clicking one of the table columns in the left pane of SQL Query Analyzer and selecting Extended properties. Figure 14.4 shows that the data category for the PatientID column is set to Medical.

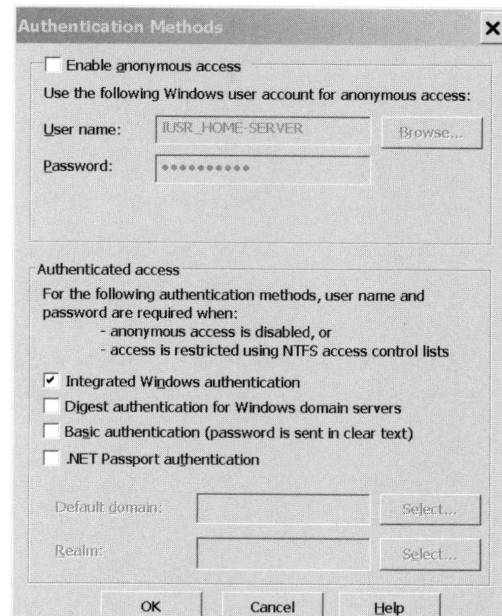

Figure 14.3 The IIS Authentication and Access Control dialog

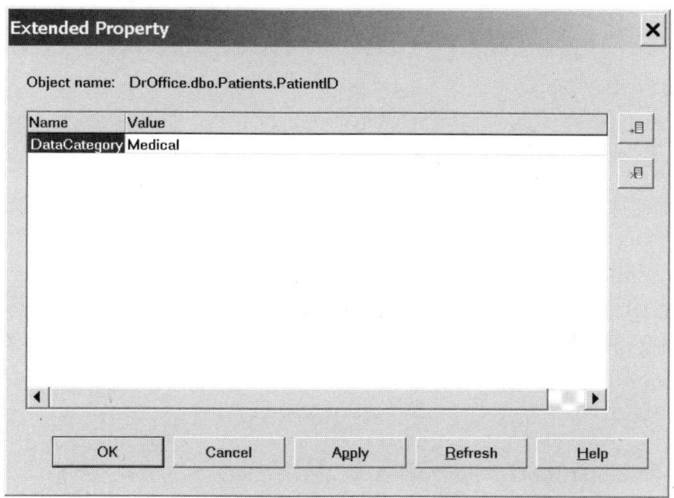

Figure 14.4 Extended Properties for PatientID column of Patients table

Retrieving the extended value for a column can be a little complex. The following set of statements, from the file patients.asp, retrieves the extended property for the social security number column of the Patients table. The value is cast to a string, because it is returned as a binary value. If the string is equal to Sensitive, the decrypt flag is set for the column. When data for the column is later retrieved from the table, it is decrypted before being displayed on the screen.

```
Set oRS = oConn.Execute("SELECT CAST([value] AS varchar) AS
➥[Value] FROM " &_
"::FN_LISTEXTENDEDPROPERTY('DataCategory', 'User', " &_
"'dbo','table', 'patients', 'column', 'SSN')")

' Ensure that encrypted columns get decrypted
If CInt(oRS("Value")) = nSensitive Then
 arrDecrypt(i) = true
Else
 arrDecrypt(i) = false
End if
```

Close SQL Query Analyzer and open the SQL Server Enterprise Manager application. Under the Action menu, select the Import Data command beneath the All Tasks menu. For the data source, select the DataMap.txt file and import it into the DrOffice database. Be sure to select the First row has column names checkbox. The columns are comma-delimited. Run the **import** command for the Patients.txt and Staff.txt files.

On the Control Panel, select the Administrative Tools command and run the Data Sources applet. Select the System DSN tab and add a SQL Server driver, naming it **DrOfficeDB**. Configure it using DBTest as the ID and DB$#4aX as the password. If this does not work, make sure the ID and password were defined for the DrOffice database. On continuing the data source configuration, make sure the DrOffice database is selected. Complete the configuration and close the Setup dialog.

Setting Up Authorization Manager

Start by creating the four users in Active Directory: Peter, Paul, Mary, and Pat. After loading the authorization store, you need to assign these users to the roles Doctor, Accounting, Administrator, and Receptionist, respectively.

The folder DrOffice should be copied to the root folder of your C drive. If you do not have a writeable C drive, or want to place the file somewhere else, modify line 12 of the file roles.asp in the Privacy folder to reflect the location where you place the file. You will need to update the security settings for the file so authenticated users accessing the application will be able to read it. Right-click the file, select Properties on the menu, select the Security tab, and then click the Add button and add Authenticated Users to the access control list. This will provide authenticated users with access to the XML file.

Start Authorization Manager (AzMan) by running azman.msc at the command line or in the Run dialog. Right-click the Authorization Manager label in the tree list in the left pane and select Open Authorization Store. Select the XML file radio button and open the file DrOffice.xml that you placed on the C drive. Expand the Role Assignments folder to expose the four roles that have been defined. Right-click each role and select the Assign Windows Users and Groups command to add one of the four users that you previously created to one of the roles, taking care to match the definitions in the Staff database table shown in Figure 14.7. You screen should look similar to the one in Figure 14.5.

Setting Up CAPICOM

The CAPICOM library is needed to support the encryption used by this application. After downloading the library, you need to copy it to a folder and unzip it. After unzipping the CAPICOM download file, retrieve the file, capicom.dll, from the capicom.cab file in the x86 folder. Using the command line, go to the folder where the DLL file is located. Register the DLL using the command **regsvr32 capicom.dll**.

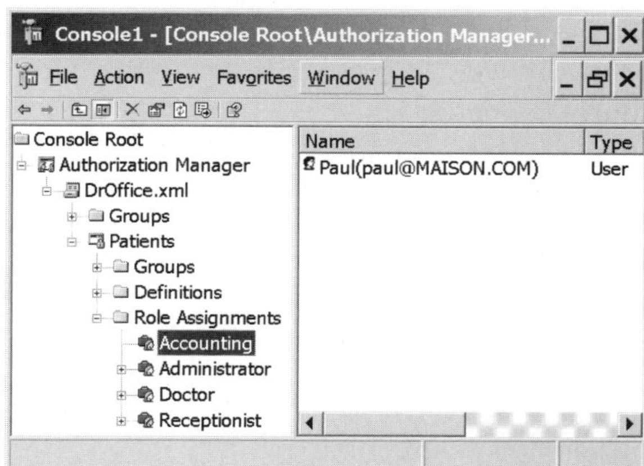

Figure 14.5 Authorization Store for the file DrOffice.xml

Testing the Database Version of the Application

At this point, everything should be ready for testing. Bring up your browser and enter the URL for the Privacy folder on your Web server. The default page should be displayed showing five commands, as shown in Figure 14.6.

Select the Application Tables link to verify that the database tables for the application were loaded successfully. There should be four tables listed. The Staff table should have four names listed along with the role of each. The Data Map table should have four entries that map the four roles to their respective data categories. The DataCategory table should list the values for the five data categories. The Column categories table is not a database table, but an extraction of the extended properties for the columns of the Patients table. Figure 14.7 displays the four tables.

Viewing Resumés

On the home page, click the Manual Login link. This will take you to a page with a combo box with four names in it. Select one of the names and click the Login button. This action runs the login.asp page, which maps the selected user to a role in the database. The DisplayData.asp page is then loaded, as shown in Figure 14.8.

From here you can display resumés or patient data. Click the Display Candidate Resumes link. This will display the list of candidates that have submitted resumés. For this sample, only a resumé for John Doe has been submitted. This can be seen on the Prospects page in Figure 14.9. Click the link to view the prospect's resumé.

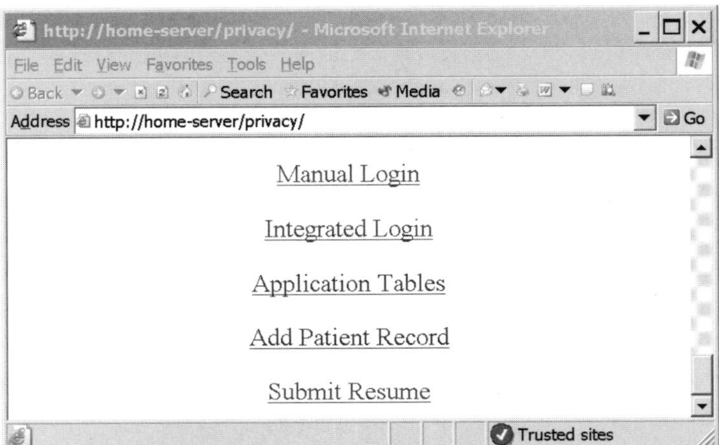

Figure 14.6 Home page for patient application

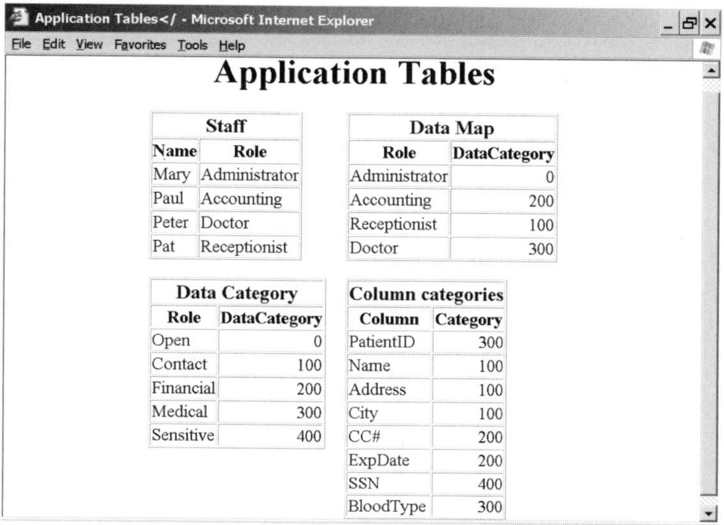

Staff	
Name	Role
Mary	Administrator
Paul	Accounting
Peter	Doctor
Pat	Receptionist

Data Map	
Role	DataCategory
Administrator	0
Accounting	200
Receptionist	100
Doctor	300

Data Category	
Role	DataCategory
Open	0
Contact	100
Financial	200
Medical	300
Sensitive	400

Column categories	
Column	Category
PatientID	300
Name	100
Address	100
City	100
CC#	200
ExpDate	200
SSN	400
BloodType	300

Figure 14.7 The database tables for the DrOffice application

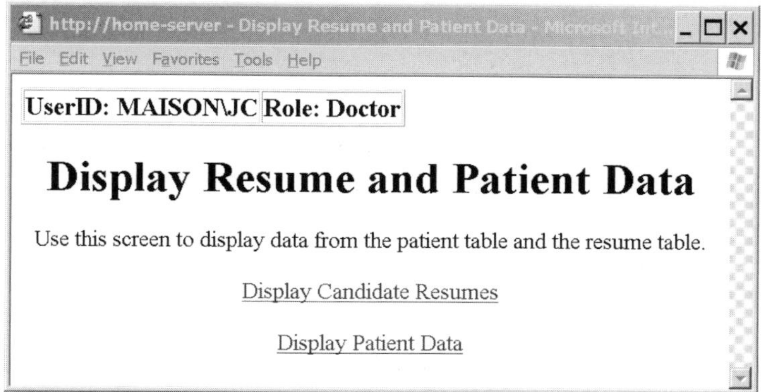

Figure 14.8 The Display Data page

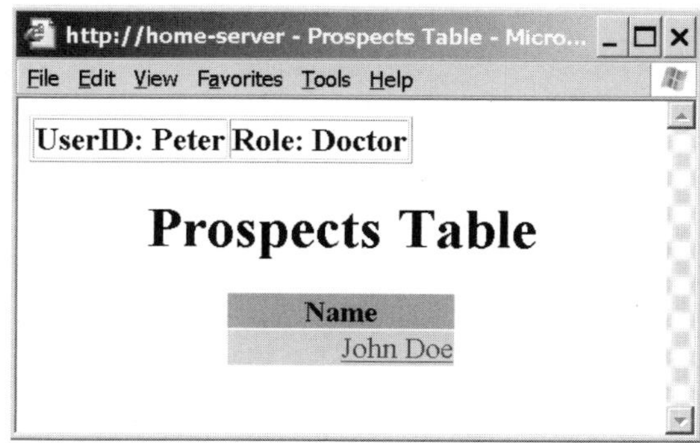

Figure 14.9 The Resumé Prospects page

Figure 14.10 shows what the resumé would look like if a doctor reviewed it. Only the medical information is visible. Go back to the login page, log in as Mary the administrator, and view the same resumé. You will notice that all of the fields of the resumé are visible now, as seen in Figure 14.11.

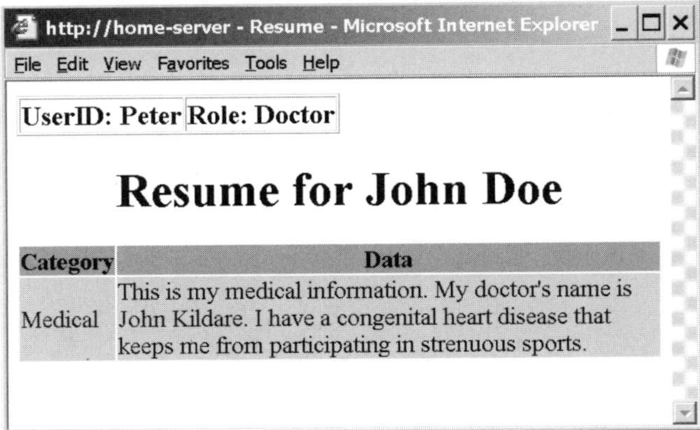

Figure 14.10 John Doe's resumé as viewed by a doctor

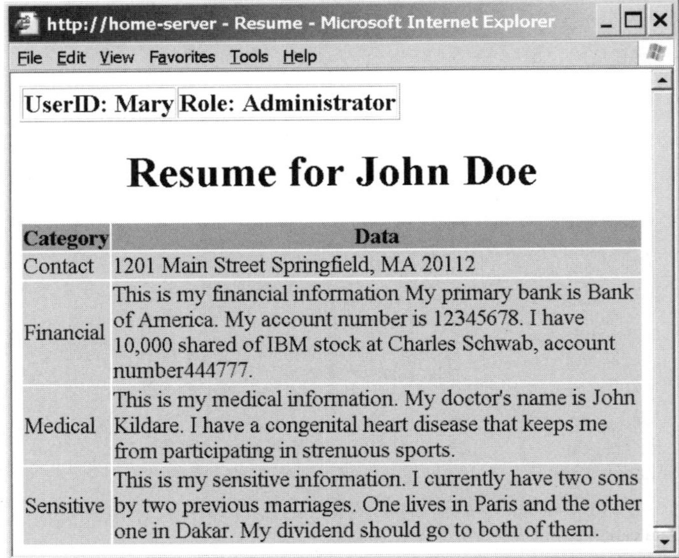

Figure 14.11 John Doe's resumé as viewed by an administrator

You can add your own resumés by going to the home page and clicking the Submit Resume link. It will cause the page shown in Figure 14.12 to display. Enter a full name in the first field. In the address box, enter a full address. This data is always tagged as contact information. In the remaining three blocks, enter any type of information that you like, and use the combo box to the left of each block to select the data category for the block. Selecting Open indicates that anyone can view the data.

Viewing Patient Information

Log in again to display the DisplayData.asp page shown in Figure 14.8. From here you can display resumés or patient data. Click the Display Patient Data link. This page will retrieve the data from the Patients table. Only the columns with a data category that matches that of the selected user will be retrieved. The remaining columns will have asterisks displayed in them. The UserID and Role of the current user will display at the top of the page. Figure 14.13 shows what the page would look like if Peter, the doctor, is the current user. If Mary the administrator were the current user, all of the columns would be retrieved.

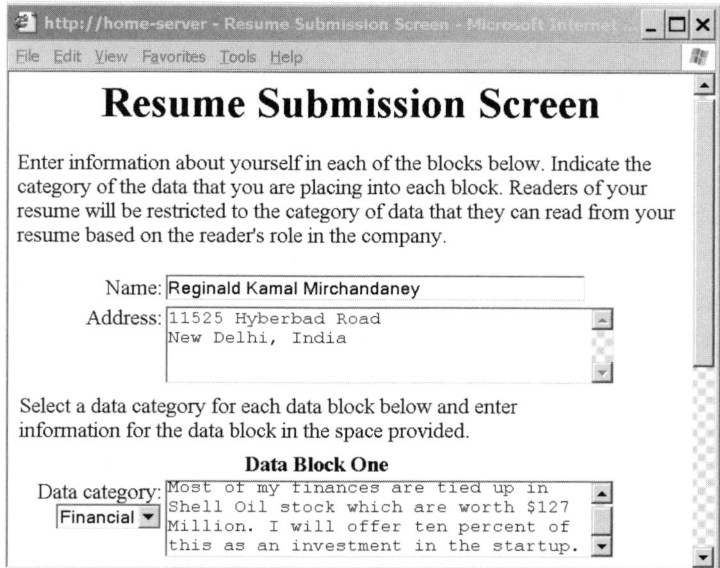

Figure 14.12 Resumé Submission Page

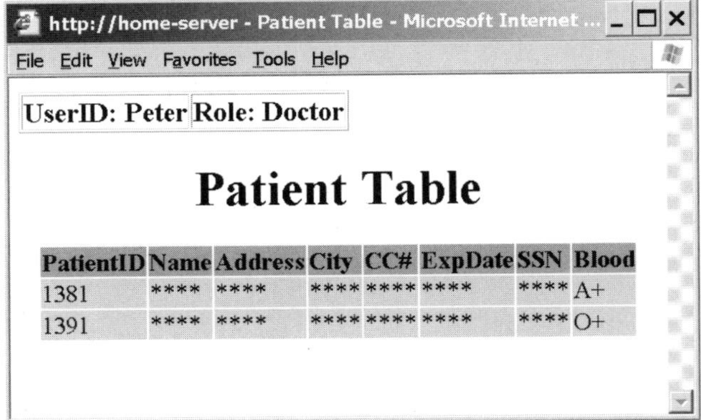

Figure 14.13 The Patient table when Peter is the current user

Select different users to see how it changes the display. Go back to the default page and click the Add Patient Record link. This will take you to a form that you can use to create a new patient record. Figure 14.14 provides an example of a completed form. No restrictions are placed on who can create a patient record. Use SQL Query Analyzer to modify the data category for one of the columns of the Patients table. If you accidentally ruin one of the values, you can rerun the ExtProp.sql file described earlier to repair it or just do a complete reinstall of the database.

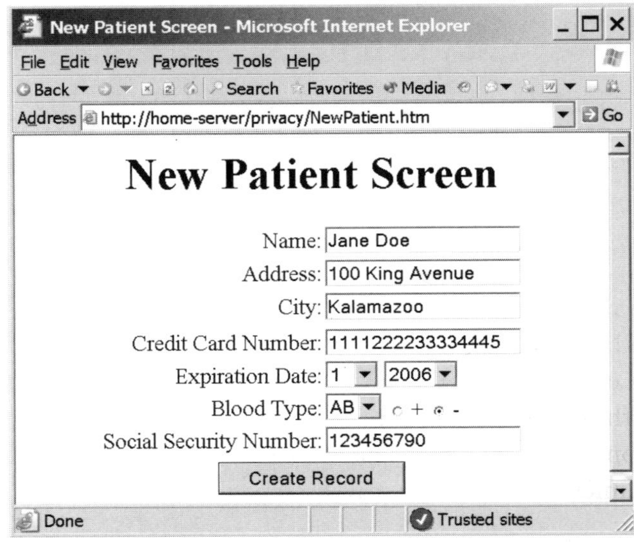

Figure 14.14 The new patient screen

Testing the Authorization Manager Version of the Application

This version of the application builds on the previous version. Instead of going to the database to retrieve a user's role, it is retrieved from the Authorization Store. Accessing the roles in an Authorization Store using VBScript takes only four lines of code, which are shown here. The first line creates the Authorization Store object and attaches it to the Authorization Store in the XML file. An Authorization Store could have multiple applications, so the desired application is selected using the OpenApplication call. The InitializeClientContextFromToken call is used to associate the Authorization Store with the security context of the currently logged-on user. The GetRoles call retrieves all of the current user's roles from the Authorization Store.

```
‘ Open the Authorization Store in the XML file
Set AzManStore = CreateObject(“Azroles.AzAuthorizationStore”)
 AzManStore.Initialize 0, “msxml://C:\DrOffice\DrOffice.xml”

 ‘ Open the Patients application in the Authorization Store
 Set App = AzManStore.OpenApplication(“Patients”)

 ‘ Load the security context for the current user
 ‘ Anonymous access to the web site must be turned
 ‘ off for this to work
 Set CCHandle = App.InitializeClientContextFromToken(0, 0)

 ‘ Read the user’s roles from the data store
 Roles = CCHandle.GetRoles()
```

Note

AzMan can also be used to define applications, tasks, and operations. Once defined, they can be used by applications in a consistent fashion. AzMan also enables the administrator to define what employees have access to without having access to or needing to understand a multitude of applications. You can find more information about using AzMan at http://msdn.microsoft.com/library/en-us/dnnetserv/html/AzManRoles.asp.

Go to the default Web page and click the *Integrated Login* link. This will send you to the roles.asp page, which will retrieve the role of the currently logged-on user from the Authorization Store. The DisplayData.asp page is then loaded. From here you can display resumés or patient data. Try both of these links to see how they work. You will notice the same functionality. The difference is that it is much easier to use the AzMan tool to modify a user's role. In addition, these changes can be viewed by any application that integrates with AzMan. Try logging on as different people or move a user to a different role and rerun the tests.

Although this version uses an XML version of the Authorization Store, it could be stored in Active Directory to make deployment simpler. The fact that it can be implemented in XML means that it can be used on other platforms. However, more code would have to be written, because the Authorization Manager would not be very practical for adding users who are defined on another platform. In general, using an Authorization Store has the following benefits:

- It is easier to share consistent roles across multiple applications.
- Application-specific databases are isolated from other applications.
- Changing a user's role is applied to each application using the Authorization Store.
- The Authorization Store provides other features such as task assignment and script creation.

The following is a printout of the DrOffice.xml file. You should be able to see the names of the roles defined in the XML file. I also included the member association that I made to show how it is attached. You will notice that the user's security GUID is used, and not his or her ID.

```
<?xml version="1.0" encoding="utf-8"?>
<AzAdminManager MajorVersion="1" MinorVersion="0"
Description="Store roles for sample patient application.">
<AzApplication Guid="72e32090-cd36-4a89-8fff-d44bbdd7431c"
Name="Patients" Description="Stores roles for the staff at a
fictious doctor's office." ApplicationVersion="1.0">
<AzTask Guid="7edb092c-1f35-4e55-ad6d-c2bb71878efa" Name="Doctor"
Description="The doctor assigned to the doctor's office."
BizRuleImportedPath="" RoleDefinition="True"/>
```

```
<AzTask Guid="9da6505c-2756-4876-ae50-630ecbe52e84"
Name="Receptionist" Description="Has access to contact
information." BizRuleImportedPath="" RoleDefinition="True"/>
<AzTask Guid="a6e83de6-4bb9-4c33-aabf-fc6f90eb3b0c"
Name="Accounting" Description="Has access to financial
information." BizRuleImportedPath="" RoleDefinition="True"/>
<AzTask Guid="1da57c66-ccbf-4429-b984-81f279b8719f"
Name="Administrator" Description="Has access to all information."
BizRuleImportedPath="" RoleDefinition="True"/>
<AzRole Guid="6e22bd25-f44c-497e-9f39-0b14105e9960"
Name="Accounting">
<TaskLink>a6e83de6-4bb9-4c33-aabf-fc6f90eb3b0c
</TaskLink>
<Member>S-1-5-21-2043930474-2994430476-1959079188-1148
</Member>
<Member>S-1-5-21-2043930474-2994430476-1959079188-1139
</Member>
</AzRole>
<AzRole Guid="8e533f34-ba21-445f-b9a0-a7aa4d6ec043"
Name="Administrator">
<TaskLink>1da57c66-ccbf-4429-b984-81f279b8719f
</TaskLink>
<Member>S-1-5-21-2043930474-2994430476-1959079188-1149
</Member>
</AzRole>
<AzRole Guid="022d64cf-0119-4522-a1dc-7fb6ccf61f8f" Name="Doctor">
<TaskLink>7edb092c-1f35-4e55-ad6d-c2bb71878efa
</TaskLink>
<Member>S-1-5-21-2043930474-2994430476-1959079188-1147
</Member>
</AzRole>
<AzRole Guid="6b9a5a3d-4f80-47ee-933d-aa8ba561031a"
Name="Receptionist">
<TaskLink>9da6505c-2756-4876-ae50-630ecbe52e84
</TaskLink>
<Member>S-1-5-21-2043930474-2994430476-1959079188-1150
</Member>
</AzRole>
</AzApplication>
</AzAdminManager>
```

Conclusion

Applications can do a lot to help the enforcement of a company's privacy policies. This simple application shows how role-based access to data can be managed. The dearth of privacy features made the program more complex than it needed to be. For example, the database does not support native encryption or data tagging. Just think if the database were smart enough to automatically encrypt data based on its data category. These are the types of features that developers need to add to applications.

This application did not include logging, which is a very important part of a data governance system. For a doctor's office, this is extremely important. A patient should be able to track everyone who has access to his or her sensitive data and know where every copy of the data is located.

Another topic that was not touched on here is the ability to tie data from different stores together. Suppose the patient's doctor created a write-up in a text document and stored it on a file server. How does the write-up get attached to the patient's record and protected using the same mechanisms? What happens when the patient uses the pharmacy in the same building or the record is transferred to a doctor using a different system? These are the types of questions that technology should be answering. It is surprising that in this age of technology, handling records in most doctors' offices is still a manual process.

15 Digital Rights Management

Digital rights management (DRM) comprises a series of technologies that are meant to protect an author's or copyright owner's intellectual property. An "author" can be an artist, musician, writer, software developer, or company. An author's intellectual property can include digital images, music, books, movies, software, video games, or industry research. However, most people view DRM as a tool that the Recording Industry Association of America (RIAA) uses to keep users from copying CDs and DVDs. This gives most people a negative feeling about DRM because they feel that it infringes upon their right to manage their own content. A person's freedom to listen to and copy content for one's own use is typically referred to as fair use. Most consumers see DRM as a restriction of their fair use rights. In actuality, both sides of the argument have their merits. Authors should be able to prevent unauthorized access to their content, and consumers should have the right to the noncommercial use of the content that they buy.

The Digital Millennium Copyright Act

The passing of the Digital Millennium Copyright Act (DMCA) concerned many people because it might give the RIAA the ability to encroach on user's *fair use* rights. One of the more ominous sections gave the RIAA the ability to obtain the identity of an accused offender of a copyright without a lawsuit, which many groups thought was a serious invasion of privacy without due process. The act could potentially enable pornographers and even criminals, who hold copyrights, to easily obtain the identity of possible copyright offenders. The RIAA argued that it would not be a trivial matter for criminals to abuse the law.[1]

1. http://news.com.com/2100-1027-5078609.html

Another section of the DMCA enables reverse engineering with certain limitations. Some companies were not happy with this section of the DMCA. Take Digital: Convergence, which came out with their free :CueCat barcode reader for scanning barcodes in magazines. After scanning, the user is taken to a Web site to obtain more information about a product. However, when some Linux programmers took the scanner apart to get it to work with the Linux operating system, Digital: Convergence cried foul. This could be because during the reverse-engineering process, the programmers found out that each device had a unique identifier that was used to track users when they went to the Digital: Convergence Web site. This is obviously a privacy violation that users weren't informed of. The ability for reverse engineering to uncover security and privacy flaws is far too beneficial to permit companies to limit its use.[2]

Lexmark, a maker of ink cartridges, also complained about reverse engineering their cartridges on grounds of copyright infringements. Unfortunately for them, on October 27, 2003, the United States Copyright Office ruled that reverse-engineering products was permitted under the exception clause of the DMCA and that permission was not needed to do so for the purposes of interoperability, functionality, and use.[3]

The Use of DRM to Defend Privacy

One area that has been overlooked by early DRM developers is individual privacy rights.[4] There are many legal documents, medical records, and financial transactions that contain sensitive data that should not be exposed to the general public. Recent legislation such as Health Information Portability and Accountability Act (HIPAA), Gramm-Leach Bliley Act (GLBA), and the Sarbanes Oxley (SOX) have mandated greater protection over individual privacy rights. However, there are few systems in place to meet the demands of this legislation. This deficiency, along with the current push for increased sharing of personal information by government agencies, should encourage the creation of more DRM-enabled solutions.

2. http://www.landfield.com/isn/mail-archive/2000/Oct/0048.html

3. http://www.businessweek.com/technology/content/nov2003/tc2003114_5174_tc024.htm

4. A recent paper by Larry Korba and Steve Kenny on using DRM for privacy rights management can be found at http://iit-iti.nrc-cnrc.gc.ca/publications/nrc-44956_e.html.

DRM, Copy-Protection Redux

Long before DRM, companies sought techniques to prevent their software from being copied. One of the most interesting from the 1980s was game manufacturers' inclusion of a code sheet with their games. It was created from a special color of paper and text to prevent copying. Every time the game was started, it would ask for the code that matched a specified number, which you had to copy from the code sheet. If you ever lost or accidentally destroyed the code sheet, you were forced to buy another copy of the game. There were many other methods of copy protection used over the years. Some of them included the following:

- Serial and parallel port license connectors
- Special CDs or floppy drives that cannot be copied
- A license file
- USB license devices
- Mandatory use of the original CD
- Online activation from a company's Web site.

Although these schemes offered some protection to the content owners, they were mostly an annoyance to honest consumers. Dishonest users were able to quickly find ways around these defenses soon after they were created. This resulted in losses to companies because of a wasted investment in a copy-protection scheme and lost customers who weren't willing to put up with the inconvenience or the feeling of not being trusted.

Here we are again with DRM as a new copy-protection scheme in which millions of dollars have been invested. And once again, consumers are annoyed, and hackers are still able to get access to any content that they want. Although copy protection is only one facet of DRM, it appears to be the feature that gets the most attention. Building loyalty starts with trust. Working directly with consumers to find an equitable solution to the piracy and fair use issue, in the end, will give both parties what they want.[5]

5. Bill Rosenblatt provides an evocative review on the state of DRM in his article, "2003 in Review: DRM Technology," http://drmwatch.com/drmtech/article.php/3294391.

Rights Management Languages

This chapter focuses on a new breed of content-protection mechanisms based on a DRM language.[6] These languages offer much more flexibility when it comes to use and control of content than typical protection schemes.

With the advent of the eXtensible Markup Language (XML), many companies and standards bodies have been coming up with definitions for XML-based languages that would facilitate the creation of interoperable, cross-platform, and Web-based applications and services. Initially, these languages were being built in to media players such as RealNetworks' RealOne Player and the Microsoft Windows Media Player. Later, they were added to other applications to enable consumers and enterprises to protect any documents they might deem as sensitive. This section looks at the major XML-based rights expression languages that are being used today.

Digital Property Rights Language (DPRL)

Digital Property Rights Language (DPRL) is an XML-based language that was created by Xerox's Palo Alto Research Center (PARC) in 1996. It was designed to enable an author to determine the terms and conditions under which digital content could be used. Like most DRM languages, it enables the author to place restrictions on who can read, modify, print, copy, or edit content. In addition, DPRL was designed to support several business models, such as subscription-based services, limited playback content, and content that deactivates itself. For example, some pay-per-view services will enable you to watch a movie as much as you want in a 24-hour period.

Although DPRL was designed to cover several business models, it was made to be extensible so that it could be adapted to still more business models. DPRL was first integrated into a product when it was used to develop Xerox-PARC's ContentGuard document management suite. DPRL was eventually superseded by the eXtensible Rights Markup Language (XrML), described later in this chapter.

eXtensible Media Commerce Language (XMCL)

In June 2001, RealNetworks announced the eXtensible Media Commerce Language (XMCL)[7] initiative. XMCL was developed to be an open XML-based framework to help manage the rights of digital media. This language

6. Some of the research for this section came from content at http://xml.coverpages.org/.

7. http://www.xmcl.org

permits the definition of business rules to support business models such as movie rentals, subscription services, online purchases, video on demand, and pay-per-view events. Companies such as Sony, Napster, Sun Microsystems, and IBM were part of this initiative. The new language was meant to permit copyright holders to determine the limits of use of media. For example, the technology can prevent content from being copied and transferred, and limit how many times content could be listened to.

RealNetworks submitted XMCL to the World Wide Web Consortium (W3C) with a suggestion that they use it as a basis for a rights expression language. XMCL has since been combined with Nokia's Mobile Rights Voucher language to form ODRL, which is discussed later in this section. RealNetworks later supported IPR Systems in their submission of ODRL to the Moving Picture Experts Group (MPEG) for their MPEG-21 Multimedia Framework.

eXtensible Rights Markup Language (XrML)

The eXtensible Rights Markup Language (XrML)[8] definition, which was designed by the ContentGuard group of Xerox Corporation, is the successor to DPRL. ContentGuard later became a separate corporation owned by Xerox, with a minority share owned by Microsoft Corporation. XrML extends DPRL beyond digital content rights management to permit the definition of the terms of use for Web services. Think of the many financial and medical service companies that are providing an online presence. They can now use XrML to define different fee-based services and place limits on how they can be used.

In May 2002, ContentGuard submitted XrML to the Rights Language Technical Committee of the Organization for the Advancement of Structured Information Standards (OASIS) standards organization. OASIS committed to use XrML as a basis for defining an industry standard rights management language.

ISO MPEG REL

The International Standards Organization (ISO) Moving Pictures Experts Group (MPEG) Rights Expression Language[9] is a derivative of XrML 2.0 that became the first standardized rights expression language. It was

8. http://www.xrml.org

9. http://www.contentguard.com/MPEGREL_home.asp

submitted to ISO by a consortium of companies including Warner Brothers, Samsung, Verisign, and the Recording Industry Association of America.[10] ISO MPEG REL is to become the basis for content management and digital asset management systems. It is designed to be used by the entertainment industry, enterprises, and consumers who are interested in protecting their digital content. This language is defined to be a cross-platform solution that is also format independent.

Open eBook Forum

The Open eBook Forum (OeBF)[11] is an organization devoted to the promotion and protection of electronic books. The Rights and Rules Working Group (RRWG) of the OeBF is using the XrML language as a basis for a rights expression language for protecting electronic books. The OeBF works with ContentGuard and MPEG-21 on the creation of this standard to help authors protect their copyrights and to give readers the freedom to manage eBooks the way they do standard books.

TV-Anytime

TV-Anytime[12] forum is an organization devoted to the creation of specifications to permit the exploitation of the digital storage found in today's consumer electronics. They work with a host of international organizations from various industries. One of their main objectives is to provide the secure dissemination of content for integrated and interoperable systems. Their goal is to be compatible with multiple delivery mechanisms. Their XML-based tvax language is yet another derivative of the XrML language.

Open Digital Rights Language (ODRL)

In September 2002, IPR Systems Ltd. submitted version 1.1 of the Open Digital Rights Language (ODRL)[13] specification. ODRL was designed to cover the use, sale, and transfer of content. It was also designed to cover the reuse of content, meaning that rights expressions applied to a piece of content can equally apply to new versions of the content. ODRL works with digital and physical content, which means that it can be used for online music as well as CDs.

---

10. http://www.msnbc.msn.com/id/4636641

11. http://www.openebook.org/about.htm

12. http://www.tv-anytime.org/

13. http://www.odrl.net

ODRL has capabilities similar to XrML. Where it differs is in the size of its implementation. Definitions that use ODRL require less space than equivalent definitions using XrML. ODRL also permits the specification of attributes, such as file formats and encoding rates, for media. This is part of the reason why the Open Mobile Alliance (OMA)[14] adopted it as its rights expression language. Nokia was one of the major influencers of getting ODRL adopted by OMA. Nokia has implemented ODRL in its 3595 model phone.

Rights Meta Data for Open Archiving

The Rights Meta Data for Open Archiving (RoMEO)[15] project hopes to use ODRL to create a mechanism for defining rights and permissions regarding content stored in institutional repositories. The Joint Information Systems Committee (JISC) is funding the RoMEO project. One of the major goals of JISC is to sidestep the restrictive aspects of copyright law and permit more open access to protected digital works. JISC would like to permit the entire community of researchers and educators to benefit from access to important papers while protecting the rights of the papers' creators to retain the right to be named as the authors of the papers. XrML was rejected as a possibility because of the vague licensing terms and lack of a Data Dictionary.

Contract Enabled Server

The Department of Information Services, at the Vienna University Economics and Business Administration, runs the Contract Enabled Server (CES) project. The department will be using ODRL as the digital rights expression language in their CES system to assist with the identification, processing and protection of digital contracts. ODRL was chosen as part of the department's strategy to build a software framework in the spirit of open source.

Making a Choice

Out of the many rights expression languages that have been mentioned here only two stand out as the clear leaders: ODRL and XrML. The remaining languages have been abandoned, subsumed by these two languages, or are derivatives of these languages.

14. http://www.openmobilealliance.org

15. http://www.lboro.ac.uk/departments/ls/disresearch/romeo/

These two languages are very similar as far as functionality goes, but they do have some subtle nuances that may influence your decision when it comes to building a solution. Some of those nuances are discussed below:

Cost

ODRL is touted as the open solution and is offered royalty-free. Although this may be appealing, it may be more appealing to go with a language such as XrML that has broader industry acceptance. Be aware that based on the wide range of patents for XrML, there may be patent-infringement issues with building solutions based on this language or going with any language that is similar to it.

XrML may charge a licensing fee for any solutions that are created using it. This is determined on a case-by-case basis. Details are sketchy at this point. It is best to contact ContentGuard directly for clarification.

Features

ODRL has a simpler implementation that results in a smaller footprint. It also has media-specific features that allow the definition of media file attributes, such as format type, encoding rate, image resolution, and compression algorithm.

XrML is a more sophisticated language that can support a wider range of solutions, especially Web services. It also has wider industry support, which will present itself in more interoperable solutions.

Supporters

ODRL was adopted by OMA, which is the standards group for mobile devices. RealNetworks, Adobe Systems, and IBM are the major backers for the technology.

XrML was adopted by OASIS, which is a standards group for XML derivative languages. ISO, Open eBook, and TV-Anytime are other standards groups that are supporting this XrML. ContentGuard and Microsoft are the major backers of this language.

Rights Management Applications

This section examines some applications that have been built using a rights expression language. If you are considering building a solution, you may want to look at what has already been created.This can help you decide which markets or languages are worth pursuing.

Electronic Media Management System

IBM's DRM technology, known as Electronic Media Management System (EMMS)[16], is a suite of components used to protect the privacy of enterprise documents. The technology provides more protection than simple authorization and encryption features. The technology is being integrated into IBM's DB2 infrastructure, which will make it available to IBM's WebSphere, Lotus, and Tivoli lines of products.

OpenIPMP

OpenIPMP[17] is an ODRL-based set of tools and services designed to provide management and secure delivery of content. OpenIPMP offers asset security and control utilizing an open framework. The *Open* portion of OpenIPMP refers to its stated goal of being developed as an open system adhering to open standards. Open systems conform to industry standards enabling interaction between various hardware and software products. They are preferable to proprietary systems because they do not lock the user into solutions from one vendor, but rather enable users to pick and choose the best of breed components from many vendors. IPMP stands for Intellectual Property Management and Protection. It is an acronym coined by MPEG to represent DRM in the classical sense of protecting intellectual property.

Windows Rights Management Services

The Windows Rights Management Services (RMS)[18] is an XrML-based server-side package that validates requests from clients to access content. The RMS server is used to first register DRM-protected content. Later, when the content needs to be accessed, it validates the request and determines the type of access that is allowed by the requester. Microsoft Office System 2003

16. http://www-306.ibm.com/software/data/emms/features/

17. http://objectlab.com/clients/openipmp/id21.htm

18. http://www.microsoft.com/windowsserver2003/technologies/rightsmgmt/default.mspx

is the most significant suite of applications that have integrated RMS within its Information Rights Management (IRM) client. RMS is a separate component that was designed to work with Microsoft Windows Server 2003 operating system.

Information Rights Management

Information Rights Management (IRM)[19] is an XrML-based component that was built for Microsoft Office System 2003 suite of applications. IRM can be used to protect access to documents created with Office System 2003 applications such as Word, Excel, or PowerPoint.

Developing DRM Solutions

Most DRM solutions were created to protect a specific type of content or output from a specific application. To protect other types of content, you need to integrate one of the technologies discussed in this chapter. For those of you interested in developing your own DRM-based solution, there are specifications and software development kits (SDKs) that can make your job easier. This section lists some major ones.

ContentGuard XrML SDK

ContentGuard offers an SDK to assist with the creation of XrML-based content protection solutions. You can find the SDK at http://www.contentguard.com/SDKs.asp.

Nokia Content Publishing Toolkit

Nokia is using the OMA version of ODRL for managing and protecting ODRL content packages. You can find the toolkit for integrating OMA ODRL into your own custom solution at http://www.forum.nokia.com/main/0,,034-57,00.html.

Open Digital Rights Language

Although there is no software development kit currently available to assist with the creation of ODRL solutions, you can find the current version of the specification at http://www.w3.org/TR/odrl/.

---

19. http://www.microsoft.com/technet/treeview/default.asp?url=/technet/prodtechnol/office/Office2003/Plan/Of03IRM.asp

Windows Rights Management Client SDK

Client-side applications that integrate with Microsoft Windows Rights Management Services or a custom server-side solution can be created using the Windows Rights Management Client SDK, which you can find at http://msdn.microsoft.com/library/en-us/drmclsdk/htm/windowsrightsmanagementclientsdk.asp

Windows Rights Management Services SDK

Server-side applications similar to Microsoft Windows Rights Management Services or a custom server-side solution can be created using the Windows Rights Management Services SDK, which you can find at http://msdn.microsoft. com/library/en-us/rms_sdk/htm/windowsrightsmanagementservicessdk.asp

Conclusion

Digital Rights Management is a powerful tool that can be used to protect copyrighted digital content, corporate intellectual property, and individual privacy. There is a lot of sensitive material in documents belonging to legal, medical, and financial institutions that could be exposed if left without the protection of DRM. Although DRM has been viewed as a means for the RIAA to infringe on consumers' *fair use* rights, this can happen only if consumers tolerate their rights being eroded. All technology suffers from the possibility of misuse. This should encourage everyone to be more involved in the development of regulations around new technology. We shouldn't trust that politicians won't be too liberal or conservative in their views. Because consumers are the ones most impacted by many technologies, they should have a voice in how they are developed and regulated.

ODRL and XrML have emerged as the two predominant rights expression languages in the industry after the demise of several languages before them. They are both XML-based languages with wide acceptance. Although the market is large enough to support both of these languages, in the end interoperability of solutions will determine how well each language survives. Consumers and enterprises should have to worry only about the technology that will fill their needs and not which protocol is running underneath. It would be unfortunate if the marketplace had to suffer because of two technologies that don't play well together.

A Privacy Section for a Feature Specification

This appendix contains a template for a privacy section that can be used in a feature specification. Use this as a guideline to create a privacy section for your feature specification document.

Privacy

This section describes the privacy impacts of this feature. These include the storage or transmission of the user's sensitive data or the tracking of the user's behavior (e.g., the user's browsing habits and product-usage history). Any data that is sent from the user's computer system over the Internet should be documented.

The following diagram is to be used as an aid to assist with fleshing out possible privacy risks within this feature. There are three environments to analyze: the user's local environment, corporate Web sites, and third-party Web sites. The lines in the diagram represent typical connections between environments.

Identify which connections are utilized by the feature and apply the analysis in the next section to each connection identified. Pay careful attention to whether a connection is secure, who can access the data collected (other users or employees), and whether this information is included in a privacy statement.

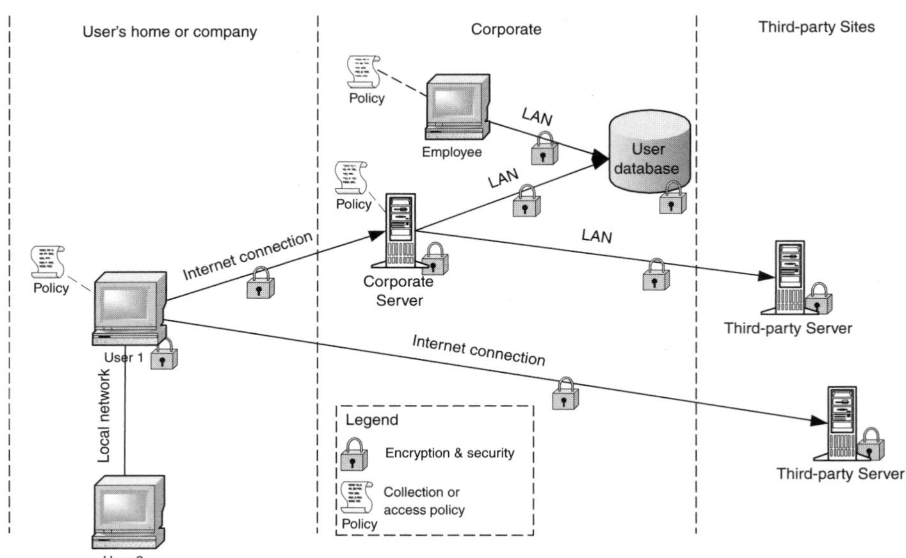

Figure A.1 Integrating privacy in each phase of development

Privacy Impact

Describe any risks to a user's privacy that may be caused by this feature. (Consider all connections identified above.) Even if there is a way to mitigate the risk, it should be described here.

Definitions

- **Personally identifiable information (PII)**—Any information that can be used to identify or find an individual (e.g., the individual's name or physical address). This includes information that can be correlated with other information to identify an individual (e.g., IP address or account number).
- **Sensitive information**—A person's medical, financial, religious, sexual, or other private information.
- **Sharing (onward transfer)**—Providing your data to a third party (i.e., not the original recipient).
- **Transmission**—Sending data out of your computer to an intended recipient (e.g., a Web service or another computer).

Impact Description

Answer these common questions that may apply to a client-side component or Web service.

- Does this feature of your client-side component or Web service store or share any PII or sensitive information? If so, for each item, explain the following:
  - What data is stored or shared?
  - How is the data used and by whom?
  - What value does the user gain from this activity?
  - Is the user's permission explicitly given before storing or sharing the data?
  - What end-user settings apply to how the data is stored and shared (point to the associated specification for these settings, where applicable)?
  - How is the data protected (e.g., are controlled access and/or encryption used)?
  - With whom is the data shared (include third parties)?
  - How long is the data stored?
  - Does the user have the ability to view and modify the stored data?

Based on your component type, complete one of the two following sections.

Client-Side Component

If this feature is part of a client-side component, complete the following:

- Does your feature send data to the Web for any reason? If so, describe in detail the contents of the data that is sent, when the data is sent, where the data is sent, and why the data is sent.
- Do users have the ability to select whether or not they want this data sent? If so, what is the default? If the default is not "off," explain why "on" is acceptable.
- Does your feature store any data in a data store for later transmission? If so, describe the contents of the data store, and when it is collected.
- If you track files, media, or other resources that are accessed, do you provide a mechanism to clear this information from the user's system? If you cache data, is there a way for the user to clear the cache or turn off the feature?

- If your application works in a peer-to-peer scenario, is PII being sent between computers? For example, a multiplayer game may send a user's profile to other players.

Web Service Component

If this feature is part of a Web service, complete the following:

- Does the Web service have a privacy statement associated with it? Where is it located? Is it registered with the corporate privacy group?
- Describe the contents of any cookies that you create and their purpose. Document any third-party cookies.
- Describe the contents of any logs that you keep. Include any unique IDs you create or use.
- Has P3P been implemented for the Web service? (For information on implementing P3P for your Web site, see Chapter 9 and visit http://msdn.microsoft.com/library/default.asp?url=/workshop/security/privacy/overview/createprivacypolicy.asp.)

B Privacy Review Template

This appendix is the placeholder for the privacy template file that can be used to document privacy issues in preparation for a privacy review. The template itself is contained in a PowerPoint file named Review Template.ppt, which can be found on the accompanying CD in the folder called, "Chapter 10."

The template file itself contains instructions on how to use the slides within the file. For further details on how to use this file, read the section *Privacy Review Template* in Chapter 10.

The file DataAnalysis.xls can be found on the accompanying CD in the folder called, "Chapter 10."

C Data Analysis Template

This appendix serves as a placeholder for the data analysis template that can be used to document the use of data by your component. The template itself is contained in an Excel spreadsheet file named DataAnalysis.xls.

The spreadsheet contains columns whose title represents a possible attribute that could be applied to the data that your application may be collecting. In the leftmost column, enter the name of a data store or data item that the application or component collects. Then place a Y or N in each of the nine attribute columns to indicate whether the attribute applies to the data. Based on the value you place in the column, you may be required to include addition disclosure in a privacy statement or add controls to your application to permit users or administrators to manage the data that your application collects.

For further information on how to use this template file, read the section *Data Analysis* in Chapter 10.

D List of Privacy Content

This appendix lists the privacy content that should accompany your product or Web site. By providing this content, you are disclosing to your customers what data you are collecting and how it is being used. In some cases, you are explaining how they can use features of your application or Web service to protect their privacy. Disclosure is an important element of customer trust. Every product or service, whether it collects data or not, should have a privacy statement that can be easily accessed by consumers.

- Privacy statement
- Privacy features document for the application
- Application help text
- Informational text above submit buttons on Web pages and dialogs
- Web site marketing and development documentation
- P3P reference file
- P3P XML privacy statement
- P3P compact policy
- Descriptive documentation
  - Registry settings
  - Logs
  - Web beacons
  - Cookies
  - Application-usage tracking files
  - Transmitted data

E Privacy Checklist

When ensuring that your product, Web site, or service is properly reviewed with regards to privacy, you should follow the seven tenets of the Safe Harbor Principles.[1] This appendix provides a checklist for each tenet to assist you with flushing out privacy issues.

Notice

- ❑ What data is stored or shared?
- ❑ How is the data used and by whom?
- ❑ How long is the data stored?
- ❑ Does the component have a privacy statement?
- ❑ What logs or history do you store?
  - Who has access?
  - Is the data protected from other users of the computer?
- ❑ What data does your component send to the Internet?
  - Which Web site?
  - When?
  - What is the purpose and customer benefit?

Choice

- ❑ What end-user settings apply to how the data is stored and shared? (Point to associated specification for these settings where applicable.)
- ❑ Is the user's permission explicitly given before storing or sharing the data?
- ❑ Do you provide a feature to clear logs and history?
- ❑ Are settings integrated with group policy?

1. More information on the Safe Harbor Principles can be found in Chapter 3.

Onward Transfer

- ❑ With whom is the data shared (include third parties)?
- ❑ Is any data transmitted outside of the user's computer?
- ❑ Is the user notified when this happens?
- ❑ Is the user able to easily access settings to control this?

Access

- ❑ Does the user have the ability to view all of the data that you store?
- ❑ Does the user have the ability to update his or her information?
- ❑ Is the user able to delete a record or unsubscribe from your service?
- ❑ Is the user able to modify his or her privacy settings?
- ❑ Is a user's access to his or her information easy and inexpensive?

Security

Related to information disclosure in the STRIDE[2] model for performing threat-modeling analyses:

- ❑ Is access to sensitive data secured?
- ❑ Is sensitive information encrypted?
- ❑ Are users of the data restricted to what they can access?
- ❑ Do you offer security features in your application?

Data Integrity

Related to Tampering in the STRIDE model for performing threat-modeling analyses:

- ❑ Do you ensure that all data is collected before using it?
- ❑ Do you have a way to determine if the data is valid or out of date?
- ❑ Are protections in place to prevent tampering?
- ❑ Do you have a data retention/deletion policy in place for each data store?

---

2. STRIDE refers to the six threat categories that are examined when performing a security threat model against an application. STRIDE stands for Spoofing, Tampering, Repudiation, Information disclosure, Denial of service, and Elevation of privilege. More information on STRIDE and performing threat modeling can be found in the book *Writing Secure Code, Second Edition* (Microsoft Press 2003).

Enforcement

- ❑ Does the user have the ability to contact you in case there are privacy issues?
- ❑ Is the contact information easy to find?
- ❑ Has a person been designated to respond to privacy issues that may occur?
- ❑ Are you signed up for the TRUSTe privacy certification program? http://truste.org

F Privacy Standard

This appendix provides a simple example of a privacy standard that can be used for directing the development of products and services for your company. More information on creating a privacy standard can be found in Chapter 10.

Overview

This privacy standard acts as a guideline for developing products and services for our company. All product teams must follow this standard. All exceptions must be vetted with your privacy lead or senior management.

Philosophy

Always provide users with prominent disclosure of and control over any of their data that is collected, stored, and shared by our products and services.

Corporate Privacy Policy

When developing privacy policies for your product or organization, make sure that they are compliant with our Corporate Privacy Policy, which can be found at http://Corporate/PrivacyPolicy.

Follow Fair Information Practices

The Federal Trade Commission (FTC) requires that companies comply with their Fair Information Practices for the treatment of personal information. Complying with these practices will help our company maintain an image of trustworthiness and avoid litigation. The Fair Information Practices include the following tenets:

Notice, Choice, Access, Security, and Enforcement

For more information on the FTC's Fair Information Practices, visit the following link:

http://www.ftc.gov/reports/privacy3/fairinfo.htm

Prominent Disclosure

All products and Web sites must have a privacy statement that is easy to find and easy to understand. The privacy statement must indicate all collection, storage, or sharing of data from users or their computers. For Web sites, the link to the privacy statement should be placed at the bottom of each Web page. For applications with a UI, a link to the privacy statement should be located beneath the Help menu. For applications that do not have a UI, its EULA or download site should contain its privacy statement. For a component that ships with an operating system, the component's privacy disclosure should be part of the operating system's privacy statement. Be sure to have each privacy statement reviewed by the corporate legal department.

Web sites must also deploy P3P if the site collects data or issues cookies. All P3P implementations must be tested against the W3C validator tool at http://ww.w3.org/p3p/validator.

Control

All products and Web sites that collect data must enable users to control the collection, storage, and sharing of their data. For products that are deployed for enterprises, IT administrators must have a means for controlling the privacy settings for these products. This control can be through group policy, a specific setup mechanism, or some other means.

Collection of Data

When collecting data from users or computers, only collect the information that is necessary to perform the business function for which it is being collected. When sharing the data, only share the information that is needed by the third party. Use a lesser granularity where possible. For example, if a user's location information is needed, only provide the city name if that is all that is needed, and not the user's entire address.

Retention Policy

All personal data collected by our company should be purged from all storage locations after six months unless there are business reasons or regulatory requirements for retaining the data for a longer period. All exceptions to the rule must be registered with the corporate data retention office with justification and a proposed retention period.

G References

This appendix contains references for links, books and other resources on privacy.

Links

Antispam Software and Information

Brightmail

http://www.brightmail.com

Junkbusters Corporation

http://www.junkbusters.com/

Mailshell

http://www.mailshell.com/mail/client/fd.html

Spamabuse.net

http://spam.abuse.net/

Spamex

http://www.spamex.com/

Stopspam.org

http://www.stopspam.org/

Anti-Spyware Software and Information

Simply the Best

http://simplythebest.net/info/spyware.html

Spyware.com

http://www.spyware.com

SpybotSpyware.com

http://spybot-spyware.com/

SpyChecker.com

http://www.spychecker.com/home.html

Kids' Privacy

FTC Kids' Privacy Site

http://www.ftc. gov/bcp/conline/edcams/kidzprivacy/index.html

LatchLogic Child Protection Software

http://latchlogic.com/childprotection/

Privacy Resources for Children from the University of Illinois, Urbana-Champaign

http://lrs.ed.uiuc.edu/wp/privacy/kidprivacy.html

SafeKids.com

http://www.safekids.com/

Privacy Advocacy and Consulting Groups

Americans for Computer Privacy

http://www.computerprivacy.org/

Center for Democracy and Technology

http://www.cdt.org/

Corporate Privacy Group

http://www.corporateprivacygroup.com/

dataPrivacy Partners Ltd

http://www.dataprivacy.com/

DelCreo, Inc

http://www.delcreo.com/delcreo/home.cfm

Electronic Frontier Foundation

http://www.eff.org/

Electronic Privacy Information Center

http://www.epic.org/

International Association of Privacy Professionals

http://www.privacyassociation.org/

Online Privacy Alliance

http://www.privacyalliance.org/

Privacy Council

http://www.privacycouncil.com/

Privacy International

http://www.privacyinternational.org/

Privacy Laws & Business

http://www.privacylaws.com/

Privacy Rights Clearinghouse

http://www.privacyrights.org/

Privaterra

http://www.privaterra.org/

TRUSTe

http://www. truste.org/

Privacy Certification Programs

BBBONLINE

http://www.bbbonline.org/business/

ESRB

http://www.esrb.org/privacy_wp_register.asp

TRUSTe

http://www.truste.org/programs/pub_how_join.html

WebTrust

http://www.cpawebtrust.org/onlstart.htm

Privacy Gatherings

The Computers, Freedom, and Privacy Conference

http://www.cfp.org/

International Association of Privacy Professionals

http://www.privacyassociation.org/html/conferences.html

Privacy Laws and Business

http://www.privacylaws.co.uk/whats-newframe.htm

Workshop on Privacy Enhancing Technologies

http://petworkshop.org/

Privacy Journals

CIO.com's Security and Privacy Research Center

http://www.cio.com/research/security/tech.html

IEEE Security and Privacy

http://www.computer.org/security/

Privacy.org

http://privacy.org/

Privacy Digest

http://www. privacydigest.com

Privacy Journal

http://www.privacyjournal.net/

Privacy Times

http://www.privacytimes.com/

Privacy Weekly

http://www.privacycouncil.com/kp_privacyWeekly.php

Privacy Surveys

An Introduction to EU Data Protection Legislation[1]

http://www.linklaters.com/pdfs/briefings/IP_040429.pdf

The Economics of Privacy

http://www.heinz.cmu.edu/~acquisti/economics-privacy.htm

Privacy Surveys from Privacy Exchange

http://www. privacyexchange.org/iss/surveys/surveys.html

Privacy Tools and Technology Companies

Anonymity Bibliography

http://freehaven.net/anonbib/

Credentica

http://www.credentica.com/

Hush Communications Corp

https://www.hushmail.com/

JRC P3P Resource Centre

http://p3p.jrc.it/

Lists of Tools from EPIC

http://www.epic.org/privacy/tools.html

Lumeria, Inc.

http://www.lumeria.com/

P3P Specification

http://www.w3.org/TR/P3P/

Zero-Knowledge Systems

http://www.zeroknowledge.com/

---

1. This is an impressive overview of the privacy legislation for the 28 countries that make up the European Economic Area.

Privacy Training

MediaPro

http://www.mediapro.com/html/products/corpComp/corpComp-main.html

Customer Paradigm

http://www.customerparadigm.com/privacyseminars.htm

DelCreo, Inc

http://www.delcreo.com/delcreo/education_training/compliance.cfm

ePrivacy Group

http://eprivacygroup.com/article/articlestatic/2/1/1/?POSTIVAID=0fa67eeb5da78273ddb7385180a81406

Internet Business Corporation

http://privacy.ibc.com.au/

Books

The Fight Against the Invasion of Privacy

Crypto: How the Code Rebels Beat the Government Saving Privacy in the Digital Age, by Steven Levy (Penguin Putnam, 2001)

The Electronic Privacy Papers: Documents on the Battle for Privacy in the Age of Surveillance, by Bruce Schneier and David Banisar (Wiley, 1997)

Identity, Privacy, And Personal Freedom: Big Brother vs. the New Resistance, by Sheldon Charrett (Paladin Press, 1999)

The Naked Employee: How Technology Is Compromising Workplace Privacy, by Frederick S. Lane (American Management Association, 2003)

Surveillance as Social Sorting: Privacy, Risk and Automated Discrimination, by David Lyon (Routledge, 2002)

Privacy Policy

Privacy Handbook: Guidelines, Exposures, Policy Implementation, and International Issues, by Albert J. Marcella, Jr. Ph.D., CISA and Carol Stucki, CISA (John Wiley & Sons, 2003)

The Privacy Payoff, by Ann Cavoukian, Ph.D. and Tyler J. Hamilton (McGraw-Hill Ryerson Limited, 2002)

Privacy Technology

Applied Cryptography: Protocols, Algorithms, and Source Code in C, Second Edition, by Bruce Schneider (Wiley, 1995)

Designing Privacy Enhancing Technologies, by Hannes Federrath (Ed.) (Springer-Verlag Telos, 2001)

Digital Cash: Commerce on the Net, Second Edition, by Peter Wayner and Morgan Kaufmann (Morgan Kaufmann Pub, 1997)

Handbook of Privacy and Privacy-Enhancing Technologies: The Case of Intelligent Software Agents, by G. W. van Blarkom RE, drs. J. J. Borking and dr.ir. J. G. E. Olk (College bescherming persoonsgegevens, 2003)

Rethinking Public Key Infrastructures and Digital Certificates: Building in Privacy, by Stefan A. Brands (MIT Press, 2000)

Translucent Databases, by Peter Wayner (Flyzone Sr Llc, 2002)

Protecting Online and Personal Privacy

Developing Trust: Online Privacy and Security, by Matt Curtin and Peter G. Neumann (APress, 2001)

Privacy for Business: Web Sites and Email, by Stephen Cobb (Dreva Hill LLC, 2002)

Privacy Handbook: Proven Countermeasures for Combating Threats to Privacy, Security, and Personal Freedom, by Michael Chesbro (Paladin Press, 2002)

Protect Yourself Online, by Matthew Danda (Microsoft Press, 2001)

Security and Privacy

Microsoft Windows Security Resource Kit, by Ben Smith and Brian Komar (Microsoft Press, 2003)

Secrets & Lies: Digital Security in a Networked World, by Bruce Schneier (John Wiley & Sons, 2000)

Writing Secure Code, Second Edition, by Michael Howard and David LeBlanc (Microsoft Press, 2002)

Index

M

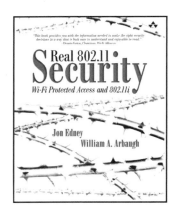

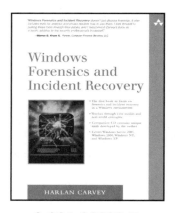

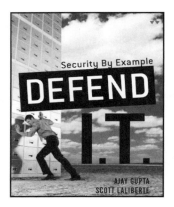

CD-ROM Warranty

Addison-Wesley warrants the enclosed CD-ROM to be free of defects in materials and faulty workmanship under normal use for a period of ninety days after purchase (when purchased new). If a defect is discovered in the CD-ROM during this warranty period, a replacement CD-ROM can be obtained at no charge by sending the defective CD-ROM, postage prepaid, with proof of purchase to:

Disc Exchange
Addison-Wesley Professional
Pearson Technology Group
75 Arlington Street, Suite 300
Boston, MA 02116
Email: AWPro@aw.com

Addison-Wesley makes no warranty or representation, either expressed or implied, with respect to this software, its quality, performance, merchantability, or fitness for a particular purpose. In no event will Addison-Wesley, its distributors, or dealers be liable for direct, indirect, special, incidental, or consequential damages arising out of the use or inability to use the software. The exclusion of implied warranties is not permitted in some states. Therefore, the above exclusion may not apply to you. This warranty provides you with specific legal rights. There may be other rights that you may have that vary from state to state. The contents of this CD-ROM are intended for personal use only.

More information and updates are available at:
http://www.awprofessional.com/